# DEDICATED TO THE MEMORY OF MY BELOVED GRANDMOTHER MATILDA WILLIAMS

This Family Tree is dedicated to Matilda Williams (1892 - 1962) who retold the story to her Granddaughter Linda, who kept it alive. The Thomas Family Tree has been compiled by Malcolm Winmill (1994 - 99) assisted by David L. Williams, Grandson of Matilda Williams (1892 - 1962).

**SOURCES OF INFORMATION**
Refer book "Rhys AP Thomas and his family" by Ralph A. Griffiths also from the file (36 years of research) by W. Cyryl Rogers, 2 Glan Brydan Avenue, Uplands, Swansea.

**Many thanks go to the following**
The archives at County Hall Swansea for supplying us with invaluable information.
The National Library of Wales, Aberystwyth.
The Golden Grove Book M.P.P (Carmarthen Record Office)
M.S.S. Pedigree Book - Compiled 1609 by W.M. Bennet of Penrice Castle, Gower.
Llwyds Parochialia (iii 122 also Truman M.S.S.)
J.H's account of Gower Pedigrees National Library of Wales.
History of the Vale of Neath by D. Rhys Philips 1925.
The printed Table of G.T. Clark of his Patrum Morganiae 1866 Lincoln Inn Fields.
INF., Rev. Ezekiel Thomas's Hand Written Book in Welsh of 1886, son of Morgan Thomas, Swansea.
Lewis Dwnn, Deputy Herald at the College of Arms (1550 - 1560).
The Holy Kingdom by Adrian Gilbert 1998.
Catherine Matilda Williams (Nee Bendle).
Margaret Eluned Lewis.
John Richard Mallon.
David Mallon

## NORMANS

Robert 2nd. (The Devil)
Duke of Normandy (Died 1035)

William The Conqueror (Reigned 1066 - 1087)

Henry 1st.
Married
Eadgyth (Died 1118)
Daughter of King Malcom of Scotland (1093)

Matilda
Married
Geoffrey Plantagenet (Died 1151)
Count of Anjou and Maine

Henry 2nd. (1154 - 1189)
Married
Eleanor of Aquitane
Niece of William the Conqueror

King Richard 1st.
"Coeur de Lion"
(Reigned 1189 - 1199)

Kind John (Reigned 1199 - 1216)
Married
Lady Isobella of Glamorgan

Henry 3rd. (Reigned 1216 - 1272)
Married
Eleanor of Provence

Edward 1st. (Reigned 1272 - 1307)
Married
Margaret of France (Daughter of Phillip 3rd)

Edward 2nd. (Reigned 1307 - 1327 Murdered)
Married
Isabella of France

Edward 3rd. (Reigned 1327 - 1377)
Married
Philipa of Hainault

John of Gaunt Duke of Lancaster
Married
Kathryn Swynford (Died 1403)

John Marquis of Somerset (Died 1401)

*Gruffydd AP Nicholas*

Harding Son of Eadmoth (1096 - 1170)

Robert Fitzharding
Married
Eva Daughter of Stestmond & Godwa

Maurice De Berkley (died 1190)
Married
Alice De Berkley

Thomas De Berkley (Died 1245)
Married
Joan De Somery

Maurice De Berkley (Died1231)
Married
Isabel Daughter of Maurice De Reoun

Lord Thomas Berkley
Married
Joan De Ferrars

Lord Maurice Berkley 3rd. (Died 1326)
Married
Eva La Zouch

Margaret Daughter of Lord Lisle

Lord Thomas Berkley (Died 1361)
Married
Margaret Mortimer Daughter of Roger Mortimer Earl of March

Elizabeth Berkley
Married
Richard Beauchamp
5th. Earl of Warwick

Richard Neville
Earl of Warwick, The King Maker

Anne Nevilla
Married
Riachrd 3rd.

Katherryn
Married
William Herbert
Earl of Pembroke

*Iestyn AP Gwrgant Arms (1068)*

*Walter Thomas Arms (1653)*

## STUARTS

Margaret Tudor (1489 - 1541)
Married
King James 4th. Scotland

James 5th. Scotland (1514 - 1542)
Married
1st. Madeline (Died 15370
Daughter of Frances 1st. King of France
2nd. Mary of Lorraine (Died 1560)
Daughter of Claude Duke of Guise

Mary Queen of Scots (Executed 1587)
Married
1st. Francis Dauphin of France
2nd. Henry Stuart Lord Darnley
(Murdered 1567)

James 1st. (James 6th. of Scotland) (1567 - 1625)
Who became first Sovereign of England of the House of Stuart (1603 - 1625)
Married
Anne (Died 1619)
Daughter of Frederick 2nd. King of Denmark

Charles 1st. (1625 - 1649 Beheaded)
Married
Henrietta Maria (Died 1669)
Daughter of Henry 4th. King of France

Charles 2nd. (Reigned 1649 - 1685)
(In Exile 1649-1650)
(1650 - 1660)
Married
Catherine of Braganza (Died 1705)
Daughter of John 4th. King of Portugal

Henry Tudor VIII
Royal Arms (1485)

## TUDORS

John Beaufort (Died 1444)
Duke of Somerset

Margaret Beaufort
Married
Edmund Tudor Earl of Richmond

Kind Henry 7th. (Died 1509)
Married
Elizabeth of York (Died 1503)

King Henry 8th.
Married
Anne Boleyn (Executed 1536)

Elizabeth 1st. (Died 1603)

Edmund Duke of Somerset
Married
Eleanor Beauchamp

Henry Duke of Somerset
Married
Eleanor Beauchamp Daughter of

Charles Somerset 1st. Earl of Worcester
Married
Elizabeth Herbert Daughter of

Henry Herbert 2nd. Earl of Worcester
Married
Elizabeth Daughter of Sir. Anthony Brown

Lady Jane Somerset
Married
Sir Edward Mansel (1531 - 1585)

Sir. Thomas Mansel
Married
Mary Daughter of Lord Mordaunt

Arthur Mansel (2nd. Son) of Britton Ferry
Married
Jane Pryse Daughter of William Pryse
of Ynysmaerdy Britton Ferry
Direct Descendant of Iestyn AP Gwrgant

*Willam Le Maunsell (1287)
(Le Mans France)
First of the Mansels*

*William Thomas (1665)
Catherine Mansel (1669)*

*Hopkin (Popkins) David Edward
of Dan-y-Graig and Ynysdawe
(1626)*

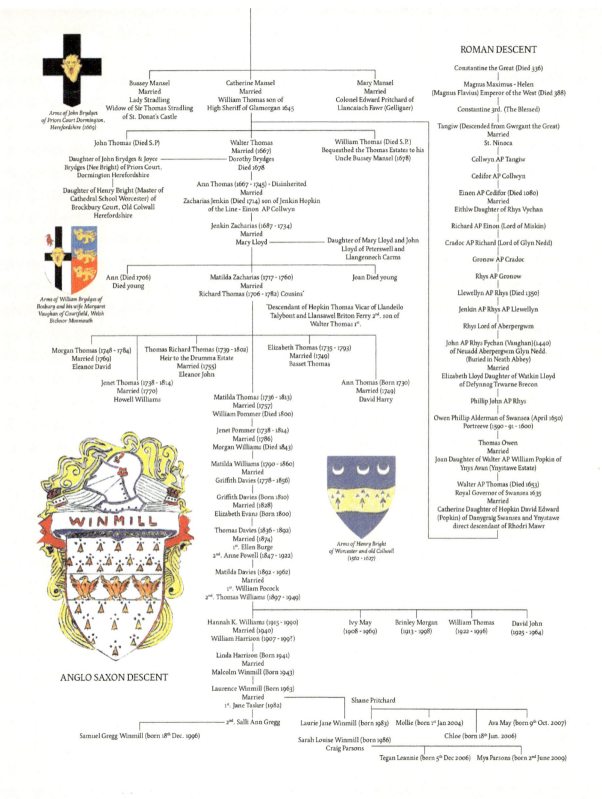

ROMAN DESCENT

Arms of John Brydges of Priors Court Dormington, Herefordshire (1669)

Bussey Mansel
Married
Lady Stradling
Widow of Sir Thomas Stradling
of St. Donat's Castle

Catherine Mansel
Married
William Thomas son of
High Sheriff of Glamorgan 1645

Mary Mansel
Married
Colonel Edward Pritchard of
Llancaiach Fawr (Gelligaer)

Constantine the Great (Died 336)

Magnus Maximus - Helen
(Magnus Flavius) Emperor of the West (Died 388)

Constantine 3rd. (The Blessed)

John Thomas (Died S.P)

Daughter of John Brydges & Joyce
Brydges (Nee Bright) of Priors Court,
Dormington Herefordshire

Daughter of Henry Bright (Master of
Cathedral School Worcester) of
Brockbury Court, Old Colwall
Herefordshire

Walter Thomas
Married (1667)
Dorothy Brydges
Died 1678

William Thomas (Died S.P.)
Bequeathed the Thomas Estates to his
Uncle Bussey Mansel (1678)

Tangiw (Descended from Gwrgant the Great)
Married
St. Ninoca

Collwyn AP Tangiw

Cedifor AP Collwyn

Ann Thomas (1667 - 1745) - Disinherited
Married
Zacharias Jenkin (Died 1714) son of Jenkin Hopkin
of the Line - Einon - AP Collwyn

Einon AP Cedifor (Died 1080)
Married
Eithlw Daughter of Rhys Vychan

Jenkin Zacharias (1687 - 1734)
Married
Mary Lloyd

Daughter of Mary Lloyd and John
Lloyd of Peterswell and
Llangennech Carms

Richard AP Einon (Lord of Miskin)

Cradoc AP Richard (Lord of Glyn Nedd)

Arms of William Brydges of
Bosbury and his wife Margaret
Vaughan of Courtfield, Welsh
Bicknor Monmouth

Ann (Died 1706)
Died young

Matilda Zacharias (1717 - 1760)
Married
Richard Thomas (1706 - 1782) Cousins*

Joan Died young

Gronow AP Cradoc

Rhys AP Gronow

*Descendant of Hopkin Thomas Vicar of Llandeilo
Talybont and Llansawel Briton Ferry 2nd. son of
Walter Thomas 1st.

Llewellyn AP Rhys (Died 1350)

Jenkin AP Rhys AP Llewellyn

Rhys Lord of Aberpergwm

Morgan Thomas (1748 - 1784)
Married (1769)
Eleanor David

Thomas Richard Thomas (1739 - 1802)
Heir to the Drumma Estate
Married (1755)
Eleanor John

Elizabeth Thomas (1735 - 1793)
Married (1749)
Basset Thomas

John AP Rhys Fychan (Vaughan)(1440)
of Neuadd Aberpergwm Glyn Nedd.
(Buried in Neath Abbey)
Married
Elizabeth Lloyd Daughter of Watkin Lloyd
of Defynnog Trwarne Brecon

Jenet Thomas (1738 - 1814)
Married (1770)
Howell Williams

Ann Thomas (Born 1730)
Married (1749)
David Harry

Matilda Thomas (1736 - 1813)
Married (1757)
William Pommer (Died 1800)

Phillip John AP Rhys

Owen Phillip Alderman of Swansea (April 1650)
Portreeve (1590 - 91 - 1600)

Jenet Pommer (1738 - 1814)
Married (1786)
Morgan Williams (Died 1843)

Thomas Owen
Married
Joan Daughter of Walter AP William Popkin of
Ynys Avan (Ynystawe Estate)

Matilda Williams (1790 - 1860)
Married
Griffith Davies (1778 - 1856)

Walter AP Thomas (Died 1653)
Royal Governor of Swansea 1635
Married
Catherine Daughter of Hopkin David Edward
(Popkin) of Danygraig Swansea and Ynystawe
direct descendant of Rhodri Mawr

Griffith Davies (Born 1810)
Married (1828)
Elizabeth Evans (Born 1800)

Thomas Davies (1836 - 1892)
Married (1874)
1st. Ellen Burge
2nd. Anne Powell (1847 - 1922)

Arms of Henry Bright
of Worcester and old Collwell
(1562 - 1627)

Matilda Davies (1892 - 1962)
Married
1st. William Pocock
2nd. Thomas Williams (1897 - 1949)

Hannah K. Williams (1915 - 1990)
Married (1940)
William Harrison (1907 - 199?)

Ivy May
(1908 - 1969)

Brinley Morgan
(1913 - 1998)

William Thomas
(1922 - 1996)

David John
(1925 - 1964)

WINMILL

Linda Harrison (Born 1941)
Married
Malcolm Winmill (Born 1943)

Laurence Winmill (Born 1963)
Married
1st. Jane Tasker (1982)

Shane Pritchard

ANGLO SAXON DESCENT

2nd. Salli Ann Gregg

Laurie Jane Winmill (born 1983)

Mollie (born 1st Jan 2004)

Ava May (born 9th Oct. 2007)

Samuel Gregg Winmill (born 18th Dec. 1996)

Sarah Louise Winmill (born 1986)
Craig Parsons

Chloe (born 18th Jun. 2006)

Tegan Leannie (born 5th Dec 2006)

Mya Parsons (born 2nd June 2009)

# The Quest

Malcolm Winmill

*For Matilda Williams (1892 – 1962) who retold the story to her granddaughter, Linda, and kept it alive.*

# CONTENTS

# PROLOGUE

**WHEN MALCOLM WINMILL WED LINDA HARRISON**, daughter of Hannah K. Williams and William Harrison, he simply did not anticipate the dynasty that he was marrying into.

Linda's maiden name and her seemingly ordinary life gave no clue of her descendants' tragically true journey from kings and princes to paupers. Upon closer inspection much later in Malcolm's retirement, a partly buried paper trail going back to Constantine the Great, Roman Emperor from 306 to 337 AD of Thracian-Illyrian ancestry, and cataloguing figures that we thought only existed on the pages of history books, was collated, thus beginning a journey that uncovered a family history dipped in deceit, murder, missing millions and mystery – an unfortunate story that has, despite many family members' vain efforts across the centuries to uncover the truth and expose the frauds at the very top of the food chain, no fairy tale ending.

Whilst many of the hundreds of thousands of people who call Wales their home have traced back their family history through several generations, Malcolm simply wasn't prepared for what he exposed on that fateful day in 1993 when he began his quest, an expedition that many of Linda's ancestors that are now long gone looked to finish and that was, for Malcolm, set to continue right up until the present day.

*This book is based on facts researched by myself between 1993 and 1998, and also those relayed to my wife, Linda, by her grandmother Matilda Williams (née Davies) from 1891 to 1962.*

Malcolm Winmill

Matilda Williams

# 1. A BRIEF HISTORY OF ANCESTRY

**TO SAY THE THOMAS FAMILY** and its descendants had no shortage of famous (or even infamous) names in its ranks is something of an understatement. A family originating from Norman and Roman descent, their bloodline can be traced all the way back to Robert II (better known as 'The Devil'), Duke of Normandy, who died in 1035, and even further back for their Roman ancestors with Constantine the Great starting proceedings.

Whilst the story we are about to explore in the succeeding chapters centres on one Walter Thomas I, an important man in his own right, to ignore the great names and key figures born before this point would be somewhat inexcusable…

The history relating to the Thomases of Danygraig has been documented across many publications, however this extract from The History and Antiquities of Glamorganshire and its Families by Thomas Nicholas in a chapter aptly entitled 'Old and Extinct Families of Glamorgan' offers an insightful overview.

*Thomas of Danygraig.* — Members of this family married with Mansels of Briton-Ferry, Middletons of Middleton Hall, Carm.; but they were of short continuation at Danygraig, having become extinct early in the 18th century. They traced their lineage, according to "J. H.'s" MS., from Einion ap Collwyn through *Owen Philip*, Portreeve of Swansea, 1600, eldest son of Philip John ap Rhys of Glyn-Nedd. In the fourth generation from

Owen, Walter Thomas *m.* Catherine, dau. of Hopkin David Edward of *Danygraig*, and had issue William, his successor, who *m.* Catherine, dau. of Arthur Mansel, Esq., of Briton-Ferry. William had several daus. and two sons, Walter and William, both of whom a. s. p., but the younger, the survivor," gave all his estate, except the customary lands in the parish of Oystermouth, to his uncle, Bussy Mansel, Esq , of Briton-Ferry, his mother's brother." It seems that William Thomas, sen., son-in-law of Arthur Mansel, was, like many of the Mansels, of strong royalist sentiments, and "suffered much for his loyalty to King Charles I. He was obliged to sell part of his estate at Llandilo-Talybont, which consisted of fee-farms, in order to prevent its being sequestered in those troublesome times, and retired to Carmarthen, where he lived some years, and then returned to Swansea. He lies buried in the south aisle of the church there, and has a handsome large monument [now gone] erected to his memory. — J. H.

The arms borne by Thomas of Danygraig, according to "J. H.'s" MS., were — *Sa., a chevron hetiveen three fteurs de lis arg.* If so, the arms of *Collwyn* ap Tangiw, of North Wales, must have been adopted by mistake for Einion ap *Collwyn*, the real ancestor.

Alongside evidence presented in the above extract, Constantine the Great is of course an inspiring name to begin with. The 57th Emperor of the Roman Empire, Constantine I, also known as Saint Constantine by the Orthodox Church, ruled from 306 AD until his death. The son of Flavius Valerius Constantius, a Roman army officer who became Caesar, deputy emperor in the west, in 293 AD, it seemed that his military roots meant that he too was destined for greatness from a very young age. Once of age, Constantine was sent east, where he rose through the ranks to become a military

CCXXXVI.

Against the South Wall of the South Isle under a —
figure in kneeling posture is seen the following inscription in
a marble pane and lines of Gold Roman Capitals. The monu=
ment also carryeth these Armes.

M.    S.

GULIELMI THOMAS ARMIGERI QVI SVB CER=
TA SPE FŒLICITER RESVRGENDI IVXTA REQVIESCIT
SACRIS REGVM CAROL PATRIS ET FILII STVDIIS
BELLO PLVSQVAM CIVILI SEMPER ADHÆSERAT
NECNON ECCLESIÆ MVNIFICVS LITERARVM ERAT
MECÆNAS
MORVM MODO NON DEERAT PROBITAS
ACHATES IN AMICITIA PACIFICVS PATERFAMILIAS
NVLLI SECVNDVS
LASCIVÆ DENIQ. LINGVÆ ELENCHVS ACERRIM⁹
DVXERAT VXOREM CATHERINAM IIᵈᵃᵐ FILIAM
ARTHVR MANSEL DE BRITON FERRY ARMIG.
E QVA PVLCHRAM ~~PROLEM~~ ET BONÆ INDOLIS
SVSCITAVIT PROLEM
OBIIT III DIE IVNII AN. SAL. MDCLXV
ET ÆTAT. S. LVIII
CATH.  C. M. P.

The next pane of marble hath also this. in Rom. Cap.

GVLIELMVS THOMAS ARMIG HIC SITVS EST
KIND READER VNDERNEATH DOTH LIE
THE TRVE PATTERN OF COVRTESIE
A LOVER OF KING CHVRCH AND LAWS
OF A SOVND PEACE THE PROPER CAVSE

CCXXXV.

Fixt to the uppermost Pillar are seen the following armes and In=
scription on marble ab in Roman capitall Character.

The paternau Coat here
shews the Field Or A
Stagg Tripping attired
and Ungulled Gules, in
a Bordure engrailed of
the second.
The Hart born in Arms
by th UPTON betokeneth
sometimes one skill'd in Mu=
sick, or such an one as delights
in Harmony:

This may be one reason for
the guise of this Coat Armor
to the name of DAVID
It sets forth also a wary ma
One unwilling to assayle an E=
nemy rashly, but rather de=
sirous to stand on his own
guard honestly than annoy
another wrongfully.

CONSECRATED
TO THE PIOVS MEMORY OF HOPKIN DAVID
ESQ DECEASED NOV ANNO DOM. MDCXXVI
ÆTAT. SVÆ LXXVII

MARVAIL NOT READER THOUGH THOU DOST SEE
This shrine so much frequented be
The Reliques of a Saynt here lye
Who spent his dayes in Piety
The Poor here come and rayse their cry
To feele their almes deeds with him die
His Freinds his Country do lament
Their Loss in him & here present
Their Tears and all Good men beside
Do weep to see how Virtue died
Then give me leave though I be but stone
To bear a part in such a publick mone

STORMS OF LAW SUITS HIS POWER LAID
THE COSTS AND DAMAGES HE PAID
FAVOVRER OF ARTS THIS WISHT, THE GRIM
DEVOVRING DEATH HAD FAVOVR'D HIM

These 4 last lines
conclude the In=
scription of the
next monument.

Copy of 'Mansel / Thomas coat of arms'
Source: Account of The Official Progress of his Grace, Henry The 1st Duke of Beaufort Through Wales in 1684.

tribune under the emperors Diocletian and Galerius before being awarded the position of Augustus, senior western emperor, in 305 AD. He was subsequently recalled to the west to campaign under his father in Britannia.

During his reign as emperor, Constantine enacted many administrative, financial, social and military reforms to strengthen the Empire, many of which were utilised long after his death. The government was restructured to separate the civil and military authorities, whilst a new gold coin, the 'solidus', was introduced to combat inflation. This coin, unbeknown to Constantine, would become the standard for Byzantine and European currencies for more than a thousand years. In regards to religion, Constantine was the first Roman emperor to claim conversion to Christianity and as a result played an influential role in the proclamation of the Edict of Milan in 313 AD, which decreed tolerance for Christianity throughout the Roman Empire.

His relationship with religion is a primary point of discussion in many historical texts, as this extract from the Encyclopaedia Britannica explores:

Throughout his life, Constantine ascribed his success to his conversion to Christianity and the support of the Christian God. The triumphal arch erected in his honour at Rome after the defeat of Maxentius ascribed the victory to the "inspiration of the Divinity" as well as to Constantine's own genius. A statue set up at the same time showed Constantine himself holding aloft a cross and the legend "By this saving sign I have delivered your city from the tyrant and restored liberty to the Senate and people of Rome." After his victory over Licinius in 324, Constantine wrote that he had come from the farthest shores of Britain as God's chosen instrument for the suppression of impiety, and in a letter to the Persian king Shapur II he proclaimed that, aided by the divine power of God, he had come to bring peace and prosperity to all lands.

Constantine's adherence to Christianity was closely associated with his rise to power.

Yet to suggest that Constantine's conversion was "politically motivated" means little in an age in which every Greek or Roman expected that political success followed from religious piety. The civil war itself fostered religious competition, each side enlisting its divine support, and it would be thought in no way unusual that Constantine should have sought divine help for his claim for power and divine justification for his acquisition of it. What is remarkable is Constantine's subsequent development of his new religious allegiance to a strong personal commitment.

Whilst his conversion seemed to aid his early career, it was his military prowess and season in battle that saw him quash two rebellions, the first by Maxentius, which erupted with a Civil War, and the second by Maximian. The latter was, three years later, depicted on a coin or gold multiple entitled 'Unconquered Constantine.'

The legacy that earned him the honorific of 'The Great' wasn't the result of his military achievements and victories alone, he was responsible for unifying the Roman Empire during his early rule and later in his reign, and ultimately reunited the provinces that had previously remained separate under one emperor.

Constantine the Great was by no means the only key figure to feature on the Thomas family tree, following him was Magnus Maximus, Western Roman Emperor from 383 to 388 AD; Constantine III 'The Blessed', Roman general and self-declared Western Roman Emperor for Britannia in 407 AD; and Tangiw, a descendant of Gwrgan Fawr (or Gwrgan the Great), the King of Ergyng, a south-east Welsh kingdom of the early medieval period. Kings, lords and princes are

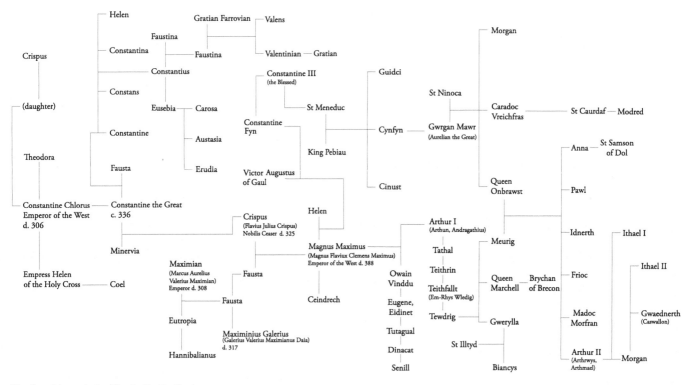

**Timeline of descendants of Constantine the Great.**

referred to from the very beginning of the bloodline with the family's connection to Iestyn ap Gwrgant, the last ruler of the Welsh kingdom of Morgannwg (now known as the counties of Glamorgan and Monmouthshire), particularly prominent.

As last ruler, Iestyn's lineage can be traced back over five centuries, spanning from the 6th century Welsh saint and king of the post-Roman Kingdom of Glywysing, Tewdrig. Despite ruling for little less than a decade, Iestyn's reign saw the building of castles throughout Cardiff and Kenfig, but he was eventually overcome by Norman invasion as following a dispute with rival Einion ap Collwyn, he invited Norman ruler Robert Fitzhamon, Lord of Gloucester, and his 12 knights to Morgannwg, who in 1090 unseated him. The Lord of Gloucester went on

to establish a lordship in Cardiff, and in time, conquered the Vale of Glamorgan (then known as the lowlands of Glamorgan), whilst the mountainous areas of the region were left in Welsh control. Ironically Caradog ap Iestyn, the eldest son of Iestyn ap Gwrgant, was the only Welsh lord to retain lands in the Glamorgan lowlands after Fitzhamon had conquered them.

As well as having links to other royal houses throughout Wales and Saint Tewdrig, Iestyn was also a descendant of the legendary Rhodri Mawr. The father of Catherine and father-in-law to Walter Thomas I, Hopkin David Edwards was a direct descendant of Rhodri Mawr (Rhodri AP Merfyn), later known as Rhodri the Great. Rhodri succeeded his father Merfyn Frych as King of Gwynedd in 844, and during

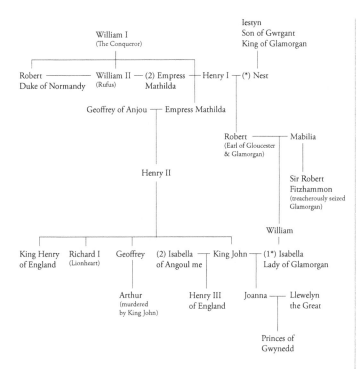

**THE NORMANS IN WALES AFTER 1091**

*The Welsh/English marriages conducted under the auspices of the Welsh Church were not recognised by the Roman Church and were therefore regarded illegitimate. Any offspring were also considered to be illegitimate. These opinions of the Bishops of Rome carried no weight in Wales itself.

King Henry of England, son of Henry II, was crowned by the Archbishop of York and ruled over England for twenty-two years whilst his father was busy in France. The Church also later ignored him, as he had the rebellious Thomas Becket killed.

his reign earned the reputation and the nickname 'King of the Britons', later in history, Rhodri is even referred to as 'King of Wales', however, in this instance it is important to note that his realm did not include southern Wales. As King, Rhodri is coined as being the master of much of modern Wales, a progression that he was able to make even in the face of pressure from the English, Vikings and Danish. He had always had an unsteady relationship with the latter, and it is thought that an event, which saw the Danish ravage Anglesey

in 854, lent inspiration to his notable victory two years later where their leader Gorm the Old, the first historically recognised King of Denmark, was killed by Rhodri's own hand. The following excerpt from The Castles of Wales reveals more about Rhodri's rule, his objective to create a unified Welsh state and the challenges he faced from the opposition:

> Rhodri's fame sprang from his success as a warrior. That success was noted by *The Ulster Chronicle* and by Sedulius Scottus, an Irish scholar at the court of the Emperor Charles the Bald at Liege. It was his victory over the Vikings in 856 which brought him international acclaim. Wales was less richly provided with fertile land and with the navigable rivers that attracted the Vikings, and the Welsh kings had considerable success in resisting them. Anglesey bore the brunt of the attacks, and it was there in 856 that Rhodri won his great victory over Horn, the leader of the Danes, much to the delight of the Irish and the Franks.

> It was not only from the west that the kingdom of Rhodri was threatened. By becoming the ruler of Powys, his mother's land, he inherited the old struggle with the kingdom of Mercia. Although Offa's Dyke had been constructed in order to define the territories of the Welsh and the English, this did not prevent the successors of Offa from attacking Wales.

Rhodri's reign was evidently not an easy one due to these pressures, and despite Rhodri being at the helm of many victories, it was at the Battle of Sunday in Anglesey in 873 that saw his demise according to the Chronicle of the Princes (Brut y Tywysogion), one of the most important primary sources of Welsh history.

Despite his connections to Rhodri Mawr's line, Hopkin David Edwards was a powerful man in his own right. A one-time Portreeve of Swansea, Hopkin's death in 1626

Seal of Richard de Clare, Earl of Glamorgan.
The shield was the same used in the Arms of Iestyn ap Gwrgant, excluding the lions.
Source: T. Nicholas, The History and Antiquities of Glamorganshire and its Families

saw a bevy of property and lands passed on to his children, including residences in Goat Street, Wind Street and Castle Street. It was Hopkin David Edward's prominence that saw the Hopkin (Popkin) family of Danygraig become one of the most significant families in Swansea, and the subject of detailed research years later, and more recently one of the subjects of Medieval Swansea, a project that was screened on BBC Wales News in 2014 and saw the city's history brought back to life.

The family's connection to Sir Rhys ap Thomas is also worth noting, as whilst this is descended through the female line, his prominence in the 15th and early 16th century saw him play a key role in the Wars of the Roses in Wales. During this time Sir Rhys remained loyal to and was an instrumental part of the victory of Henry Tudor, also known as Henry VII, at the Battle of Bosworth – rumour has it that he even delivered the deadly blow that killed King Richard

III – a position that saw him rewarded with lands and offices throughout South Wales.

Rhys' special relationship with Henry Tudor was documented in Sir Rhys AP Thomas and His Family: A Study in the Wars of the Roses and Early Tudor Politics by Ralph A. Griffiths:

The accession of Henry Tudor heralded a revolution in Rhys ap Thomas's fortunes in Wales and offered him a prominent role on an even broader front in Tudor service. It is sometimes said that Henry VII failed to fulfil the promise made to Rhys before Bosworth that the Welshman would become 'chief gouernour of Wales', and enjoy its 'perpetuall lyvetenantship.' Yet apart from the king's own uncle, Jasper Tudor, no one received such commanding authority in large parts of Wales as Rhys did, and he, like Jasper, normally resided in south Wales and therefore took full opportunity to exercise his new powers. The chroniclers who recorded the king's promise also acknowledged this reality when they noted that Henry 'afterward when he had obtanyd the kingdom he gave liberally to Rhys.' Throughout his reign, Henry VII appreciated unswerving loyalty and he retained a particularly strong attachment to those who had sustained him in or before 1485. To expect a king who shrank from creating new peers to have ennobled his steadfast Welsh squire on Bosworth Field is unrealistic. To expect him to have conferred on Rhys the kind of all-embracing power in Wales and the English borderland that Henry Stafford, duke of Buckingham, enjoyed briefly under Richard III is to ignore the obligations which Henry owed to others with interests in Wales – his uncle Jasper and his stepfather, Thomas, Lord Stanley, amongst them – as well as the reluctance of a circumspect new king to follow the precedent of Buckingham's extraordinary commission. In these contexts, it would seem that Rhys ap Thomas had good reason to be content with his treatment after 1485.

Rhys demonstrated his continuing loyalty to Henry by suppressing a Yorkist rebellion at Brecon in 1486, and taking part in the campaign against the pretender Lambert Simnel in 1487 as well as assisting with the subsequent campaigns against Perkin Warbeck. As in the Battle of Bosworth, his loyalty was continually rewarded, and in addition to procuring lands and offices as mentioned before, he was Constable and Lieutenant of Breconshire, Chamberlain of Carmarthenshire and Cardiganshire, Seneschall and Chancellor of Haverfordwest, Rouse and Builth, Justiciar of South Wales, and Governor of all Wales.

Rhys married twice, and was known to have several mistresses, however his only legitimate son, Gruffydd ap Rhys ap Thomas, pre-deceased him in 1521. Sir Rhys ap Thomas died in 1525, and his estates and offices were bequeathed to his grandson and heir, Rhys ap Gruffydd, before being taken by the Crown and given to Lord Ferrers after the aforementioned was accused and beheaded for treason by Henry VIII in 1531.

# 2. WALTER THOMAS I

**WHILST IT IS THE FAMILY'S** impressive ancestry that really commandeers the headlines, the real story – which is, we remind you, factual and based on many years of research – begins in the 17th century and centres on one Walter Thomas of Swansea.

Walter Thomas I was a powerful and prominent figure in the creation of what many in those days referred to as the making of 'Modern Wales', a country that until now was the stomping ground of Welsh gentry and upstarts, a premise central to this story as the hunt for lands and titles, and the desecration of any prey or person that stood in their way, became not just a part of what shaped society into the country we know today but everyday life for Walter Thomas' descendants. Walter Thomas himself was a descendant of John AP Rhys, Lord of Glyn-Nedd, and whilst his own timeline came to an end in 1653 at his residence in Danygraig St Thomas, Swansea, his life events sent ripples far into the future, repercussions that determined the fate of family members alive today and those deceased.

Trade was important to the Welsh economy from rather early in history, even today the Port of Swansea has a capacity to handle cargo weighing more than 30,000 DWT, and whilst the capabilities of the port weren't always this wide ranging, Walter was integral to the development of the early docks towards the close of the 16$^{th}$ century. As with more developed ports, trade in Swansea was seasonal, and due to the dark nights and short days of the autumn/winter months (from November to February inclusive) operations were in bulk confined to summertime when conditions were more favourable for those at sea and on land. Despite its underdevelopment the Port of Swansea was still frequented by ships from importing ports and local harbours, the Jonas of Swansea for example, which had a 40 ton capacity, made half a dozen round trips from Swansea to Rochelle between 1587 and 1588. During this time, long before Walter was named portreeve, the coal pits, which were small in size compared to those documented much later during the Industrial Revolution, were able to cater to the demand presented by the increasingly busy port. One factor that meant supply met demand was the coal pits' proximity to the sea, and even during a time when mining technology was rudimentary, coal could be mined and transported easily by water, a fact that cut out problematic and primitive road transit. It was during this time that the Thomases of Danygraig alongside the Mansels of Margam put their cards on the table to become prominent family names associated with mining.

Walter's work on the docks and quays assigned him a reputation for being forceful in character and, more definitively, a man of local influence. Walter's fervour was another trait well celebrated in the limited edition publication *History of the Port of Swansea* by W.H. Jones, as this extract details:

> Possessing a breezy enthusiasm in municipal affairs with which he managed to inspire the records of the Corporation throughout his long life. We would like to relate all that this prominent man did for his native town, but that must be recorded elsewhere.

> Walter Thomas – who signed his Christian name 'Wallter' – comes upon the scene in relation to the harbour during the years of his portreevalty, 1615-16. The minutes of the proceedings of his year in office are recorded in the town books in his own clerkly handwriting, which

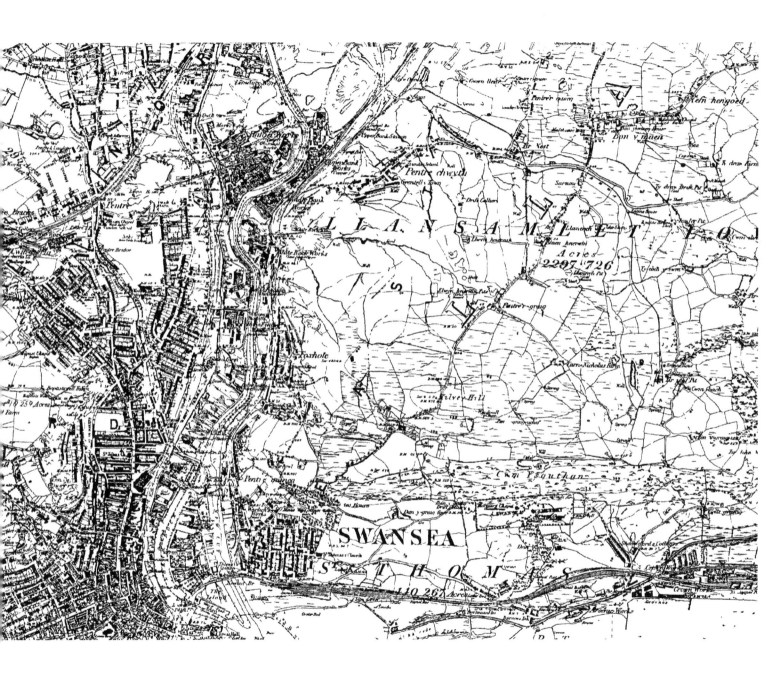

distinguishes him as a man of unusual education.

This extract relates to the summary uncovered in the Book of Orders, an account of his undertakings and achievements that very much directly relates to the model used by the borough officials following him.

Walter's interest in the harbour, its development and subsequently the future of Swansea was no secret locally however, but despite his zeal the accounts found in the Book of Orders weren't particularly lengthy, a fact that many historians had wished were otherwise. An entry made on 30 May 1616 however shows particular promise and reveals Walter's eagerness for advancing the town into the modern age through trade.

> The daie and yeare aboue written the newe Keye lyinge Right over against the store house of Robert Phillips, yt was begone to be made and builded by me Wallter Thomas, Portreve for the tyme beinge of the sayde towne of Swanzy, and by the consent and assent of the aldermen and burgesses of the sayd towne. The charge of what was builded now at the begininge, in this my yeare, came to seven pounds and twoe shillings, and I hope yt he w'ch shall succeede me in my office will be ameanes [amenable or agreeable] yt this good woorke, beinge begoone, shall be sett forewards and finished
>
> p'me Wallter Thomas, portrefe

The build of the new quay was necessary to the progression of trade in the Port of Swansea, especially as the existing quay, the second of its kind for the docks, had fallen into disrepair in 1597. The dock and the influx of trade had since suffered and for a man so heavily involved in the transport of coal from his own works and the trading of other prized materials, such as feathers and wool, the lack of provisions available for discharging and unloading were more than just a concerning town affair.

During his year as portreeve, Walter made it his business to erect a new quay and even did so at his own expense, a concept unheard of until his time in office. Whilst the brief Book of Orders extract confirms this, what it doesn't tell you is that Walter actually owned the land in and around the new quay, named locally as 'The Mount', at the bottom of Wind Street. His determination to reposition Swansea as a leader in maritime trade, ahead of the Bristol Channel and the south coast of England, is revealed across a number of accounts.

Over the next two years, work continued on the quay at the portreeves' own cost with large expenditure detailed as late as 1619. Unfortunately after this date the fate of the quay would be left as before in the hands of succeeding portreeves, who, as history explains, did not have the same passion or acumen as Walter, and the portreeves that served and developed the quay at their own expense, regarding the advancement of the port. That's why for many the development of Swansea as a major port resumed during the early 18th century, a whole two centuries after Walter Thomas' early regime, when the expansion of local coal mining and iron production, teamed with the introduction of new and more innovative smelting and tinplate manufacturing techniques, forced the port to expand its capabilities and provide more permanent harbour facilities. Even in the first half of the 17th century however, thanks to Walter's efforts to develop the quay and wider port, the Port of Swansea was making a name for itself as the 1990 book Swansea: An Illustrated History by Glanmor Williams reveals:

> In Oliver Cromwell's charter to the town, he could refer to it with more than a little pride as 'an ancient port town and populous, situate on the sea-coasts towards France, convenient for shipping and resisting foreign invasions.' For a century beforehand the municipal authorities had been paying more minute attention to the state of the harbour and the welfare of shipping. Careful

regulations had been laid down for the repair of the quay and the disposal of ballast so that the waterways should not become cluttered up. Enterprising individuals like Walter Thomas of Danygraig had been engaged on improving the quay and building small docks.

Despite as previously mentioned Walter's successors not having the same level of enthusiasm for the improvement of Swansea as a trade influencer, the new quay was finished in 1652, one year before his death, with the quay the subject of numerous repairs and extensions in subsequent years. The completion of the quay, and the construction of the graving dock some years earlier, saw, as Walter had predicted and hoped for, a growth in trade with the marked increase resulting in the resurgence of riverside activity, such as boat and shipping building. Commerce traditional to the Middle Ages – i.e. salt, wine, corn, fruit and fine cloth – could be imported in bulk, whilst the improved amenities meant that products made in South Wales, such as butter, cheese, hides,

Maces secured by Walter Thomas 1st, 1615.
Photograph by Ken Dickinson 2008. Glyn Vivian Art Gallery GVT1904.3

leather, wool, feathers and, more notably, coal, could be exported. Compared with the annual export of 3,000 tons of coal between 1591 and 1600, Swansea was now exporting more than 12,000 tons per year from 1631 to 1640, a four-fold increase. As supply increased so too did demand, and the status of Swansea as the coal capital of Wales would capture the crown's gaze also, particularly as the Civil Wars drew nearer.

There was no doubt that trade and the progression of his beloved Swansea was important, and as well as improving facilities at his own expense, Walter also invested in locally made goods even in rival trade city Bristol as this extract from the Glynn Vivian Art Gallery Collection shows:

> Maces are emblems of superior office to be carried before the Mayor in official processions and placed on the table at meetings. These silver maces were made in Bristol in 1615 at the instigation of the Portreeve, Walter Thomas. In the 'Common Hall Book' of Swansea Town records, Walter Thomas tells how he took the old 1573 silver maces to a goldsmith to be melted down and re-fashioned into a new pair at a cost of £4.1s.0d. (£4.05). Like the maces before and after, these were decorated with the town crest and the maces crossed behind it. The maces went missing after another set was made in 1752, but were rediscovered by George Grant Francis in 1840, repaired and returned to the Town Hall. The crowns surrounding the maces were removed at the time of Cromwell.

Walter Thomas wasn't just noted in history for his involvement in the development of trade at the Port of Swansea, he also held office as the Royal Governor of Swansea and High Sheriff of Glamorgan in 1635 under Charles I of England. The monarch of three kingdoms after he became heir apparent to the English, Irish and Scottish thrones following the death of his elder brother Henry Frederick, Prince of Wales, in 1612, Charles' and Walter's timelines would become intertwined and equally as damned with the approach of the Civil Wars. During his time as Royal Governor and High Sheriff, Walter owned large areas of

Sir Thomas Mansel 1st Baronet of Margam, and his wife Jane, 1625.
Artist: Unknown.
Image courtesy of Heritage Images.

Sir Thomas Mansel Baronet's tomb. He died in 1631.

land in Swansea, specifically in the Llansamlet and Neath Abbey wards, tracts which included some 24 dwellings in Wind Street as well as farm lands in Carmarthenshire, Cardiganshire and Breconshire.

His role as High Sheriff of Glamorgan was particularly notable. Sheriffs of Glamorgan, of which there was many between the 16th and 20th centuries, served under and were answerable to the independent Lords of Glamorgan, that is until this lordship merged with the crown. The Sheriffs were often compared with English shires, referred to as 'officers of the crown' throughout history. Due to their appointment by the crown this role, which was previously held by the likes of William Herbert of Cogan Pill and Sir Edward Stradling of

St Donat's Castle in the 16th century and Sir Thomas Mansel of Margam Abbey for a second term in the 17th century, witnessed a period of great unrest during the Civil Wars.

Whilst the Civil Wars are often referred to singularly as the 'English Civil War', tensions began to escalate between all parties long before mid-1642, when both sides began to arm and Charles I raised his army. Known as the 'Wars of the Three Kingdoms' conflicts across England, Ireland and Scotland from 1639 onwards would accumulate in the events of the Civil Wars and the concluding execution of the kingdoms' monarch by the English Parliament in 1649.

• • • • • •

## THE IRISH REBELLION AND DEMISE OF CHARLES I

Managing three separate kingdoms all of which had opposing views on both religion and the monarchy was of course not an easy task. Alongside battling with unpopularity overseas – Charles was initially part of an unsuccessful and detested attempt to marry him to a Spanish Habsburg princess which subsequently culminated in an eight month visit to Spain in 1623, a trip that demonstrated the futility of the marriage negotiations – on home soil his quarrelling with the Parliament of England meant that many were disillusioned shortly after his succession.

Believing in the divine right of kings, Charles, much to Parliament's disapproval, strongly thought that the three kingdoms should be governed by him, and him alone, a notion that the majority of Parliament and even the common people thought was the beginning of a tyrannical absolute monarch. Religion-wise Charles was also not currying any favour, his religious policies plus his marriage to a Roman Catholic, the Bourbon princess Henrietta Maria of France, planted the seeds of mistrust for many groups, including the Puritans and the Calvinists. During his early reign, Charles attempted to impose his religious policies in Scotland, which, despite being from Scotland, being born and spending all of his childhood there, were met by rebellion. It was across the Irish Sea, where the situation was most disaffected however.

A country already split into three socio-political groups – Gaelic Irish (Catholic), Old English (Catholic) and New English (Protestant) – Charles' support for the Catholics, along with his heavy-handed approach towards improving the Irish economy saw him and Strafford, Lord Deputy of Ireland, known more commonly as Charles' right-hand man, train a large army, which would both raise the royal standard and provide a juxtaposing authority to weaken the Irish Parliament, a process Charles had failed to achieve

**King Charles I (1600-1649) after Sir Anthony Van Dyck.
Image Courtesy of National Trust Images.**

in London. Despite his support of the Catholic, all three groups rallied against Charles and his imposing order, and Strafford's fall from the top cemented Charles' weakened, if not non-existent, influence. As a result there were a long list of disputes that led to the Irish Rebellion, but issues concerning the transfer of land ownership between native Catholics and Protestant settlers, namely those in relation to the plantation of Ulster, were the final nail in the coffin for Charles, both in Ireland and England, as this extract from the BCW Project shows:

The failure to capture Dublin turned what was intended to be a swift, bloodless coup into full-scale war. Sir Phelim O'Neill issued a proclamation declaring that the insurgents had taken up arms only for the defence and liberty of themselves and the native Irish; the insurgency was not intended to harm the King or any of his subjects. However, the resentment felt by the Ulster Irish against the settlers soon erupted into violence. Protestants were robbed and evicted from their lands, farms and houses were burnt, cattle stolen. As the violence escalated into widespread killing of settlers, a notorious massacre took place at Portadown in County Armagh in November 1641 where around 100 men, women and children were thrown off the bridge to drown in the River Bann.

Thousands of Protestant settlers were killed in the uprising and many fled as refugees to England. Reports of wholesale massacres and atrocities spread rapidly through England and Scotland, provoking fears of an international Popish conspiracy. At Westminster, John Pym used the situation to political advantage, implicating the King's ministers in the conspiracy and suggesting that the King himself was not to be trusted with control of the army that would be required to quell the rebellion.

The Irish Rebellion was no doubt a bloody chapter in the history of the country, and its existence cemented Parliament's and much of the nation's fears regarding Charles I. The situation following the Irish Rebellion quickly escalated with rumours circulating that Parliament even intended to arrest Charles' wife for supposedly conspiring with the Irish rebels, a move that led the king to take drastic action.

• • • • • •

Following the Irish rebellion in 1641, Charles begun to suspect that some members of the English Parliament, later named 'Roundheads', were plotting against him and colluding with the invading Scots. Five members in particular – Pym, John Hampden, Denzil Holles, William Strode and Sir Arthur Haselrig – and one peer – Lord Mandeville – were named on grounds of high treason, and Charles himself directed Parliament to give up these members, a request met by refusal. One botched arrest attempt later, Parliament was able to seize the capital with Charles fleeing to Hampton Court Palace and then to Windsor Castle as a result.

Charles I however was not about to remain in exile and after sending his wife and eldest daughter abroad to safety, Charles began his campaign, raising the royal standard in Nottingham and gaining control of Wales, alongside the Midlands, the West Country and northern England, whilst Parliament held London, the south east of England and East Anglia.

Walter's status as a rich merchant who exported iron to Bristol and agricultural by-products, including skins and feathers, plus his two terms serving as portreeve in 1615 and 1625, made him a key figure worthy of Charles I's attention. In search of men and money in his bid to regain control of the three kingdoms and overthrow the Parliament that had exiled him from the capital and many parts of the south of England, Charles gave Walter the right to mine for coal in certain areas of Swansea and Llangyfelach, estates recently sequestered from John Dorington, there were however conditions.

For every wey mined and sold by Walter, the King would receive 18d. It was no secret that Charles I's financial needs were extremely pressing during the first Civil War, in fact it was the King's main issue, and as a vehement supporter of the royalist cause, the county of Glamorgan assisted heavily by contributing some £1,000 to the war chest.

Whilst Charles' demand for money was met graciously, the royal demand for men – some 60 from Swansea, 20 from Llangyfelach and 40 from Neath – was met with rebellion. Once royalist, the town of Swansea was about to do a U-turn regardless of the inclination of leading aldermen or their lord, the Earl of Worcester. The Earls of Worcester were a major but declining source of influence when it came to Swansea's loyalty to the royal cause, as W.S.K. Thomas explains in this extract from *The History of Swansea*:

> Though the control which the family exercised over the town had been weakened by the early decades of the seventeenth century, it had by no means been completely removed. It was not in the best interests of the town to sever all connections with its lord, for he, and especially one like the Earl of Worcester who had considerable influence at Court, could do much to promote the prosperity of the borough. Thus, on the eve of the Civil War, the wishes of the Worcester family – especially as they would have been made known to the town through the deputy-steward Walter Thomas – while not a decisive force, perhaps, would certainly have weighed heavily in the determinations of the corporation.

At the start of the Civil Wars, the Earl of Worcester was Henry Somerset. Besides his title as the fifth Earl and first Marquis, the lord's Catholicism and staunch support of the royals saw him favour the King.

Both Walter and his son and heir, William Thomas, were High Sheriffs during this period, and the royal demand for men was quickly followed by a protest, however, it was in 1644 when Swansea was called to surrender by a parliamentary skip stationed in Milford Haven, that the High Sheriff and majority of the 'Gentlemen of Glamorganshire' cemented their status as royalists.

The summons, signed by Robert Moulton, read as follows:

To the Mayor and Gentlemen of Swansea

Gentlemen,

These are to will and require you, in the name of the Right Honourable Robert, Earl of Warwick, Lord High Admiral of England, Wales, and Ireland, and his Majesty's Navy Royal at Sea, that you forthwith yield the town and garrison into the obedience of the King and Parliament, and in so doing you shall be received into the protection and the associated Covenant, and shall be defended against all Irish rebels, Papists, and those who seek to subvert liberties, and to destroy religion, which, at this time, all the Papists and rebels in the three Kingdoms are in arms to overthrow.
Therefore, consider of it, and submit; for if you shall obstinate, and spill any blood in resisting, you may not expect such favour as your neighbours have had. And this is the advice of your friend, who endeavours to preserve you, if you accept of his proffer; if not, I shall endeavour to keep you without trade till your forced obedience bring you to the mercy of him that tendereth you grace and favour. I shall expect your answer by the bearer.

Rob(ert) Moulton

The call to surrender was met by rejection in the form of a letter, which had the names of its subscribers omitted, however according to W.S.K. Thomas' research it is safe to assume that among them would have been eminent barrister and judge, David Jenkins of Hensol (also known as 'The Judge of the Mountains'), Bussey (Bussy) Mansel of Briton Ferry and William Thomas of Danygraig.

The aforementioned letter went as follows:

To Robert Moulton, subscriber to the Paper directed to

the Mayor and Gentlemen of Swansea.

We cannot understand how we may, with any justice or loyalty, return you the name of gentleman to your rude and rebellious paper, in the front whereof you have the boldness and presumption, in the name of the right honourable (as you term him) (whom we do and must account a dishonourable and most insulting rebel) Robert, Earl of Warwick, (by you styled) High Admiral of England, Wales and Ireland, and his Majesty's Navy Royal at Sea (the which we do and ought to protest he hath most traitorously betrayed and rebelliously possessed) to will and require us forthwith to yield the town and garrison of Swansea into the obedience of the King and Parliament (a most foul treason, masked under a fair and specious show of a most loyal and just adherency and subjection to his Majesty and his Parliament at Oxford), in defiance of which, your traitorous summons, we send you this our fixed resolution, that we will neither yield town or garrison, nor any the least interest we hold of life or fortune (under the protection of his Sacred Majesty) but will defend the same and our county against your proud and insolent menacings (wherein your proper trade is exhibited), and in the account of a rebel and traitor we leave you to your fearful destruction.

Subscribed by the High Sheriff, and most of the Gentlemen of Glamorganshire.

Whilst no action was documented as being taken by Parliament in response to the refusal detailed in the letter above, despite Swansea's further celebrations during the defeat of Sir William Waller at Copredy Bridge near Banbury, the aftermath of the Civil Wars, the fall to power under Oliver Cromwell's Roundheads, and the trial and beheading of Charles I brought along a series of events that would set the course for both the Thomases of Danygraig and the Mansels

of Briton Ferry for centuries to come.

As one of the signatories of King Charles I's death warrant, Oliver Cromwell, an intensely religious man, self-styled Puritan Moses and Parliamentarian supporter was an instrumental figure in the fall of the royalist cause, and the subsequent sequestration of lands from Walter Thomas I and his son William Thomas. Due to the King's pressing needs across the border in England, Sir Charles Gerard, a professional solider and prominent figure in the defence of the royal cause was recalled, leaving Swansea perilously exposed. Cromwell's Roundheads took this as an opportunity to move against the local royalist leaders, and on 1 August 1645, the town shifted from being in royalist hands to that under Parliamentarian control. By mid-October of the same year, more royalists were cleared out of Pembrokeshire and then Carmarthen, and as forces advanced into Glamorgan, it was clear that the subscribers' insolent reply to the Moulton's summons would not be forgotten.

In Cromwell's eyes Walter and William, along with the Mansels, were, in one word, a problem, and whilst upon the defeat of Charles I and his forces co-conspirer Jenkins was imprisoned by Parliament from 1645 to 1660, the fates of the Mansels and Thomases were very different.

Under Oliver Cromwell's short lived reign as Commonwealth of England, William Thomas was firstly deprived of his status as alderman, one that had made him and his father figures of influence in Swansea and the rest of South Wales. Along with his title, William's estates were also sequestered. Custody of the castle held by Walter Thomas as part of his role as Royal Governor was taken and handed to Richard Donnell then to Philip Jones – the son of a farmer at Penywaun in Llangyfelach, Cromwellian governor of Swansea, and soon to be Comptroller of Cromwell's household and one of the most powerful figures in the whole of Glamorgan – upon his appointment to office by

Parliament as highlighted in the royalist composition papers relating to Glamorganshire, originally published in 1646, and republished on 13 October 1888.

No. 688 – WALTER THOMAS, OF SWANSEY, IN THE CO. OF GLAMORGAN, ESQ

His Delinquency : that he was Commissioner of array and Governor of Swansey Castle for the Kinge against the Parliament.

He had taken the National Covenant and Negative oath before the committee in the county as they certified. He compounded upon a particular sent up from the county and a second one delivered in under his own hand by which it appeared.

That he was seized in fee to him and his heirs in possession of and in certain lands and Tenements lying and being in Killybebill, Llangevelach, Oystermouth, Bushopston, Loughor, Lanridrian, Langenith, and Swanzey, in the co. of Glamorgan, and particularly expressed in the particular of his estate. The rents amounted to the yearly sum of £140 6s 8d. That he was also seized of a Frank tenement during the term of his life, the remainder in fee to Katherine, the wife of William Thomas, of and in certain other lands and tenements lying and being within the Manor of Kilway, in the said county, of the yearly value before the troubles of... £34.

The document continues to describe the value of Walter's estate, and proceeds to publicise, in detail, his humble petition.

Sheweth,

That about the beginning of theis wars and when the King ha considerable forces in ye country, the King appointed

**Weobley Castle, Llanrhidian. Home of Sir Rhys ap Thomas.**

**Portrait of Colonel Philip Jones of Fonmon Castle (about 50 at the time).**

Swansea Castle occupied by Royal Governor Walter Thomas 1635.

the petitioner a Commissioner of Array with others whom he freely acknowledgeth to have met and sat with upon ye said Comision concearninge that otherwise he might have exposed himselfe at that tyme to danger and ruine by the King's partie. That notwithstandige the said Commission, the peticoner did put noting in execution in ye said county besides his meetinge with the other Commrs as aforesaid, only hee ingeniously confesseth, that beinge made about the same time Governor of the Towne of Swansey he did arme and array ye inhabitants of ye Towne and none else besides, wherein heacknowledgeth his error, and offence, and with all submission craves pardon by ye Parliament having submitted himself before ye first of December to ye Parliament.

And therefore humbly prayeth you would be pleased to admit him to his composicon and in regard of his great weakness and age unable so much as to sturr in his bed without ye helpe of two; you would be pleased to be attended by some other in his behalf about ye making of his composicon.

And as touching his estate he humbly offereth to returne up a true particular thereof under his hand and therewith if yr honors think fit to have ye same certified by major Generall Laugharne or ye committee of ye country: he is ready to submit thereunto

And he shall pray, etc

WALTER THOMAS.

The sequestration of the estates was a common form of punishment during this period, as those deemed to be 'delinquents', royalists or even recusant Catholics (i.e. individuals who did not attend services of the Church of England) by Parliament were deprived of lands that had been in the family for generations before. Records of delinquent royalists and their lost fortunes are evidenced throughout various state papers kept in the National Archives, but no matter how unfound or unjust the punishment appeared to be, following the seizure of the estates, royalists and non-combatant Catholics did have rights, as would Walter and William Thomas. The right to appeal or compound, having their lands restored in return for a hefty fine valued at a fraction of the capital value of their estate, was pursued by many. However, the process was not easy and as well as being able to produce evidence regarding the condition of the estate, the charges against it and further details that may help to reduce the fine in the form of 'Composition Papers', the procedure was extremely costly, with many of the accused unable to afford to take things much further after the inventories of the estates were apprehended.

Bussey Mansel, youngest son of Arthur Mansel and Jane, the daughter and heiress of William Pryce of Briton Ferry, on the other hand was awarded a very different punishment, as this extract from The History of Swansea illuminates:

He [Bussy Mansel] averted possible imprisonment and

confiscation of his property by deserting the royal cause some time between September and November 1645. It is quite possible that among
the subscribers there were many others who, like Bussy, were not unprepared to change sides.

November 1645 was a notable year for Bussey Mansel, despite his reputation as royalist stalwart earlier. During this month, he was named commander-in-chief of the parliamentary forces in the county of Glamorgan, and more surprisingly, since Bussey had publicly renounced his royalist links, he was promoted to this position of power at the ripe old age of 22, a statement that reflected his undisclosed possession of powerful influence in high quarters. Bussey's changing allegiances hadn't gone unnoticed as the following letter from Charles I to William Thomas I demanding the apprehension of Bussey Mansel and other Parliamentarians proves.

Bussey's shift from royalist to decorated parliamentary commander-in-chief took place over a matter of months. Even in a letter to Sir Jacob Astley, Baron of Reading, written on 13 September 1645, Bussey had been clear about his support of the royalist cause, a stance that changed on the day of his promotion. The motives behind his 'change of heart' are still unknown, but his role as proud Parliamentary supporter was short lived as the cause behind Charles II's succession gained strength.

• • • • • •

## LIFE UNDER CROMWELLIAN RULE

Known for having no formal training in military tactics, you'd think that Oliver Cromwell's chances of winning the First Civil War were pretty much non-existent, but his prowess and the formation of the New Model Army saw him defeat the King's major army in a number of battles, including a critical meet in the field at the Battle of Naseby in 1645. Now one of the most famous characters in history, there is no doubt that Cromwell, while never having the title of king, ran England and the ruling Parliament from his point of view, notably from the years 1649 to 1653. He subsequently served as 1st Lord Protector of the Commonwealth of England, Scotland and Ireland from 1653 to 1658, but what was life like for figures like Walter Thomas and William Thomas under the Roundhead regime?

As Protector, Cromwell had the power to call and dissolve parliaments but was obliged under the instrument to seek the majority vote of a Council of State. Nevertheless, Cromwell's power was bolstered by his continuing popularity among the army. He is said to have had two key objectives as Lord Protector. The first was 'healing and settling' the nation after the chaos of the Civil Wars and the regicide, which meant establishing a stable form for the new government to take. Although Cromwell declared to the first Protectorate Parliament that, 'Government by one man and a parliament is fundamental', in practice social priorities took precedence over forms of government. Such forms were, he said, 'but ... dross and dung in comparison of Christ.' The social priorities did not, despite the revolutionary nature of the government, include any meaningful attempt to reform the social order. Cromwell declared, "A nobleman, a gentleman, a yeoman; the distinction of these: that is a good interest of the nation, and a great one!" Small-scale reform such as that carried out on the judicial system was outweighed by attempts to restore order to English politics. Direct taxation was reduced slightly

Fonmon Castle, former home of Colonel Philip Jones.

and peace was made with the Dutch, ending the First Anglo-Dutch War.

The spiritual and moral reform was also part of Cromwell's plans for England and Wales, and with the help of 15 major generals and deputy major generals, commonly known as 'godly governors', he began his crusade to reform the nation's morals. These generals not only supervised militia forces and security commissions, but collected taxes and ensured support for the government in the English and Welsh provinces continued. The fallout from the First Civil War after all meant many were disillusioned, and to support his new moral outlook, Cromwell was no stranger to making examples of individuals, and even sacrificed many of his own men to the opposition – a factor that did not strengthen his position but reopened the wounds of the early days of the Civil Wars.

The aforementioned spiritual and moral reform of Wales, like elsewhere throughout the three kingdoms, wasn't something that Cromwell could achieve overnight however, regardless of the examples he made of his own people and opposing parties as this extract from *The History of Swansea* explains:

But in Wales as a whole, despite the powerful preaching of eloquent Welsh Puritan ministers, and the missionary zeal of the London churches which brought new men to the border, Puritanism made only slow progress. Important among the factors accounting for this situation were the spiritual inertia and ignorance of the mass of the Welsh people, their subservience to the gentry, and the continuingly firm grip of the unejected royalist clergymen. Those who exercised supreme authority in England were not oblivious of the peculiar claims of Wales and, in July 1649, Major-General Thomas Harrison, a convinced millenarian, and one of Cromwell's best cavalry officers, was appointed to the south Wales command. His impressions, together with the persuasive arguments of that most dynamic of crusaders, the Cornishman, Hugh Peter, the perceptive advice of the courageous and mercurial activist, Vavasor Powell, the impact of a cascade of petitions emanating from both north and south Wales calling for church reform, and the readiness of Rump Parliament to listen sympathetically, led to the passing, in February 1650, of the Act for the Better Propagation and Preaching of the Gospel in Wales. This legislation was to remain in force for three years. By its terms, a body of 71 commissioners was appointed, any five of whom, acting together, could examine ministers and, if they thought fit, eject them from their livings. Within three years they had removed in all 278 clergy; 82 in north Wales, 151 in south Wales, and 45 in Monmouthshire. Among those turned out of their parishes was Hopkin Morgan*, vicar of St. Mary's, Swansea, on the ground of 'insufficiency.'

*Hopkin Thomas, second son of Walter Thomas I, vicar of Llandeilo Talybont and Llansawell (Briton Ferry).*

During his time as head of government, he also made it

his task to 'tame' the Irish, and had a particular hatred for Irish Catholics. He sent an army there and despite promising to treat well those who surrendered to him, he slaughtered the people of Wexford and Drogheda who did surrender to his forces. He used terror to 'tame' the Irish, and no one was spared, he even ordered that all Irish children should be sent to the West Indies to work as slave labourers in the sugar plantations. He knew many would die out there – but dead children could not grow into adults and have more children. Cromwell left a dark stain on the history of Ireland.

In 1657 the more conservative of Cromwell's supporters made another attempt to make him king in an effort to place him under the restraining influence of ancient rules and restrictions. He again refused the title, but did accept a redefinition of his powers in 'The Humble Petition and Advice.' He had always led a minority government, and the coalition of interests he represented disintegrated with his death, opening the way to restoration twenty months later. By the end of his life, Cromwell and his major generals had become hated people, with almost the entirety of the population tired of having strict rules forced upon them, and Swansea was no different.

• • • • • •

During the restoration of the monarchy under Charles II, long after the climax of the English Civil War at the execution of his father Charles I on 30 January 1649, it seemed that Walter Thomas I and William Thomas' fates were changing. It wasn't all plain sailing for Charles II however, as whilst the three kingdoms became a de facto republic under Oliver Cromwell, a period often referred to as the English Interregnum, Charles II was defeated at the Battle of Worcester in 1651, resulting in his escape to mainland Europe.

King Charles II (1630-1685) by Sir Peter Lely.
Image Courtesy of National Trust Images.

Exiled to France, the Dutch Republic and the Spanish Netherlands for a number of years, Charles II spotted an opportunity to regain control of his birth right after the death of Cromwell and the succession of his son Richard as Lord Protector of the Commonwealth of England, Scotland and Ireland, an event that caused a political crisis across the kingdoms. The restoration of the monarchy wasn't the product of blood and brawn as you may expect, instead Charles was invited to return to Britain to lead the restoration of the monarchy and he was subsequently

*Charles R.*

Whereas wee have lately Issued a Commission vnto Bushy Maunsell Esqr and thereby have constituted him Colonell Generall of our County of Glamorgan for wise consideracions vs mouving: wee revoke the said Commission and make voyde all powers thereby graunted and from the same derived. and wee require the high Sherriffe of that our County to publish the same in all convenient places within his Bayliwick and this shalbee his sufficient Warrant in that behalfe - Given under ô Sign Manuall at ô Court at Abergauueney the 11th of September 1645

To ô Trusty and Welbeloved William Thomas Esqr high Sherriffe of ô County of Glamorgan

By his Maᵗⁱ Command

Edw Walker

A letter from Charles I to William Thomas, son of Walter Thomas 1st. Died 1653. Source: Cardiff Archives.

received, to rapturous applause, in London on his 30th birthday on 29 May 1660. With documentation finalised much later, Charles II officially succeeded his father in 1649.

With Charles II now in his rightful place on the throne and at the head of the English Parliament, the lands once confiscated from Walter Thomas and his son and heir William Thomas were returned. Bussey Mansel also returned to the fold, with his temporary betrayal under the 12 year rule of Oliver Cromwell's Roundheads being described as nothing more than a 'trimmer.'

Bussey's betrayal did not halt his ascent through the political ranks. After the restoration, he was elected Member of Parliament for Glamorgan in 1679 on two separate occasions, and again in the years 1689, 1690, 1695 and 1698. Bussey even replaced his 'more cautious cousin', most probably by agreement, as county Member at the dissolution of the Cavalier Parliament, which, to this day, is still the longest English Parliament, enduring nearly 18 years of the quarter-century reign of Charles II of England.

At the 1681 election, Bussey took an altogether different tact and actually stood down in his cousin's favour for the county. He was however later displaced by Robert Thomas. After this date Bussey left no trace on the records of the Oxford Parliament, but evidence suggests that he was removed from local office in 1682, before facing a short period of imprisonment during Monmouth's rebellion. His repute for rebellion continued for a number of years as Bussey was included among the opposition to James II, marking him as considerable both for interest and estate. He regained the county seat in 1689, but records of this cannot be distinguished from that of Thomas Mansel II. Bussey was however listed as a supporter of the disabling clause in the bill to restore corporations, and continued to sit for the county as a court Whig until his death.

Oliver Cromwell, Lord Protector (1599-1658) by Samuel Cooper.
Image Courtesy of National Trust Images.

# 3. A TALE OF TWO BROTHERS

**WILLIAM THOMAS, SON OF WALTER THOMAS I**, married Catherine Mansel, daughter of Arthur Mansel and Jane Pryce and sister of the now notorious Bussey Mansel. Despite relations being somewhat fraught between the two families following Bussey's past as Cromwell's youngest commander-in-chief, the pair went on to have 11 children.

The eldest daughter Catherine went on to marry Christopher Middleton of Middleton Hall, Lanarthne. Anne, William's second daughter, married Jeremiah Dawkins of Kilvourough Manor, Gower, whilst Jane married her cousin Morgan Aubrey of Ynyscedwin. Catherine, Anne and Jane were the only daughters that did not die young and unmarried. William and Catherine had many more sons, Edward Thomas died young and unmarried, whilst John Thomas died 1667, also unmarried, but the story takes an interesting turn when we draw our attentions to son and heir Walter Thomas II and his younger brother William Thomas II.

Named after his grandfather, the inspiring and iconic Walter Thomas I, it was Walter's dalliances that are more integral to the story compared with his namesake's involvement in the Civil Wars and the advancement of the Port of Swansea.

Upon the death of his father William I in 1665, as bequeathed by his proven Will with the exception of certain other monetary legacies to his siblings, the Thomas estates were entailed to Walter II, his eldest son and heir, by means of a life interest in much of the estate to his wife Catherine. William's Will also contained directions for his third son John, whose role it was to convey the messages, houses and tenements the latter had received to his eldest Walter, in exchange for which Walter would surrender to John all sure, free and customary land in William's possession in the Parish of Oystermouth. Unfortunately John pre-deceased Walter by several months in 1667, a scenario that meant these instructions could not be carried out as intended. The details of William's Will – dated 3 March 1650, with Codicil of 8 March 1658 and proven by Carmarthen Registry on 4 August 1665 – resulted in Walter Thomas II being in possession of vast properties and lands at the time of his death. The capital message constituting of the Danygraig St Thomas tenements of Llysnewydd and Gwern'lleste in the Parish of Llansamlet, Llandremore in Llandeilo Talybont, tenements in the town of Swansea and customary lands in the Manor Oystermouth. Due to John's early death without legal issue all of the estates bequeathed to him by his grandfather in the Parish of Oystermouth and elsewhere were passed on to Walter.

These lands included meadows, pastures and woods in Llangenith; the moity and half of the Water Grist Mill; the houses, lands, weirs, pastures, barns and orchards of Llanrhydian; several parcels of land at a place called Poppet Hill in Swansea, situated at the top of Mount Pleasant Hill; all houses and gardens situated in Towns End in Swansea near the White Walls; one mansion and houses in Fisher Street; a number of properties in Wassail Street; one mansion in St Mary Street; one house in Goat Street and a second in Carr Street; lands in Pennard; all the woods and underwoods at Tyr-y-Gwl and Therwast in the Parishes of Swansea and Llansamlet; a parcel of land called Erwprisgedwin in Llandeilo Talybont; houses and land situated at the Mount in Wind Street, Swansea; and also lands in Kilvey.

Walter Thomas' marriage to Dorothy Brydges was his last and most defining union, despite many historians right up until the modern day outrightly denying that any such ceremony took place. As the following extract from *A*

*Short Treatise on the Ownership of Land in the Parishes of Cadoxton Juxta Neath and Kilybebyll in the County of Glamorgan* by Richard J Thomas, former Steward of the Manor of Neath Ultra and Kilybebyll, proves:

> William Thomas of Danygraig, Swansea, Son of Walter Thomas and Brother of Catherine Seys, married Catherine, a Daughter of Arthur Mansel of Briton Ferry. William Thomas had two Sons by his Wife, Walter and William, who both died without legal issue. William, the Survivor, devised his Property, which included (amongst other Properties) the Rhydding Estate, to his Uncle, Bussy Mansel, his Mother's Brother.

This is just one instance and publicly published accounts whereby the marriage between Walter Thomas II and Dorothy Brydges is not acknowledged, and the denial of their children implied.

Oystermouth Castle

Marriage Settlement

W. Thomas Dorothy Brydges

Indenture dated 2nd day of April in the 19th year of the reign of our Sovereign Charles II

Between Walter Thomas of Swansea Glamorgan in the presence of Catherine Thomas, mother and widow of William Thomas deceased, Bussey Mansel of Britton Ferry, William Brydges of Tiberton Hereford, Herbert Aubrey the younger of Clehonger Hereford, Thomas Carpender of Chilston Hereford, David Evans of Cadoxton Juxta Neath and John Brydges father of the said daughter Dorothy Brydges.

A sum of 2,000 lawful money to be paid to John Brydges, includes settlement to male heirs or daughters 3,000.

The co-heir and second daughter of John Brydges (who died in 1669) and Joyce Bright of Prior's Court, Dormington near Hereford, Dorothy's name and standing have been somewhat tarnished by the claims that her union with Walter Thomas II did not take place and the two children she subsequently shared with him were illegitimate. Before, during and after the 17th century illegitimacy was the most shameful secret, with the rights of such bastard children non-existent. During these periods, a child's status as an illegitimate or 'basechild' would be specified at their christening.

Like in England, illegitimacy in Wales was slowly increasing and the incidental costs for the parish, who were often rendered the only form of support for the 'deceived maiden', were great. If a marriage between the maiden and the father of the unborn child could not be arranged, despite the financial advances of the parish, the father, or even his parents, would be forced to enter into an indemnity bond to pay for the maintenance of the child. As well as indemnity

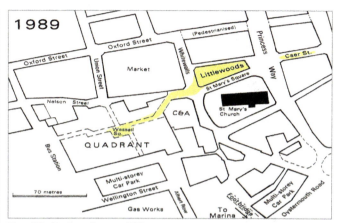

Map of The Quadrant, Swansea 1989.

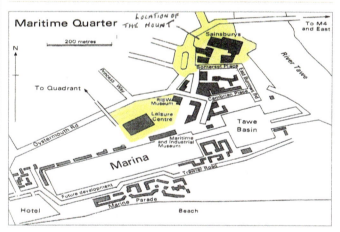

Map outlining the Maritime Quarter, Swansea 1989.

bonds being forcefully applied, the church courts, which were particularly powerful from the 16th to the early 18th century, would step in. As with instances of fornication and adultery, bridal or prenuptial pregnancy would be brought to the attention of the churchwardens and both parties would be publicly named.

Illegitimacy was, even in the 17th century when the gap between rich and poor was at its largest, a classless phenomenon, meaning the mere notion these children were

·SOLI· GLORIA· DEO·

Anglo Saxon Church in Dormington, Hereford, where Walter and Dorothy wed.

born to people with standing like Walter Thomas II was not completely incomprehensible. This may also explain why so many historians have labelled Dorothy and her two children, Joan and Ann, in this manner. New evidence, uncovered by Malcolm Winmill and The Walter Thomas Inheritance Association, however could turn this preconception on its head…

Walter Thomas married Dorothy Brydges in 1667, also the year of his death and the birth year of their second child, Ann. Their eldest daughter Joan died young and unmarried, making Ann a defining character as Walter's only surviving child. Five months after his marriage, Walter was struck down by the plague. Nevertheless the births of both Ann and Joan were officially documented at their baptisms at Birghill Parish Church, Hereford, in 1672.

• • • • • •

## THE PLAGUE

The plague, often referred to as the Black Death, is one of the most devastating pandemics in human history, resulting in the deaths of an estimated 75 to 200 million people. The spread of the disease itself peaked in Europe during the 14th century, more specifically the years 1346 to 1353, but the disease was to return several decades later to take the lives of many more, with the world's population not officially recovering from pre-plague levels until the end of the 17th century. From the initial spread to its recurrences, the plague created a series of religious, social and economic upheavals, which had profound effects on the course of European history. It was also responsible for striking a number of key figures, including Walter Thomas II, down in their prime.

The Great Plague returned in 1665, and is reported to be the last major epidemic of the bubonic plague to occur in England, killing a quarter of London's population.

An account published online at Historic UK gives a powerful insight into the Great Plague and its effects on those of all class levels:

Incubation took a mere four to six days and when the plague appeared in a household, the house was sealed, thus condemning the whole family to death! These houses were distinguished by a painted red cross on the door and the words, 'Lord have mercy on us.' At night the corpses were brought out in answer to the cry,' Bring out your dead', put in a cart and taken away to the plague pits. One called the Great Pit was at Aldgate in London and another at Finsbury Fields. The King, Charles II and his Court left London and fled to Oxford. Those people who could sent their families away from London during these months, but the poor had no recourse but to stay.

In his diary, Samuel Pepys gives a vivid account of the empty streets in London, as all who could had left in an attempt to flee the pestilence. It was believed that holding a posy of flowers to the nose kept away the plague and to this day judges are still given a nose-gay to carry on ceremonial occasions as a protection against the plague! A song about the plague is still sung by children. 'Ring-a-ring of roses' describes in great detail the symptoms of the plague and ends with 'All fall down.' The last word, 'dead', is omitted today.

The plague spread to many parts of the country, and in turn brought devastation to Wales. Whilst the initial epidemic killed one third of the Welsh population, it wasn't until the late 17th century that the country was largely free from the plague as a number of relapses left countless dead.

Birghill Parish Church

● ● ● ● ● ●

Following the death of Walter Thomas, Dorothy returned to her parents' estate, where all was well until the death of both her mother and father in 1669, two more victims of the plague. The scene was set for the first of many deceptions that saw Walter's only surviving daughter and rightful heir defrauded out of her birth right. A woman of standing in her own right thanks to her distinguished family name and vast estates, Dorothy's parents' estates were equally divided between Dorothy and her two sisters, Joyce and Margaret, giving each a life interest to be passed onto their respective heirs. Margaret went on to marry Thomas Carpender of Chilston, before dying in 1666 and leaving behind a daughter named Theodosia, who married Lemuel Kingdon of London before being widowed in 1688. Joyce on the other hand stayed a little closer to home marrying Herbert Aubrey of Clehonger, Hereford.

There was no doubt that Dorothy's father, John, was

an important man whilst his brother James became the first Duke of Chandos. The first of fourteen children of Sir James Brydges, third Baronet of Wilton Castle, Sheriff of Herefordshire, eighth Baron Chandos; and Elizabeth Barnard, James became the ninth Baron Chandos, and was created first Viscount Wilton and first Earl of Carnarvon upon his father's death in 1714. Whilst the titles Marquessate of Carnarvon and the Dukedom of Chandos were created for him later in 1719. James was also a prominent political figure, and stood as Member of Parliament for Hereford between 1698 and 1714. Educated at Westminster School and New College, Oxford, as well as being a man of learning, James was also an avid traveller and served as paymaster-general of the force abroad during the War of the Spanish Succession. His head for business also saw him accumulate great wealth during this period, though a number of investments made after he became Duke of Chandos failed to make the mark as this account from Baroquemusic.org chronicling James' rise and fall, as well as his dealings with German-born British

Baroque composer Handel, explores:

The rise and fall of HENRY JAMES BRYDGES, first duke of Chandos, provides as worthy a subject as any for a film or television drama. Within the space of ten years, from say 1710 to 1720, he rose to fame and riches, only to descend into relative obscurity following the loss of his wealth which was equally as dramatic as the gaining of it. Along the way he created one of baroque London's most palatial mansions, and was responsible for bequeathing to posterity the inestimable gift of Handel's Chandos Anthems.

In 1717 Brydges was created first Duke of Chandos 'for no apparent reason', and in the same year on August 4th, he secured the services of Handel who joined the Chapelmaster Dr. Pepusch as composer-in-residence. The Duke maintained an excellent musical establishment of up to thirty first-class players among whom were named Francesco Scarlatti, brother of Alessandro, and Johann Christoph Bach, cousin of J.S.

The Church of St. Lawrence on the Canons Estate had been almost entirely rebuilt in 1715 by Brydges. Only the tower of the original medieval church remained. A lavish patron of the arts, Brydges employed the fashionable artists of his day to decorate his great mansion of Canons, and those same artists – Antonio Bellucci, Louis Laguerre, Francesco Sleter – created the dramatic interior of the church. Walls and ceiling were covered with paintings of biblical scenes, some brilliantly coloured, others in sepia and grisaille. "Trompe - l'oeil" was used to considerable effect. The splendid woodwork included an organ case carved by Grinling Gibbons, and Handel would certainly have played on this organ.

In certain respects the life-style of "Princely Chandos"

was, as contemporaries recognized, as grand as that of a German electoral prince. In 1720 however, the year in which the rebuilding of the palace was completed, the almost miraculous rise in the fortunes of Chandos (as Brydges was styled from April 1717) crashed abruptly in what became known as the South Sea Bubble financial disaster.

When the South Sea Company had been set up in 1711, it was granted a monopoly on trade with all Spanish territories, South America and the west coast of North America. In 1720, the government encouraged investors to trade government stocks for South Sea Company shares and as these boomed, more and more people speculated in them, forcing the share price higher. In much the same way as many internet stocks today, the price was "talked up" based on nebulous, largely unfounded future prospects, and the price of nominal £100 shares rose to almost £1,000. In July 1720, with company shares at a vastly inflated, unrealistic and unsustainable level, confidence collapsed, and with it the share price. Investors lost considerable amounts and some even committed suicide. Chandos himself suffered major losses, signaling the end of his princely lifestyle. Needless to say, Handel left to seek his fortune elsewhere.

James survived the aforementioned financial crisis and, like John, had a bevy of estates and other assets to pass on upon his death in 1744. He was succeeded by his two surviving children from his first marriage to Mary Lake, daughter of Sir Thomas Lake of Cannons, Middlesex, and Rebecca Langham. Eldest son John became Marquess of Carnarvon, whilst youngest son Henry became the second Duke of Chandos. James subsequent marriages to Cassandra Willoughby, daughter of Francis Willoughby and Emma

Barnard, and Lydia Catherine Van Hatten, daughter of John Van Hatten and Lydia Davall, bore no children.

Like the Thomases, the Brydges had their own reputation to uphold and an equally impressive lineage to follow in the footsteps of. The family arrived in England with William the Conqueror another renowned historical figure connected to the Thomas family. Links to the Thomases don't end there, another member of the Brydges family, Anne, actually married into the Mansel family.

Dorothy subsequently married again to William Hall of Peterchurch, Herefordshire, a union that had no issue. Her death in 1678, a time in which Ann was only 13 years of age, should have resulted in Ann inheriting the same third of the Herefordshire estate – which she did not receive. Dorothy's share was instead sold by her husband William in 1684 to one Francis Woodhouse of Larport Court near Mordiford, Hereford. William died in 1716, and Ann is not mentioned in his Will.

The following extract taken from a letter to Malcolm Winmill from John Harnden, dated 29 April 1998, reveals more about how the extensive estate of John Brydges was dealt with following his death and that of his daughter.

From the enclosed sheet you will see that I have been investigating some of the more relevant deeds in order to try and find out more about Dorothy and her second husband William HALL.

The set of deeds G87/32/1-29 covers the fate of Court y Park from the 13th century until the 1800s, but it is only nos. 4 to 17 that concern the BRYDGES family. John BRYDGES built up his holdings between 1638 and 1643 (Nos 4-7) as far as the Court y Park area is concerned, although other purchases in other parishes may have come later.

He died in 1669, and there is then a schedule of his

Priors Court, principal residence of John and Joyce Brydges.

deeds, most of which concern the renting of various parts of his properties (No. 8A)

The later deeds (Nos 8B-11, 13, 14, 16 & 17) show that the husband of Joyce, and son-in-law of Dorothy were working in concert, but apparently not with Dorothy.

It is not until 1684 that Dorothy is mentioned. In deed No. 15 we learn that Dorothy has died and that William HALL has married an Ann.

Due to the survival of his younger brother, William Thomas II, and Ann's age, Walter's estates as bequeathed to him by his father William and to him by his father Walter Thomas I, were still subject to a life interest and guardianship as awarded to his mother Catherine Mansel. According to extracts taken from the Magna Carta, the role of the guardian, in this case Catherine and later Bussey, was as follows:

If any such heir be under age and a ward he shall when he becomes of age have his inheritance without relief or fine.

The guardian of the land of any such heir shall take thereon only reasonable revenues, customs, and services, without destruction and wastes of men or property, and if we shall have committed the wardship of any such land to a sheriff and he commits destruction, we well take amends from him and the lands shall be committed to two lawful and discreet men of that fee, who shall be answerable to the issues to us.

The guardian so long as he shall have the wardship of the lands shall keep up and maintain the houses, parks, fishponds, mills, everything pertaining thereto, out of the issues of the same and shall restore the whole to the heir when he comes of age stocked with ploughs and grain as the season requires and the issues of the land can reasonably bear.

All fines unjustly and unlawfully given to us, and all fines levied unjustly and against the law of the land shall be entirely remitted of the matter settled by the judgement of the twenty four barons, together with the aforesaid Stephen Archbishop of Canterbury if he himself can be present.

As Walter Thomas died without having male issue, younger brother William become heir entail under the terms of Walter's Will, a role that, due to William's minority at the time, would be overseen by guardian, and Walter and William's mother, Catherine. A legally enforceable wish highlighted in this extract taken from his Will, dated 1667, as witnessed by Bussey Mansel and his son Thomas Mansel.

And withal I doe appoint and humbly desire my said dear mother to be tutor and guardian over my children and over my said brother William Thomas and my nephew Morgan Awbrey during their minority. And if my said mother happened to dye before they accomplish their full age of one and twenty years then I appoint and desire my loving uncle Bussey Mansell and cosen Thomas

Mansell his sonne or else the survivor of them to be their guardians to be accomptable for the meane proffet of my estate, received by them or any of them in case of the death of any of these infants before they attaine to their full age of one and twenty years, to the next of kyn of my family and ... takeing out letter of administration excluding my wife and her relations from any advantage of benefit thereof.

Signed in the presence of Bussey Mansel, James Turberville, William Jones and Morgan, Walter's Will provides definitive evidence of Catherine's expected role as a guardian, based on the premise that Catherine passed away after either William, Morgan or a surviving heir of his own body came of age. Upon further reading, the terms of Walter's Will give younger brother William and his male heirs rights to become tenants in tail, however as William never married, had no issue and was also a minor at the time of Walter's untimely death the line of inheritance should by law revert back to Walter's surviving heir once it was legally acceptable to do so under the terms of the Will and associated guardianship.

Referred to as 'heirs of his body' in the Will, this phrase was commonly used in probate cases throughout history and related to 'descendants of one's bloodline, such as children or grandchildren, until such time as there are no direct descendants. If the bloodline runs out, the property will 'revert" to the nearest relative traced back to the original owner.'

The use of the statement in Walter's Will, proved in 1668, however offers a vital nugget of evidence that his estate was to be entailed to a male heir thus proving he was more than aware of Dorothy's pregnancy, a pregnancy that resulted in the birth of his only surviving heir, Ann Thomas.

The legal rights of female heirs are something that has morphed throughout history. Primogeniture was rife not just in England and Wales but in most of Europe, in particular realms with established monarchies seemed to favour males in succession. Primogeniture is the right, by law or custom, of the firstborn male child to inherit the family estate, in preference to siblings. In the absence of children, inheritance passed to collateral relatives, usually male, in order of seniority of their lines of descent, hence why Walter's estate was passed to his younger brother William and would be entailed to any male heirs of his body also, despite the existence of Ann. By law, the eligible descendants of deceased elder siblings take precedence over living younger siblings, and with that inheritance is settled in the manner of a depth-first search.

Primogeniture was so significant that its history stems back to biblical times with the earliest account recorded relating to one Issac and his sons Jacob and Esau. Despite being first born Esau sold his birth right to Jacob for food. There are also various accounts recorded and even drawn reference to now throughout Roman law and during the re-emergence period in medieval Europe, the origin of which is explained here in an extract from An Inquiry into the Nature and Causes of the Wealth of Nations by 18th century Scottish moral philosopher, pioneer of political economy and key figure in the Scottish Enlightenment Adam Smith:

Court y Park, home of John Brydges.

> When land was considered as the means, not of subsistence merely, but of power and protection, it was thought better that it should descend undivided to one. In those disorderly times, every great landlord was a sort of petty prince. His tenants were his subjects. He was their judge, and in some respects their legislator in peace and their leader in war. He made war according to his own discretion, frequently against his neighbours, and sometimes against his sovereign. The security of a landed estate, therefore, the protection which its owner could afford to those who dwelt on it, depended upon its greatness. To divide it was to ruin it, and to expose every part of it to be oppressed and swallowed up by the incursions of its neighbours. The law of primogeniture, therefore, came to take place, not immediately indeed, but in process of time, in the succession of landed estates, for the same reason that it has generally taken place in that of monarchies, though not always at their first institution.

As all accounts relating to primogeniture show, the order of succession wasn't just a sequence that those of noble or royal birth had to concern themselves with, but, as the inheritance of the Thomas estates proves, a matter for those holding all and any types of lands and titles to consider.

ye Gene of fideliter Administrando eadem ad Sancta Dei Evangelia
Jurat &c

# In the Name of God Amen

The Sixteenth day of October in the Second year of the reigne
of our Soveraigne Lord George King of Great Britain &c and
in the year of our Lord One Thousand Seven Hundred and
Sixteen I William Hall of Peterchurch in the County of Hereford
Esquire being Sick and weak in Body But of sound and perfect
mind and memory Praise be given to Almighty God do make
this my last Will and Testament in manner and form following
(That is to say) ffirst and principally I commit my Soul into the
hands of Almighty God my Creator hoping thro' the
meritorious death and passion of my Saviour Christ Jesus to
have remission of my Sins And my Body I commit to the Earth
to be decently interred at the discretion of my Executors hereafter
named and as touching the disposition of such Temporal
Estate as it hath pleased Almighty God to bestow upon me
I give and dispose of as follows ffirst I Will that all my Debts
and ffuneral charges be paid and discharged Item I give and
bequeath unto my Servant Mary Skinner in consideration of
her good Services to me done the sum of One Hundred and
ffifty pounds of lawfull money to be paid her within Six months
after my decease and also the Bed on which she lies with its
appurtenances and all other the ffurniture of her said Chamber
and also all my wearing Linnen Item I give and bequeath unto
David Wilton the sum of ffive pounds to be paid him immediately
after my decease Item I give and bequeath unto Elizabeth
Wilton Wife of the said David Wilton the sum of One
Hundred and ffifty pounds to be paid her in one year after my
decease Item I give and bequeath unto my Servant ... Dowell
the sum of Tenn pounds besides all Wages due to him to be
paid him in Six months after my decease and also all my
Woolen wearing apparell except my best Suit and also my Gray
Horse Item I give and bequeath unto Sylvanus Lloyd the sum of Six
pounds for to lay a Grave Stone upon of my own Stone to be paid
him in Six Months after my decease and also ffour of my Rings
Item I give and bequeath unto the poor of the parish of Dorstone
the sum of ffifty pounds to be setled upon good Security as a
Stock for their use for ever and the Interest thereof to be divi d
amongst the said poor at the ffeasts of Easter and Christmas
by ye Minister Church wardens and principal inhabitants of the
said parish of Dorstone Item I give and bequeath unto the poor
of the parish of Peterchurch the sum of One Hundred pounds
and this with the ffifty pounds above bequeathed to the poor
of the parish Dorstone to be paid in one year after my
decease to be setled upon good Security and the Interest
thereof to be divided amongst such of the said poor as doth
not receive Alms from the said parish of Peterchurch and
this distribution to be made at the ffeasts of Easter and

Christmas by the minister Churchwardens and principal
inhabitants of the said parish of Peterchurch Item I give and
bequeath unto William Morgan formerly my servant the sum of
two Pounds to be paid him immediatly after my decease Item I
give and bequeath unto my Nephew Benedict Wall Esquire the
sum of one Pound to be paid him in one year after my decease
Item I give and bequeath unto my Brother Francis Wall my
best Suit of Clothes and also my Mare with the Bridle and
Sadle and also my second best Horse Item I give and bequeath
unto my Nephew Francis Wall the sum of five Pounds to be
paid him within six months after my decease Item I give and
bequeath unto my Nephew Henry Wall the sum of tenn Pounds
to be paid him in six months after my Decease and also my best
horse and the remainder of my Horses Item I give and
bequeath unto my Neice Mary Wall daughter of my Brother
Francis Wall the sum of tenn Pounds to be paid her in six months
after my Decease and also the Bed with its appurtenances and
all the furniture that is in the New Chamber and also a sett of
Diaper Table linnen Item I give and bequeath unto my Godson
Edward Bennington the sum of fifty Pounds and also my Violin to
be paid in one year after my decease Item I give and bequeath
unto Mr James Pritnard the sum of five Pounds to be paid
him in six months after my Decease Item I give unto those
that sing at my ffunerall the sum of Two Pounds to be paid
them immediatly by my Executors who are to pay the severall
Legacies above mentioned Item I give and bequeath unto my
Servant Dorothy Mitchell the sum of five Pounds to be paid
her within six Months after my Decease all the rest and
residue of my real and personal Estate Goods and Chattles
whatsoever I give and bequeath unto my very good ffriends
Henry Lewis of Llina in the County of Monmouth Esquire and
Charles Thompson of the parish of Madley in the County of
Hereford Gent both which I doe hereby nominate constitute
and appoint full and sole Executors to this my last Will and Testant
And I do hereby revoke disanull and make void all former
Wills and Testaments by me heretofore made In Witness hereof
I have hereunto sett my hand and Seal the day and year above
written Will: Wall Signed Sealed Published and Delivered
in the presence of us with the words (use my) being first interlined
Jon Hillin Gh Tho Powell Jon Aus:fo

## Probatum

fuit hujusmodi Testamentum apud London
... Decimo ... et Egregio viro Johanne Bettesworth Legum
Doctore Curia Prærogativa Cantuariensis Magistro ... toto sive
Commissario legitime constituto Nono die mensis Novembris Anno
Domini Millesimo Septingentesimo Trigesimo Sexto Juramento
Caroli Thompson unius Executorum indicto Testamento nominat' Cui
Commissa fuit Administratio omnium et singulorum bonorum
jurium et Creditorum dicti defuncti De bene et fideliter Administrando
eadem ad Sancta Dei Evangelia jurat' reservata potestate similem
Commissionem faciendi Henrico Lewis Armigero alteri Executori in

# 4. THE DISINHERITANCE OF ANN THOMAS

THE PREVALENCE OF THE PHRASE 'heirs of his body' as noted in Walter's Will was explained further in the document entitled Commentary on Counsels' Opinion by The Walter Thomas Inheritance Association, as too was the use of barred the entail, an action that the Association suspected was ultimately used by William Thomas to disinherit Ann Thomas from her father's estate.

The opinion provided by Mr O'Sullivan on 24 February 1998 explained that:

> An entail differed from a fee simple because whilst a fee simple could be passed by inheritance to anyone, an entail could only pass by inheritance to a lineal descendant of the original donee.

In response the members of The Walter Thomas Inheritance Association provided poignant historical background to not only uncover the importance of the phrase 'heirs of his body' once more but further explain the legislation used to prevent Ann Thomas from claiming her rightful inheritance.

Whilst the contents of Walter's Will make it clear that the estate should be passed on to his younger brother William, under the guardianship of his mother Catherine, until the aforementioned comes of age, it also states that should William not produce any male heirs then the line of inheritance would revert back to Walter's, regardless of whether his heir was male or female. In property law, a conveyance by the owner or grantor to the grantee and heirs of the body creates a fee tail for the grantee with a reversion in the grantor should the natural, lawful descendants of the grantee all die out. Each person who inherits according to this formula is considered an heir at law of the grantee. Since the inheritance may not pass to someone who is not a natural, lawful descendant of the grantee, the heir is necessarily also 'of the body' of the grantee. Collateral kin, who share some or all of the grantee's ancestry, but do not directly descend from the grantee, may not inherit.

Under the terms of William Thomas II's Will (1677) however it was obvious that a separate legal action had been taken to bequeath all of the Thomas estates to his uncle Bussey Mansel, despite Bussey's original role, as set out under the terms of Walter's Will, as trustee and guardian, as the following translation verifies. The Will of William Thomas II was proven despite approaches made by sisters Catherine Middleton and Ann Dawkins, Morgan Aubrey and several others to contest.

> In the name of God Amen having been heard, seen and understood and fully and carefully discussed between us Richard Lloyd, knight and doctor of law, surrogate for the venerable and excellent Master, Leolin Jenkins, knight and also doctor of law of the concerning the merits and circumstances of the matter of the wills or probate for testaments or last wills and codicils in the writing of William Thomas, recently of Dan y Graig in the Parish of Lansamlett in the county of Glamorgan and province of Canterbury, armiger deceased having while he lived and at the time of his death goods, rights or credits in different dioceses or peculiar jurisdictions within the province of Canterbury aforesaid.

> Because before us in court Bussy Mansell armiger and one of the executors named in the said testament or last will of the said defunct instituting a cause on the

Margam House

4th Baron Lord Bussy Mansel the 2nd with wife Lady Barbara Blackett (Daughter of the 2nd Earl of Jersey – William Villiers). Their daughter Lisa Barbara Mansel married Lord Vernon of Sudbury Hill.
This Portrait can be seen at the Glynn Vivian Art Gallery – GV1951.1099

one part and Catherine Middleton alias Thomas and Ann Dawkins alias Thomas, natural and legitimate sisters of the defunct, and also Morgan Awbrey armiger, nephew (son of sister) of the said deceased particularly representing all and singular the other right title and interest in the goods, rights and credits of the said deceased and all those having or hoping to have interest in such on the other part. The same business instituted by the party and others judicially at a certain time and was turned over and considered and is still being turned over and considered proceeding to the correct and legitimate decision as aforesaid.

Bussy Mansell executor before named through his procurator appeared before us legally and satisfactorily and the aforesaid Catherine Middleton alias Thomas, Ann Dawkins alias Thomas and Morgan Awbrey armiger representing all and singular the other rights and interest in the goods, rights and credits of the said deceased which had been had or hoped to be had and it was known and sufficiently sought on the part of the aforesaid Bussy Mansell executor aforesaid.

Sentence having been proclaimed as justice having been made on the one part as had been sought and demanded and to the remaining party to all and singular of them who in no way appeared but were contumaciously absent despite being sought and with the whole matter of the said business conscientiously recounted before us, decision has been made according to the law, in this part. To our definitive sentence or our final proclamation in this business we have caused proceedings to be taken and have proceeded in this in a way which follows, on account of the act enrolled, deduced, alleged, exhibited, proposed, proved fairly and confessed we find and conclude on the part of the aforesaid Bussy Mansell, Knight, the executor before stated and on the side of his accusation in this allegation and in the testament and codicil and otherwise against the other part in this matter given and exhibited and, regarding the decision in this court of registry (by means of the fact that we wished to have and have this certain, alleged testament and codicil which was respectively read and introduced) we are satisfied sufficiently and fully that the below pronouncement, finding, decision and proof have not been affected by one party or the other party or on behalf of aforesaid party or in any way except what was deduced from the aforesaid allegation or probate which was intended by the aforesaid Bussy Mansell armiger

# 𝕸𝖆𝖌𝖓𝖆 𝕮𝖆𝖗𝖙𝖆 1215

'...2 *(lines 7-9)* If any of Our earls, barons, or others who hold lands of Us by knight's service shall die, and at the time of his death his heir shall be of full age and owe a relief, he shall have his inheritance, on payment of ancient relief.

3 *(line 9)* If, any such heir shall be under age and a ward. He shall, when he comes of age, have his inheritance without relief or fine.

4 *(lines 10 - 12)* The guardian of the land of any such heir shall take therefrom only reasonable revenues, customs, and services, without destruction and waste of men or property; and if We shall have committed the wardship of any such land to a sheriff and he commits destruction, We will take amends from him, and the land shall be committed to two lawful and discreet men of that fee, who shall be answerable for the issues to US.

5 *(lines 12 - 13)* The guardian, so long as he shall have the wardship of the land, shall keep up and maintain the houses, parks, fishponds, pools, mills, everything pertaining thereto, out of the issues of the same, and shall restore the whole to the heir when he comes of age, stocked with ploughs and grain as the season requires and the issues of the land can reasonably bear.'

executor aforesaid in this part, not put out or in any way altered. For that reason we Richard Lloyd, knight and doctor of law, surrogate aforesaid in the name of Christ firstly and in the sight of the one and only God using the before mentioned information and having with the advice of legal expertise in this part have considered fully and deliberated concerning the aforenamed William Thomas armiger, deceased and have decided that while he lived he was of sound mind and sane memory and that the will and codicil in his writing containing his last will being dated 3rd day of the month of October in the year of our Lord 1677, otherwise in this matter (as stated above) exhibited and remaining within the registry of this court which certain testament ad codicil we wished to have and have read and entered, and he

(William Thomas) has made appointed and declared the aforesaid Bussy Mansell armiger his executor named, ordained made and constituted etc. and has willed given bequeathed relinquished and disposed in all and through all respectively his sad testament and codicil or last will aforesaid (as aforesaid) exhibited and containing the attached legal probate before us in the said matter and we make pronouncement, determine and declare that it has legality on account of the clea and strong validity of the said testament or last will and codicil aforesaid (as aforesaid) exhibited and held in the registry of this court and we pronounce determine and declare the probate and approbation and registration of the will and codicil of the said William Thomas armiger deceased otherwise in common form made and bound and presently approved determined and confirmed trough this our definitive sentence or this our final decree which, indeed, has been made and declared in these writings.

Before his death there was doubt that William Thomas and his uncle Bussey were close, in fact, it is written in a historical document currently stored in the Swansea Archives that William left Swansea in 1666 far disposed and very much in debt to his uncle. As reflected in the extracts from the Magna Carta, Bussey's duties as trustee and guardian extended to more than just providing a helping hand to his nephew whenever he may need it, legal duties that Bussey never fulfilled thus committing serious fraud. His actions and complete disregard for his duties as a trustee and guardian saw Ann Thomas, who was only 11 years old at the time and unable to understand the intricate nature of succession, disinherited. Could it be that William was in so much debt to his uncle that he barred the entail to Walter's estate thereby bequeathing Bussey all associated lands? The historical background certainly suggests that this was the case.

The Settled Land Acts were a series of English land laws

**Sir Thomas Mansel 1ˢᵗ Baron of Margam, father of Lord Bussy 2ⁿᵈ (1667-1723) by Michael Dahl.**
**Image Courtesy of National Trust Images**

that make for essential reading when reviewing the case of Walter's missing millions. The legislation itself concerned the limits when creating a settlement, referred to legally as a conveyancing device used by a property owner who wants to ensure that future generations of his family are provided for. Throughout history there are generally two types of settlement – a 'trust for sale' where land or goods are transferred by the owner by deed or will to trustees and a 'strict settlement' whereby the landowner would keep the aforesaid land within his family. The latter was used in relation to the division of limited freehold estates over time.

A fee tail is referenced throughout much of the evidence relating to the disinheritance of Ann Thomas, and the estates in question were notably limited with succession confined to the direct descendants of the original holder of the estate – descendants determined according to ancient heirship rules which always lean in the favour of the eldest son. Whilst the Settled Land Acts meant that many cases looking to resolve disputes regarding the division of lands or goods could be fairly deciphered and a verdict decided on, there were a number of disadvantages often connected to the legislation. These difficulties were compounded by the fact that very often the settlement would continue on ad infinitum through the process of resettlement. The son's eldest son who was entitled to the fee tail could by barring the entail create a fee simple and bring the settlement to an end. He was not entitled to his interest in possession until his father died, however while his father lived he could not bar the entail unless his father consented to it. His father would be reluctant to give his consent as this would mean the land would pass outside the family. Obviously the son would be in need of money to sustain him until he became entitled in possession, meaning often a compromise would be reached which would enable the land to remain in the family but at the same time satisfy the son's need for cash. The father and son would bar the entail but there would be a resettlement of the land which usually took the form of a conveyance to the father for life, to the eldest son for life remainder and to his eldest son in tail, whilst the fee tail was passed back another generation. As part of the settlement the eldest son would be granted an immediate annuity on the land or a lump sum. These resettlements meant that the deterioration of the land and the impoverishment of the landowners continued generation after generation.

The definition of barring the entail is precisely summed up here in an extract from The Fee Tail and the Common Recovery in Medieval England by Joseph Biancalana.

> The common recovery was an especially strong device for barring entails. Its strength lay not only in its being effective but also in its being easy to use and certain to work. The greater ease and sureness of the recovery becomes apparent when it is compared to other means of barring entails available in the mid-fifteenth century.

> To bar an entail meant to prevent anyone with an otherwise good and valid claim under an entail from successfully enforcing his interest under a grant in fee tail. A claimant under an entail who brought an action to enforce his interest might be barred in three ways. First, an heir under an entail might be barred because his ancestor under the entail had granted the land to another with warranty. If the heir under the entail was also that ancestor's heir general, which was frequently the case, the ancestor's warranty would descend to the heir. At common law, the descent of the ancestor's warranty would bar the heir completely from undoing his ancestor's grant. But under De Donis, the heir under the entail was barred only to the extent that lands in fee simple had descended to him from his ancestor. This was the doctrine of assets by descent. Secondly, an ancestor of claimant might have granted or released his right to the land with warranty.

As the details above suggest once the estate was entailed the owner of the property is severely limited in regards to management, for example the rights of his issue could not be defeated by Deeds of Gifts or sale, not directly affected by more limited transactions, such as leases and rent charges. The result – 'the stranger' (in this case uncle Bussey) would emerge as owner in fee simple, leaving all other claimants (in this case, Walter's rightful and only surviving heir, Ann) barred and left to console themselves with a valueless judgement.

By becoming an owner in fee simple, Bussey then had two options – he could reconvey the land to the tenant entail or pay a fine to purchase the land himself. As the members of The Walter Thomas Inheritance Association explain here:

> A fine was the formal agreement which was entered in the Court records to show the terms on which, with the Court leave, the action was discontinued. The practice of 'levying a fine' was of early origin than the common recovery, and was much used in early times as a mode of conveyance owing to its sanctity as a compromise approved by the Court and registered in the records. Originally a title acquired by fine was impregnable if not contested within a year and a day. This was modified by legislation which made fines binding immediately on the parties and allowed other persons 5 years in which to make their claims.

> Because the Statued De Donis expressly prohibited the barring of entails by fines, legislation was necessary for this purpose. The Statue of Fines 1489, which dealt with fines generally, provided a pre-text for holding that a fine would hence forth bar the issue entail; and an Act of 1540 confirmed this construction, so that the fine was immediately effective to bar the issue.

> A fine had the advantage that it could be levied without the concurrence of the tenant in possession. But it was not so effective as a common recovery, for although it barred the rights of the issue entail, it did not bar the

the nature of a writt of right, and the steward is to have for his ffee vppon every such plaint xij*d.* and for the copy of the plaint and ꝑtestac̄on viij*d.*; and if there be not to be had (by challenge or otherwise) twelve men within the said Mannor, the steward may by warrant sum̄on soe many as shall be needfull out of any other Lordshipp within the Seignory of Gower to join with the other, and noe customary tenants by the custome may implead a customary tenant in any other court for any cause vnder x*s.* vppon paine of an amerciam$^{t}$ to the Lord of the said Mannō if courts be duely kept.

For herryotts both free and customary, tenants pay them as is menc̄oned in the Surveys of Oystermouth.

---

## THE MANNOR OF KILVEY

### a member of the said Seignory.

The Extent and Boundaryes of the said Mannor.

The said Mannor extendeth to y$^{e}$ river Tawe on the west the brooke of Crymlin and a way called the Geven ffordd vppon Mynydd Drymme leadinge to Cissevaen—on the east, the brooke of Crynach and Glaisse on the north, and the sea on y$^{e}$ south.

The Demeazn lands of the said Mannor.

Forrest vychan aīs Forrest yssa lett to Phillipp Jones Esq$^{r}$.

| | *Contents of acres.* | | *Val. p$^{r}$. annum.* | | |
|---|---|---|---|---|---|
| | *a.* | *r.* | *li.* | *s.* | *d.* |
| A manc̄on house without buildinges thereto belongeinge and severall closes of arrable pasture and meadow ground lyeinge togeather about the said house and abuttinge vppon the river called Mynrod on the east and the river Tawe on the west, the freehould of Hopkin Popkins called Fforrest ycha on the north and on the south thereof both the said rivers which inclose the said | | | | | |

*KILVEY.*

These small Tenem$^{ts}$ followinge are returned by the Jury to be lett at will to the severall tenants after named, but I had noe notice of them when I was vppon the place.

| | *Contents of acres.* a. r. | *Rents payable.* li. s. d. |
|---|---|---|
| Walter Thomas Esq$^{r}$ for lands called Tir Dauid Taylor in the hands of Watkin Dauid | 00.0 | 01.00.00 |
| William Thomas Esq$^{r}$ for Coed hir draeth | 00.0 | 00.01.04 |
| The same for Erw maes y barr in the hands of Morgan Lleñ | 00.0 | 00.03.00 |
| The same for other lands called Trychwarter hirion | 00.0 | 00.05.00 |
| The same for Tir vach Eynon ddee in the hands of Jo$^{n}$ Leyson | 00.0 | 00.16.10 |
| M$^{r}$ William Evans for lands in the Gwnglyn | 00.0 | 00.02.04 |
| Hopkin Popkins for Erw'r vallen | 00.0 | 00.01.00 |
| Morgan Leyson for Tyle garow | 00.0 | 00.05.00 |
| Hopkin Thomas for a parcell of land called Bryn y Garth hên | 00.0 | 00.01.00 |
| Thomas William Hopkin for Tir Madocke vondda | 00.0 | 01.00.00 |
| Thomas John Thomas for lands in the Close | 00.0 | 00.10.00 |
| Hopkin John/Gwynn for Henkerregg vach | 00.0 | 00.06.08 |
| | 00.0 | 04.12.02 |

---

The Freehoulders of the said Mannor with the rents they pay.

| | *li. s. d.* |
|---|---|
| Walter Thomas Esq$^{r}$ for lands called Erw vawr | 00.00.08 |
| The same Walter for Tir y gwl | 00.00.06 |
| The same for lands called Therwes | 00.00.01½ |
| The same for a wear | 00.01.00 |
| William Thomas Esq$^{r}$ for lands called Gwern y llyeste | 00.00.04 |
| The same for lands called Tir Engharad V$^{ch}$ W$^{m}$ | 00.03.04 |
| The same for Tir W$^{m}$ ap Evan ap Henry | 00.00.10 |
| The same William for Tir Nest vrase | 00.02.00 |
| The same William for Tir Gwillim ap Lewis | 00.00.03 |
| The same William for Hickes wear | 00.00.06 |
| The same William for Glopert wear | 00.00.06 |
| The same William for Sillwear | 00.00.06 |
| The same William for Lleesnewidd | 01.00.00 |
| The same William for Morva r cyrsse | 00.10.00 |
| The same William for Morva rhythallt | 00.06.08 |
| The same William for Gored vach | 00.02.00 |
| The same William for Tir Edmund and Gelly gravog | 00.00.07½ |
| The same William for lands in the hands of John Leyson | 00.00.07½ |
| The same William for lands in the hands of W$^{m}$ Bevan Jenkin | 00.01.00 |
| The same William for lands in the hands of Thomas Bowen | 00.01.00 |
| The same for lands in the hands of Dauid W$^{m}$ Morgan | 00.01.05 |
| The same for lands called Keel y bwry in the hands of W$^{m}$ Bevan | 00.01.10 |
| The same for lands in the hands of John Bevan Jenkin | 00.01.01½ |
| The same for lands called Llwyn crwn ysha in the hands of Morgan ffen | 00.00.08 |
| The same for other lands in the hands of John Morgan Llewelin | 00 00.04 |
| The same for lands called Talshoba in the hands of Owen Thomas Rees | 00.00.07½ |
| The same for lands in the hands of Edward Morgan | 00.00.07½ |
| The same for lands in the hands of Owen Morgan Llewelin called Pant y blawd | 00.00.09 |

Juro$^{rs}$ in that behaulfe, in answear to the Articles hereunto annexed given in Charge unto them the said Juro$^{rs}$.

*The names of the said Jurors.*

| | | | |
|---|---|---|---|
| Lewelin Rogers, Gent.<br>Thomas Popkins, Gent.<br>John Popkins, Gent.<br>Jenkin Nicholas, Gent. | Jur' | William Pritchard, Gent.<br>Roger Morgan, Gent.<br>Morgan Rosser, Gent.<br>William Jones, Gent. | Jur' |

TO THE FIRST ARTICLE—The said Jurors doe say—and present uppon their Oathes—That the severall persons hereafter named doe hould by soccage tenure, the Lands & Tenements hereafter specifyed, from and under His Grace the said Duke of Beaufort, in right of this his said Mannor, at and under the yearely Chieffe Rents hereafter specifyed, payable on the Feast of S$^{t}$ Michael the Archangel yearely, & collected by the Reeve (being a Free Tenant) of the said Manor or his (sworne) Deputy, to the use of the Lord of the said Mannor:—The names of which Free Tenants and of the respective Tenements aforesaid, and Rents, are hereafter particularly menconed, viz$^{t}$

| | |
|---|---|
| BUSSY MANSELL, Esq$^{re}$, for Tiry Gwl now in the hands of John Popkins, Gent. | vj$^{d}$ |
| The same for Therwes now in the hands of the s$^{d}$ John Popkins | j$^{d}$½ |
| The same for Gwernyllyeste now in the hands of William Robert | iiij$^{d}$½ |
| The same for Tir Engharadverch William | iij$^{s}$ |
| The same for Tiry Gwayth & Tir W$^{m}$ ap Evan ap Henry | x$^{d}$ |
| The same for Tir Neast vrase | ij$^{s}$ |
| The same for Tir Gwillim ap Lewis aīs Danygraig vach in the hands of Daniel Vaughan | iij$^{d}$ |
| The same for Llisnewydd now in the hands of Thomas Price, Gent. | xx$^{s}$ |
| The same for Morvaer Kyrse now in the hands of the said Thomas | x$^{s}$ |
| The same for Morvarhythallt now in the hands of the said Thomas | vj$^{s}$ viij$^{d}$ |
| The same for Tir Edmond 4$^{d}$½ for Gellygravog 3$^{d}$ now in the hands of Walter Edward | vij *ob.* |
| The same for lands late in the hands of W$^{m}$ Bevan Jenkin and now W$^{m}$ Dowle | xij$^{d}$ |
| The same for lands late in the hands of Thomas Bowen, and now of Richard Robert | xij$^{d}$ |
| The same for lands near Lansamlett Church now in the hands of Margarett John Thomas | xvij$^{d}$ |
| The same for lands late in the hands of John Lyson and now of James William Jenkin | vij$^{d}$ *ob.* |
| The same for Kilbury now in the hands of David John Lyson | xxij$^{d}$ |
| The same for Lloyntrwn y cha late in the hands of John Morgan Llewelin, and now of John David Vaughan | iiij$^{d}$ |
| The same for Lloynkrwn y sha now in the hands of Evan John Bevan | viij$^{d}$ |
| The same for Lands neare Lanwerne late in the hands of John Bevan Jenkin, and now of Thomas William Hopkin | xiij$^{d}$ |
| The same for Talshoba 3$^{d}$ & for Tir Evan Llygyty 4$^{d}$½, now in the hands of Thomas Rosser & Tobyas Rosser | vij$^{d}$ *ob.* |
| The same for Lands at Kevenhenvoed late in the hands of Edward Morgan and now of Charity Vaughan | vij$^{d}$ *ob* |
| The same for Panty blawd now in the hands of David Woodwall | ix$^{d}$ |
| The same for Lands at Kevenhenvoed late in the hand of Jenkin W$^{m}$ Rees and now of Robert Powell & Matthew William | ix$^{d}$ |
| The same for Tir Morgan Cadwgan, now in the hands of Edward Rees | ij$^{d}$ |
| The same for Tilerdengil Boneymaen & Kae Mawr, now in the hands of Robert Thomas Bowen | xvj$^{d}$ |
| The same for Lands late in the hands of David Jenkin and now of Margarett David | ij$^{d}$ |
| The same for Tir y ddyan late in the hands of Tho. William and now of Morgan Howell | ix$^{d}$ |
| The same for Tir y vord now in the hands of William Jenkin Bowen | viij$^{d}$ |
| The same for Pant y gevile & Pwll mawr now in the hands of Joan John, Widdow | xj$^{d}$ |
| The same for Pude glase late in the hands of Edward William and now of Hopkin Griffith. | ix$^{d}$ |
| The same for Lands at Dan y graig late in the hands of William David ap David & Lyson Jenkin & now of William ap William | vij$^{d}$ *ob.* |
| The same for Lands now in the hands of Thomas Watkin | iiij$^{d}$ |
| The same for Waine Wen now or late in the hands of Anne Steven. | iiij$^{d}$ *ob.* |
| The same for Lands late in the hands of William David Thomas and now of Edward David & Eliz$^{h}$ William, Spinster | xij$^{d}$ |
| The same for Lands now in the hands of Evan David and William Lewis | xij$^{d}$ |
| The same for Lands late in the hands of Owen David Bowen and now of Watkin Elias | iij$^{d}$ *ob.* |
| The same for Lands late in the hands of William Rosser and now of Evan William | xij$^{d}$ |
| The same for Tir Evan Llewelingoth now in the hands of Morgan David | ij$^{d}$ |
| The same for Gellyegassegg now in the hands of William Robert | ij$^{d}$ |
| The same Lloyn herim now in the hands of Richard Owen | x$^{d}$ |
| The same for Trergrove 12$^{d}$, & for Tir Evan Jenkin Treharne 2$^{d}$ now in the hands of Hopkin David Vaughan | xiiij$^{d}$ |
| The same for Lands late in the hands of Thomas John Thomas, and now of Rees Woodwall and Morgan Llewelin | ix$^{d}$ *ob.* |

| | *li.* | *s.* | *d.* |
|---|---|---|---|
| The same for lands in the hands of Jenkin William Rees | 00 | 00 | 09 |
| The same for lands called Tir Cadwgan in the hands of Morgan Jo⁰ Thō | 00 | 00 | 02 |
| The same for lands called Tyle 'r dyngil and Bone y mane in the hands of Dauid Wᵐ Dauid | 00 | 01 | 04 |
| The same for lands in the hands of William Thomas Griffith | 00 | 00 | 09 |
| The same for lands called Tir y ddyan in the hands of Thomas William | 00 | 00 | 09 |
| The same for lands called Tir y vord in the hands of Evan Jenkin | 00 | 00 | 08 |
| The same for lands called Pont y gevile and Pwll mawr in the hands of Owen Richard and Robert Richard | 00 | 00 | 11 |
| The same for lands in the hands of Edward William | 00 | 00 | 09 |
| The same for lands in the hands of Wᵐ Dauid ap Dauid and Leyson Jenkin | 00 | 00 | 09 |
| The same for lands in the hands of Wᵐ Dauid Thomas | 00 | 01 | 00 |
| The same for lands in the hands of the wife of Wᵐ Dauid Jo⁰ Richard | 00 | 01 | 00 |
| The same for lands in the hands of Owen Dauid Bowen | 00 | 00 | 03 |
| The same for lands in the hands of William Rosser | 00 | 01 | 00 |
| The same for lands called Gelly 'r gasseg | 00 | 02 | 00 |
| The same for lands called Llwyn hernin in the hands of Hopkin John Gwynn | 00 | 00 | 10 |
| The same for lands called Tir Evan ften goch in the hands of Dauid Rees | 00 | 00 | 02 |
| Sume | 03 | 12 | 03½ |
| Walter Thomas Esqʳ for lands in the hands of Hopkin Dauid Vaughan called Tregove and Tir Evan Jenkin Treharn | 00 | 01 | 02 |

| | *li.* | *s.* | *d.* |
|---|---|---|---|
| The same Walter for lands in the hands of Thomas John Thomas | 00 | 00 | 09½ |
| The same Walter for lands in the hands of Morgan John Morgan | 00 | 00 | 03 |
| The same Walter for lands in the hands of Watkin Dauid | 00 | 00 | 06 |
| Mʳ William Evans for lands called Gelly gynven | 00 | 00 | 09 |
| The same William Evans for lands called Tir Phillipp Tew | 00 | 00 | 05 |
| The same William for lands called Tir Evan bach | 00 | 00 | 03 |
| The same William for lands called Tir Tom Griffith | 00 | 01 | 04 |
| The same William for lands called Gwayn Evan ddee | 00 | 00 | 03 |
| The same William for lands called Gwern vare | 00 | 00 | 03 |
| The same William for lands called Tir Tom lya | 00 | 00 | 07 |
| The same William for lands called Tir Madocke bach and Evan Goch ap Richard | 00 | 04 | 05 |
| The same William for lands called Tir Meyricke yshan and Evan Jenkin Tryharne | 00 | 04 | 10 |
| The same William for lands in the hands of Rosser Dauid Llewelin | 00 | 01 | 10 |
| Dauid Nicholas for lands called Ynis dderow | 00 | 01 | 03 |
| The same Dauid for lands called Ty dy ats mawr | 00 | 02 | 06 |
| The same Dauid for lands called Ty 'r y llwyn | 00 | 00 | 05 |
| The same Dauid for lands called Tir Madocke goch | 00 | 00 | 05½ |
| The same Dauid for lands called Tir y brown | 00 | 00 | 05½ |
| The same Dauid for lands called Tir drymme | 00 | 01 | 09 |
| The same Dauid for lands called Tir y prydidd | 00 | 00 | 06 |
| The same Dauid for lands called Tir y bwla | 00 | 00 | 01½ |
| The same Dauid for lands called Tir verch ften ycha | 00 | 00 | 04½ |
| Hopkin Perkins for lands called Fforrest ycha | 00 | 02 | 02 |
| Thomas Perkins for lands called Tir tanglust | 00 | 01 | 04 |
| Richard Leyson for lands called Glyn y gorse | 00 | 00 | 08 |
| The same Richard for lands called Gorselwyn | 00 | 00 | 03 |

| | *li.* | *s.* | *d.* |
|---|---|---|---|
| The same Richard for lands called Parke y bryn rose y velin | 00 | 01 | 00 |
| The same Richard for lands called Tir Evan Gwynn | 00 | 00 | 04 |
| The same Richard for lands called Croft yr Gethin | 00 | 00 | 03 |
| The same Richard for lands called Tir Tom Griffith | 00 | 00 | 07½ |
| The same Richard for lands called Tir Madocke goch, Tir y mynidd and Gwern bwll | 00 | 00 | 05½ |
| The same Richard for lands called Pant y ffynon late in the hands of Thomas Dauid Vaughan | | | |
| Morgan Jones for lands called Knape coch | 00 | 01 | 05 |
| The same Morgan for lands called Keven benvod | 00 | 01 | 00 |
| The same Morgan for lands called Gwern y maen llwyd | 00 | 00 | 01½ |
| The same Morgan for lands called Gelly dywill | 00 | 01 | 00 |
| The same Morgan for lands called Glan mynrod | 00 | 01 | 05 |
| Vxor Roger Jones for lands called Blaen brane | 00 | 00 | 09 |
| The same for lands called Kilvrane | 00 | 00 | 10 |
| The same for lands called Tir y milwr | 00 | 01 | 07 |
| The same for lands called Tir Meyricke yshan | 00 | 00 | 11 |
| The same for lands called Lletty mane | 00 | 00 | 02 |
| Jenkin Griffith for lands called Gelly dêg and Llechredd drymme | 00 | 01 | 08 |
| The same Jenkin for lands called Cwm Crynach and Tir y prydidd in the hands of Richard John | 00 | 01 | 00 |
| John Jenkin for lands called Tir reynallt | 00 | 01 | 01 |
| The same John Jenkin for lands called the Vonddar and Ynis arlla | | | |
| The same John for lands called Tir Thomas Meyricke | 00 | 00 | 04 |
| The same John for lands called Tir Evan Jenkin Tryharne | 00 | 00 | 02 |
| The same John for lands called Tir Evan Lloyd in the hands of Hopkin Thomas | 00 | 00 | 05 |

| | |
|---|---|
| The same for Lands late in the hands of Watkin David & now of Cecill Hopkin | vjᵈ |
| The same for the late Lands of Morgan David now in the possession of the said Morgan | iiijᵈ |
| The same for Tir Madocke whith Goedhirseth and Tir Gwillim Gronow ddu, being the late Lands of Mʳ Gibbs | vjᵈ o |
| The same for Tir Evan Lloyd now in the hands of Hopkin David Woodwall | vᵈ |
| The same for Tir Thomas Griffith David ddu being the late Lands of Thomas William Hopkin now in the hands of John David | ixᵈ |
| The same for Tydr ats Mawr being the late lands of the said Thomas now in the hands of the said John David | xijᵈ |
| The same & Elizabeth Thomas, Widdow, for Gelly dowill afs Tir Wᵐ Rees Griffith being the late Lands of Thomas Morgan, Gent. | xijᵈ |
| DAVID EVANS, Esqʳˢ, for Gellygynoen now in his possession | ixᵈ |
| The same for Tir Phillipptew in his possession | vᵈ |
| The same for Tir Evan bach in his possession | iiijᵈ |
| The same for Tir Tom Griffith ap Hopkin Lloyd in his possession | xvjᵈ |
| The same for Gwayn Evan ddu in his possession | iiijᵈ |
| The same for Gwernvare in his possession | iiijᵈ |
| The same for Tir Tom lya now in the possession Gwenllian Morgan, Widdow | ·υ |
| The same for Tir John Llewelin ap Owen, Evan Madocke bach and Evan goch ap Richard now in the hands of Evan Jenkin Bowen, Edward Rosser & also John ... Widdow | |
| The same for Tir Meyricke y chan 4ˢ 8ᵈ and for Tir Evan Jenkin Treharne 2ˢ, now in the hands of David Hopkin | iiijˢ xᵈ |
| The same for Lands late in the hands of Rosser | |

| | |
|---|---|
| David Llewelin and now of Evan Rosser and Robert Rosser | xxijᵈ |
| The same for Tir Trymme now in the hands of Mault Thomas Widdow | xxjᵈ |
| The same for Tir y prydidd now in the hands of Llewelyn John William | vjᵈ |
| The same for Glynygorse now in the hands of Paul John Bevan | viijᵈ |
| The same for Tiry Corseloyn now in the hands of the sᵈ Paul | iij |
| The same for Parke y brin Rhose y Velin now in the hands of the said Paul | xijᵈ |
| The same for Tir Evan Gwynn now in the hands of the said Paul | iiijᵈ |
| The same for Crofty kethin now in his possession | iijᵈ |
| The same for Tir Thomas Griffiths ap Hopkin Lloyd now in his possession | vjᵈ |
| The same for Tir Evan Madocke goth Tir y Mynydd and Gwern bwll now in the hands of Griffith John Awbrey and Richard Jerdin | vᵈ ob. |
| The same for Pant y Fynnon lase, now in the hands of Richard Jerdin | vᵈ |
| The same for Gellydeg now in the hands of Evan Rosser and others | xxᵈ |
| The same for Cwm kyrnach 8ᵈ for Tiry prydidd 4ᵈ in the hands of Lyson Prees and others | xijᵈ |
| The same for Tir Jenkin ap Gwillim & Lloyn y vr wydir in the hands of Katherine John | xxiijᵈ |
| The same for Tir Llen lase now in the hands of Edward Rosser | vᵈ |
| The same for Clyn Cadwgan now in the hands of Zacharias Jenkin | vjᵈ |
| The same for Tir Hopkin Rosser Vaine in the hands of the said Zacharias | iiijᵈ |
| The same for Tir Howell ap Evan Jenkin now called Trymme ycha being the late Lands of | |

owner of the subsequent reversion, that is to say the person who would be entitled to the land on failure of the heirs of the body of the original tenant entail.

The estate produced by a fine was known as a 'base fee.' In effect a base fee was a determinable fee simple; it endured for as long as the entail would have continued if it has not been barred, and determined when the entail would have ended. Though less effective, fines has a much wider scope than recoveries. A fine could be levied by one who had no entail but merely a hope of being the heir or who had merely a contingent or executory interest entail, i.e. an entail to which he would be entitled only if some specified event occurred.

Only the person seized could suffer a recovery; and if they would not collaborate, a fine was the only device available for barring an entail which had not yet fallen into possession.

As with most legislation affecting English and Welsh settlements, the 18th century brought amendments that changed the role of fines and recoveries, making them purely a formality that was seen as complicated and expensive. The introduction of the Fine and Recoveries Act much later in 1833 saw the process of barring the entail play an integral role in the mechanism of family settlements, with simpler methods now called upon in court.

Alongside other evidence, the *Survey of the Manor of Kilvey A.D. 1686* denotes Bussey Mansel as freeholder, however the areas described in the following excerpts taken from page 344 to 347 were the aforementioned lost Thomas estates.

BUSSY MANSELL, Esq, for Tiry Gwl now in the hands of John Popkins, Gent...

The same for Trergrove 12d, & for Tir Evan Jenkin

Treharne 2d now in the hands of Hopkin David Vaughan.

The same & Elizabeth Thomas, Widdow, for Gelly dowill als Tir Wm Rees Griffith being the late Lands of Thomas Morgan, Gent

DAVID EVANS, Esq, for Gellygynoen now in his possession.

The same for Tir Meyricke y chan 4s 8d and for Tir Evan Jenkin Treharne 2s, now in the hands of David Hopkin.

The Survey of the Manor of Kilvey A.D. 1650 and the Survey of the Manor of Kilvey A.D. 1688 also document the holdings of William Thomas I and Bussey Mansel, evidence that highlights the great deal of land and properties at stake.

According to documents from the Cardiff Record Office, Bussey and his son Thomas also leased a great deal of Walter Thomas' estates, some of which are shown below:

Counterpart 1663/4 from Bussy Mansel of Britton Ferry to John Griffith of Llangyfelach, yeoman of a message lands called Tir William David y vicar in the tenure of Katherine Thomas, widow, expecting timber, quarries and mines. Term 99 years of lease. CL/BF

Lease from Bussey and Thomas Mansel Gwagnreyrch in Langeflach in 1668 and in 1669 Tire pen yr Hewle also in Llangyfelach. CL/BF

Bussey and Thomas Mansel a May 1 1670 lease to Thomas Griffiths concerning Pant y Guire in Lanswitt Juxta Neath. CL/BF

Bussey Mansel a lease dated October 10 1670 to Llewillin Bevan lands in Llangyfelach called Yddoy Tyrwn Twll y Gwthie. CL/BF

Bussey and Thomas Mansell a lease 1 November 1671 to Mary Poniran called Ystrad Owen.

Thomas Mansel 12 June 1672 lease to Thomas Williams Trehar in Lantwit Juxta Neath.

20 August 1673 Bussy Mansel for land called Tir y Merchr in Lanridin. D 32838

Bussey Mansel to Evan Leyson for Aberdylas Fach for 10 October 1673 in Lantwit Juxta Neath.

Whilst, as The Walter Thomas Inheritance Association communicates, it is easy to understand why the estate was originally entailed to his brother, after the experiences of his father and grandfather during the temporary forfeiture of their estates during the aftermath of the Civil Wars, and there is no doubt that William's barring the entail was perfectly legal, its succession by William and Walter's uncle and the progression through the Mansel line was a matter of fraud under the terms of Walter's Last Will and Testament. But this instance wouldn't be the end but the start of a series of deceptions faced by Ann Thomas and her descendants.

**Registration of Marriage, Zacharias Jenkin and Ann Thomas late 1680's (date unknown), Llangyfelach Parish Church.**

# 5. THE MURDER OF JENKIN ZACHARIAS

**ANN WAS JUST 11 YEARS OLD** when William passed away in 1677 and Catherine became the guardian and trustee of not just her but her father's estate. Whilst it would have been communicated to her that the line of succession would favour her father's younger brother William and any male heirs he produced later on in his lifetime, William's death and the bequeath of estates to his uncle Bussey would be difficult for any teenager to understand, regardless of Ann's personal standing. We cannot know just how much Ann was aware of from the historical documents that the case behind the Walter Thomas' estates draws evidence from, but there is no doubt that Ann, once of age, moved on with her life.

As the great-granddaughter of the legendary Walter Thomas I, and even in the face of what many presumed was her suspected illegitimacy, Ann would have had no shortage of suitors. Ann however was married in the latter part of the 1680s to Zacharias Jenkin, son of Jenkin Hopkin of the Einon AP Collwyn line and of the same line of decent as Walter Thomas I himself.

The marriage between Zacharias and Ann bore three children, Jenkin Zacharias (Zachary or Zachariah) being the eldest. Documents do show however that Jenkin had an elder brother, Evan, however despite following Evan's baptism in 1680, he disappears from records.

According to historical documents gathered on behalf of The Walter Thomas Inheritance Association, Jenkin first appears in 1715, a time where he lived in lower Llansamlet. As these records only usually document the presence of the heads of household, Jenkin appears one year after the death of his father, however, it is now known that Zacharias Jenkin lived with his son's family on the basis that he married before 1714, an arrangement common during this era.

An important figure in his own right being in the employ of the Duke of Beaufort, Jenkin first served the second Duke of Beaufort – the only son of Charles Somerset, Marquess of Worcester, and Rebecca Child – Henry Somerset, up until his death in 1714, then the third Duke of Beaufort, Henry Somerset-Scudamore, for the remainder of his career alongside fellow housekeepers Edward Thomas, Thomas Morgan and David Morgan. It was only during the years 1726, 1728, 1730 and 1731 that Jenkin isn't referred to in the Parish of Llansamlet records, which is a strange phenomenon for the Elizabethan era. Under Elizabethan law, more specifically The Poor Relief Act 1601, no individual could move to another parish without permission unless they were gentry or had a contract to work elsewhere.

The 1601 Act states that each individual parish was responsible for its 'own' poor. Arguments over which parish was responsible for a pauper's poor relief and concerns over migration to more generous parishes led to the passing of the Settlement Act 1662 which allowed relief only to established residents of a parish – mainly through birth, marriage and apprenticeship. A pauper applicant had to prove a 'settlement', and if unable to, they were removed to the next parish that was nearest to the place of their birth, or where they might prove some connection, as a result some paupers were moved hundreds of miles. Although each parish that they passed through was not responsible for them, under other legislation they were supposed to supply food and drink and shelter for at least one night. Individual parishes were keen to keep costs of poor relief as low as possible and there are examples of paupers being shunted back and forth between parishes. The Settlement Laws allowed strangers to a parish to be removed after 40 days if they were not working, but the cost of removing such people meant that they were often left until they tried to claim poor relief. In 1697 Settlement Laws were tightened with people barred from entering a parish unless they produced a Settlement certificate.

The introduction of the Poor Relief Act – also known throughout history as the Settlement Act or, more honestly, the Settlement and Removal Act – by the Cavalier Parliament of England affected all when it came to their inclusion in the parish records, records that have often been the only source of information available to shape proceedings when major historical events were perhaps thin on the ground. The increase of the poor across England and Wales was also particularly influential and acted as a primary reason for why such an Act was passed as explained here in this extract from Statutes of the Realm: Volume 5, 1628-80, originally published by Great Britain Record Commission:

Rectial of the increase of the poor, and that the same arises from Defect in the poor Lwas and want of Employment

Reasons for passing this Act.; Justice of the Peace may remove Persons coming to settle in Ten´ement under £ 10 per Annum to last Settlement.

Whereas the necessity number and continual increase of the Poore not onely within the Cities of London and Westminster with the Liberties of each of them but alsoe through the whole Kingdome of England and Dominion of Wales is very great and exceeding burthensome being occasioned by reason of some defects in the Law concerning the setling of the Poor and for want of a due Provision of the regulations of releife and imployment in such Parishes or Places where they are legally setled which doth enforce many to turn incorrigible Rogues and

others to perish for want togeather with the neglect of the faithfull execution of such Lawes & Statutes as have formerly beene made for the apprehending of Rogues and Vagabonds and for the good of the Poore For remedy whereof and for the preventing the perishing of any of the Poore whether young or old for want of such supplies as are necessary May it please your most Excellent Majestie that it may be enacted and be it enacted by the Kings most Excellent Majesty by and with the Advice and Consent of the Lords Spiritual and Temporal and the Commons in this present Parliament assembled and by the Authority of the same That whereas by reason of some defects in the Law poore people are not restrained from going from one Parish to another and therefore doe endeavor to settle themselves in those Parishes where there is the best Stocke the largest Commons or Wastes to build Cottages and the most Woods for them to burn and destroy and when they have consumed it then to another Parish and att last become Rogues and Vagabonds to the great discouragem[en]t. of Parishes to provide Stocks where it is lyable to be devoured by Strangers Be it therefore enacted by the Authority aforesaid That it shall and may be lawfull upon complaint made by the Churchwardens or Overseers of the Poore of any Parish to any Justice of Peace within Forty dayes after any such Person or Persons coming so to settle as aforesaid in any Tenement under the yearely value of Ten pounds for any two Justices of the Peace whereof one to be of the Quo§ of the Division where any person or persons that are likely to be chargeable to the Parish shall come to inhabitt by theire warrant to remove and convey such person or persons to such Parish where he or they were last legally setled either as a native Householder Sojourner Apprentice or Servant for the space of forty dayes at the least unlesse he or they give sufficient security for the discharge of the said Parish to bee allowed by the said Justices.

In addition to influencing settlement before and during the 18th century, as it would have for individuals like Jenkin Zacharias, the Poor Law also influenced the seasonal provision of workers, the nature of workhouses and the apprehension of individuals described as rogues and vagabonds.

Despite his service to the Beauforts being fraught with loyalty, once of age and even before that, Jenkin was fully aware of his mother's disinheritance, a fraud that troubled him greatly. The troubles of his and his family's past came back to haunt him once more as the estates that should have been passed down to him by grandfather Walter, his uncle William and then his mother Ann were sold off to the Popkin family, the Tenant family and many more, once Bussey's line of succession and then the Earl of Jersey's came to a brutal yet expected halt.

Having been bequeathed a vast bulk of the Thomas estates by William Thomas II in 1677, it is believed that Bussey Mansel conveyed a proportion of the lands during his lifetime. Particularly following the death of his son, Thomas Mansel, who predeceased his father in 1684. Thomas is buried in Westminster Abbey, as were several members of the Mansel family. In the north aisle of the nave of the Abbey is a white marble monument to Thomas Mansel (joined together with one for William Morgan of Tredegar), possibly created by sculptor William Stanton, with the Latin inscription which can be translated as:

Near this place lie, in certain hopes of a resurrection, the ashes of Thomas Mansell, eldest son of Bussy Mansell, Esquire of Briton Ferry in Glamorganshire. He took to wife Elizabeth, daughter and heir of Richard Games, Esquire of Penderin in Brecknockshire, by whom

Oxwich Castle

he had one son Thomas, and two daughters Mary and Elizabeth. He died 13 December 1684 aged 38.

The coat of arms showing a 'chevron between three maunches, a crescent for difference' for Mansel and the arms of Games can also be seen.

To keep the estates in the family, upon his death in 1699, the lands and properties were bequeathed by Bussey to his godson, also named Thomas Mansel, as whilst son Thomas had two daughters, both were illegitimate. Thomas held the estates for just six years before dying without legal issue in 1705. As well as being a Member of Parliament for Cardiff, Thomas was buried in Westminster Abbey near his father, however, his grave has no marker. The estates were then handed to cousin Thomas Mansel of Margam, an action that fraudulently goes against William Thomas' intentions for his family estates. It clearly states in William's Will that should there not be a lineal continuation of heirs in the Mansel male line then the ownership of the estates should revert back to the Thomas family, a statement that should have put Ann Thomas centre stage as rightful heir once more. Instead the Thomas and Briton Ferry estates were passed to his son,

Louisa Barbarina Mansel, Lady Vernon (1732-1786) by Thomas Gainsborough RA.
Image Courtesy of National Trust Images

Bussey Mansel of Margam when he died in 1723. The Pryce-Mansel Estates of Briton Ferry, Danygraig, which included Briton Ferry House, were particularly vast and according to Hanes. Morg., 227 it contained 40,000 acres scattered across 40 parishes.

The history of the Mansel family is particularly well documented, and even today relics found in Penrice and Margam Abbey form the basis of several thousand documents in the National Library of Wales, in addition to being the subject of many books, including A History of Margam Abbey by Walter de Gray Birch, Descriptive Catalogue of the Penrice and Margam Abbey Manuscripts also by De Gray Birch, History of the Family of Maunsell (Mansell, Mansel) by C. A. Maunsell and E. P. Statham, and Limbus Patrum Morganiae et Glamorganiae by G. T. Clark. Needless to say no document, either privately or publicly published, mentioned the deception that this great house was at the centre of.

Bussey Mansel of Margam, the fourth Baron Mansel, married in 1729 to Lady Barbara Blackett, a union that saw the estates pass from the Mansel family to that of the Earl of Jersey as Lady Barbara was the daughter of the second Earl, William Villiers, known as Viscount Villiers. From 1697 to 1711, William was an English peer from an infamous family. The son of Edward Villiers, the first Earl of Jersey, and his wife Barbara (née Chiffinch), William forged a successful career on the political scene, representing Kent in the House of Commons from 1705 to 1708 before succeeding his father in the earldom. His role earned him an international reputation, and during a trip to Italy in 1703 he famously commissioned a bronze medal from renowned Florence-based Italian sculptor Massimiliano Soldani-Benz. Lady Barbara was the eldest of his three children with Judith Herne, daughter of Frederick Herne and Elizabeth Lisle. Son William Villiers became the third Earl of Jersey, whilst his younger son Thomas because the first Earl of Clarendon. Barbara's marriage to Bussey wasn't her first, as her name suggests she was firstly married to Sir William Blackett, a British politician who sat in the House of Commons from 1710 to 1728 and the second Baronet of Newcastle-upon-Tyne, in 1725. They had no children, leaving Barbara free to marry again when Sir William died three years later.

The marriage between Bussey and Lady Barbara bore one child, a daughter named Louisa Barbara, thus ending the Mansel male line. But it was Louisa's marriage to Lord Vernon of Sudbury Hall that saw the estates deceitfully

Vernon House, Briton Ferry. Home of Arthur Mansel and Jane Pryce. Parents of Bussy Mansel and sister Catherine, who married William Thomas of Dan-y-Graig. Mother and Father of Walter Thomas 1667. Image Credit: The National Library of Wales.

### ANCESTRY OF THE FAMILIES OF YNYSYMAERDY MANOR AND VERNON HOUSE

IESTYN ap GWRGAN . . . Lord of Glamorgan until Norman times.
CARADOC ap IESTYN . . . Lord of Afan Wallia.
MORGAN ap CARADOC . . .
MORGAN GAM . . . d. 1240.
LEISON ap MORGAN GAM . . . Leison was succeeded by his brother.
MORGAN FYCHAN . . . d. 1288 . . . Morgan Fychan's son Rhys was the founder of the Baglan branch of the family.
LEISON (D'Avêne)        RHYS  d 1330
LEISON
EVAN LAS.
WILLIAM . . . Ancestor of the PRICE (ap Rhys) family of Ynysymaerdy.
LEISON PRICE of YNYSYMAERDY . . . Builder of the "fair new house" which later became known as Vernon House.
WILLIAM.
JANE . . . d. 1638 . . . Married Arthur Mansel, 3rd son of Sir Thomas Mansel, 1st Baronet of Margam.
THOMAS (died when young)
BUSSY . . . m. Catherine, Lady Stradling in 1646 . . . He died in 1699
THOMAS (son) . . . Died in 1684. Buried in Westminster Abbey.
THOMAS (Bussy's grandson) . . . inherited the Briton Ferry Estate. He died in 1705 without heir, so the estate passed to his god-son Bussy Mansel of Margam.
BUSSY MANSEL (The second) . . . m. Lady Barbara Blacket in 1729. (She was the daughter of the 2nd Earl of Jersey). They lived in Briton Ferry from 1705 until 1740 when he inherited the title of 4th Lord Margam. Vernon House was rebuilt; probably during this period. Bussy died in 1750 and his daughter inherited the Briton Ferry Estate.
LOUISA BARBARA (Daughter) . . . m. Lord Vernon of Sudbury Hall, Derbyshire. Louisa Barbara died in 1786 and willed the property to her god-son William Augustus Henry Villiers, second son of the 4th Earl of Jersey.
WILLIAM AUGUSTUS HENRY . . . Inherited the estate. He died unmarried in 1813 and the estate then passed to his brother, the 5th Earl of Jersey.
GEORGE CHILD VILLIERS . . . Fifth Earl of Jersey . . . d. 1855.
GEORGE AUGUSTUS FREDERICK VILLIERS . . . Sixth Earl of Jersey . . . d. 1859.
VICTOR ALBERT GEORGE VILLIERS . . . Seventh Earl of Jersey . . . d. 1915.
GEORGE HENRY ROBERT CHILD VILLIERS . . . Eighth Earl of Jersey . . . d. 1923.
GEORGE FRANCIS VILLIERS . . . Ninth Earl of Jersey. The present Earl.
The Estate was sold in 1951.
The Vernon House was demolished in 1974.

A copy of 'Ancestry of the Families of Ynysmaerdy Manor and Vernon House.

remain in the hands of the House of Jersey. Upon her death in 1786, and due to the fact that she had no children with Lord Vernon, she bequeathed her estates to godson William Augustus Henry Villiers, second son of the fourth Earl of Jersey. Dying unmarried in 1813, Villiers bequeathed the estate to his brother, the fifth Earl of Jersey, and the estates were passed on in this fashion consecutively until the ninth Earl of Jersey, a progression that we will explore later in this book.

Aware of the continuing deceit whilst estates that should be rightly his mother's and then his, living in close quarters with one Robert Popkin, his cousin by law and contemporary, was the final nail in the coffin for Jenkin Zacharias. As we mentioned earlier much of the Thomas estates were sold to the Popkin family.

John Popkin was just one family member who took up residence on the estate, living at a farm known as Tyr-y-Mynydd, which sits north east of the Drymma mountain property that was originally held by the Thomas family. The extract below from The History of the Vale of Neath by

D. Rhys Phillips however demonstrates that his family's ownership of said estates was a fact that Robert wasn't afraid to boast about at his local drinking hole.

**Ynystawe House, drawn by Eluned Lewis 2000.**

The author of *Hanes Morganwg* (pp. 346-8) states that after the death of Phillip Hoby in 1678, his widow Elizabeth appointed Phillip Williams as Steward of the Neath Abbey Estate ; that the whole of the title deeds and court rolls of the manor passed into his hands at Elizabeth's death ; and that after Phillip Williams's death in 1717, his son Llewelyn Williams of Duffryn succeeded to the stewardship.

The indenture D.D. 849, given on a previous page shows that on 25 March 1731, Thomas Williams [solicitor, Neath] was described as "the steward of the said Griffith Rice and Edward Rice in their life time." This statement of Lucy Rice, widow of Edward, throws some doubt on D.W. Jones's dates and facts, for he implies in *Han. Morg.* p. 347, that Thos. Williams did not succeed Llewelyn of Duffryn till 1748-49, when –

"The estate was sold to John Popkin, Esq ... second son of Thomas Popkin, Esq., who was the Sheriff of Glamorgan in 1718. John Popkin lived in the Drumau,

and he was called 'the old lord of Drumau' : his wife was Sophia, daughter of Herbert Herbert of Lletty'r Awel, Glynneath. When John Popkin bought the estate, the old steward Llewelyn Williams gave up all the deeds, maps, etc. to Thomas Williams, solicitor, Neath, who had been appointed steward under the new proprietor. Thomas Williams lived at Cwrt Herbert, and there also his son and grandson, Thomas Williams, dwelt – each acting as steward under John Popkin and his successor. A daughter of the last Thomas Williams married John Edwards, Esq., Rheolau. John Popkin (the old lord of Drumau) owned extensive iron works, and his father before him, and his forge was so perfect that one of its chief operations was the manufacture of muskets. Having buried all his children he made a Will in 1758 bequeathing all his property to his nephew Phillip, the second son of his sister Catherine, who had married (Sept. 28, 1704) a Mr. Evan Bowen of Maes Eglwys, Parish of Llangyfelach.

In addition to the Neath Abbey Estate falling into the hands of the Popkin family, Margam MS. 5695 contains evidence that the next stage of history regarding the Furnace also found its way to Thomas Popkin.

Heads of a Lease by the Rt. Hon. Bussy, now Lord Mansel, to Thomas Popkins, Esqre., of Melin-y-Court Furnace, from 25th March last for eleven years. Dat: 25th November, A.D. 1736.

Rumour has it that Robert was partial to bragging about the very story of Ann Thomas' disinheritance and his subsequent possession of her estates. Jenkin decided to take matters into his own hands after enduring years of booze fuelled taunts by Robert.

Jenkin confronted Robert at his home at Ynystawe (Ynistawe) House, a skirmish that led to a violent exchange and Jenkin's death. During the struggle Jenkin was pushed down the stairs, a matter that was quickly brushed under the carpet thanks to the affluence of Robert's father, Thomas Popkin of Fforest Uychan Estate, Ynystawe, and Sheriff of Swansea in 1718. Thomas Popkin was related to Hopkin David Edwards (Popkin) of Danygraig, Swansea and Ynystawe, the father of Catherine and father-in-law to Walter Thomas I.

The following extract from The History and Antiquities of Glamorganshire and its Families by Thomas Nicholas, found in a chapter entitled 'Old and Extinct Families of Glamorgan', provides an overview into the lineage of the wider family, denoting a presence that may have well resulted in the affluent nature of Thomas Popkin himself.

**Maes Gwernen Hall, part of the Popkin Estate.**

*Popkin of Ynys-Tawe and Forest.*

There were Popkins of Ynys-Tawe and Forest, both of the same lineage, the former the senior line, and both now extinct. They claimed descent from Rhodri Mawr, King of Wales, through his eldest son, Prince Anarawd (*succ.* A.D. 877). Gruffydd Gethin, the first named in the pedigrees as of Ynys-Tawe, ninth in descent, had a son Hopkin ap Gruffydd, and he a son David *ap Hopkin* of Ynys-Tawe, who *m.* Eva, dau. of Jenkin ap Leyson of Avan, of the race of Iestyn ap Gwrgant. Hopkin ap David ap Hopkin followed, and had a son David ap Hopkin, whose son, *Hopkin David* of Ynys-Tawe, had an elder son, ——

David *Popkin*, who finally fixed the patronymic as a surname. He *m.* Jennet, dau. of Robert William, Esq., of Court Rhyd-hir, and, with other children, had a son and successor, John [*sc.,* son of] David Popkin, of Ynys-Tawe, who, adhering to the favourite family name, called his eldest son Hopkin [*sc.,* son of] John David Popkin, who was also of Ynys-Tawe. By his wife Luce, dau. Of Harry

Rees ap Gruffydd, he left an elder son, his successor, David Popkin, who *m.* Jane, dau. of Thomas Morgan Cadwgan, Esq., and was succeeded by his son, Hopkin David Popkin, living 1678, whose wife was a dau. of John David Rosser of Trewyddfa. The account of this elder branch here ceases in our MSS.

The Forest *junior* line begins with Hopkin, second son of the above Hopkin David of Ynys-Tawe, and continues at Forest, near Neath, for ten generations. This line seems to have held a higher position in the county than the senior. Thomas Popkin of Forest was Sheriff of Glamorgan in 1718, and his grandson Thomas held the same office in 1755. They intermarried with the families of Dawkins of Ynystawlog, Evans of Peterwell, Card. ; and the last-mentioned Thomas *m.* Justina Maria, dau. of Sir John Stepney of Llanelly. The last male representative was Bennet Popkin, Esq., of Forest, "who went to reside at Kittlehill in pursuance of a limitation in the will of his aunt, Mrs. Bennet." He *m.* Mary, dau. and co-h. of David White, Esq., of Miskin, and *d.s.p.* (See *Bath of Ffynone.*)

The arms of the Popkins were — *Or, a stag passant gu., attired and hoofed sa. ; a bordure engrailed gu.*

The murder of Jenkin Zacharias is likely to be just one defining event that was seemingly suppressed by the Popkin family in a bid to keep their honour and reputation firmly intact. Like events with limited historical evidence always attract, the murder of Jenkin Zacharias and the mayhem that ensued was kept alive from generation to generation via word of mouth, and whilst over time some details have got lost or evolved, there is evidence to suggest that Jenkin and Robert's relationship as cousins by law may have been troubled long before the public house bragging that led to the violent struggle at Ynystawe and Jenkin's untimely demise…

Many accounts relate to one Rebecca Evans as being the first wife of Jenkin Zacharias, and whilst no documentary evidence of the marriage between the two can be found, as many of the parish records for the period have been destroyed, there is much family evidence, particularly from the early 19th century, that suggests a number of the rumours relating to the era, and more particularly their union, may in fact have some truth to them. Jenkin is said to have met up with Rebecca on a hunting trip at her grandfather's estate in Llangennech Carms near Llanelli. A marriage arranged by proxy by their respective parents, whilst there is evidence to support that the marriage did go ahead, the partnership was never solemnised – despite some sources claiming that the pair lived together at Ynystawe Hall and went on to have three daughters – leaving Rebecca and Jenkin to marry their respective partners, Robert Popkin and Mary Lloyd.

Mary Lloyd, daughter of Mary Lloyd and John Lloyd of Peterswell and Llangennech Carms, was actually the step-sister of Rebecca Evans, a product of her mother's first marriage to Daniel Evans, a prominent barrister of the day who in his lifetime accumulated vast estates. Daniel's nephew was actually Benjamin Franklin, who he educated

X. DAVID ap Hopkin of Ynis Dawe, m. Margaret, d. of Thomas Havard of Cwrt-sion-Yonge, Brecknock. Issue: 1. *Hopkin*. 2. *John*, whence POPKIN OF FFOREST. 3. *Edward*, whence a BRANCH. 4. *Thomas*. 5. *Crisly*. 6. *Jenet*, m. John Thomas Vach[ychan], of Cilvae. 7. *Wenllian*, m. Morgan ap John Gibbon of Llanvihangel by St. Fagan's. 8. *Margaret*, m. Thomas Lloyd ap John of Glyn Nedd. 9. *Elizabeth*, m. David Landegg of Gower. Of base issue : 10. Sir *Thomas*, parson of Llanilad. 11. *Thomas*. 12. *Margaret*, m. John Hopkins of Llanrhidian. Also, by Margaret Carter of Duffyn-Clydach : 13. *Catherine*, m. Lewis ——, a tailor.

XI. HOPKIN of Ynis-Dawe and Fforest, m. Denis, d. of William ap John ap Rhys of Glyn Nedd, and had: 1. *David*. 2. *Roger*, m. Margaret, d. of Thomas ap Griffith ap Owen Gethyn. 3. *John*. 4. *Ellen*, m. William ap Llewelyn John of Bryn Coch. 5. *Jenet*, m. Evan ap William of Cwrt-Sarth in Briton Ferry. 6. *Wenllian*, m. Howel ap Cadwgan of Abergorky. 7. *Margaret*, m. Rhys ap David Jenkin.

XII. DAVID, m. Jenet, d. of Robert ap William of Cwrt-Rhyd-hir, and had: 1. *John*. 2. *Robert*, m. Margaret, d. of John ap Evan David of Llanguig [Glyn Llwchwr], and had (a) *Hopkin*, (b) *Isabel*. 3. *Edward* of Swansea, m. Jenet, d. of Rhys ap Thomas Hir of Llangevelach, and had (a) *Hopkin*, (b) *John*, (c) *William*, (d) *Thomas*, or David, m. Blanch, d. of Rees Hopkin Jenkin of Llangevelach ; (e) a dau., m. Morgan John Morgan; (f) *Margaret*, (g) *Jenet*. 4. *Margaret*, m. Thomas Rosser of Altvannoc. 5. *Wenllian*, m. 1st Henry Grono of Pennard ; 2nd John ap Thomas Franklen. 6. *Catherine*, m. John Llewelyn of Gardine (?). 7. *Alice*, m. Hopkin Rosser of Blaen Crymllyn [Llancerymlyn]. 8. *Jenet*, m. David ap Rosser ap Owen ap Jevan-làs. 9. *Catherine*, m. Griffith ap Evan Morgan of Cilybebill.

XIII. JOHN of Ynis-Dawe and Fforest, living 1621, m. 1st Eva, d. of Thomas Powel ap John Goch of Lloydarth ; 2nd Mary, d. of Thomas Vychan. By the first: 1. *Hopkin*. 2. *Thomas*.

XIV. HOPKIN of Ynis-Dawe and Fforest, m. Lucy, d. of Henry Price ap Griffith ap Evan Melyn. Issue: 1. *David*. 2. *Roger*, m. Catherine, d. of Griffith Jeffrey of Ystrad-Gynlais.

XV. DAVID ap Hopkin of Ynis-Dawe, m. Jane, d. of Thomas ap Morgan Cadwgan. Issue : 1. *Hopkin*. 2. *John*, m. a d. of Evan Powel of Llangevelach. 3. *Robert*, m. a d. of Rev. Samuel Acton.

XVI. HOPKIN HOPKINS of Ynis-Dawe in 1678, m. a d. of John David Rosser of Trewyddfa.

---

## POPKIN OF DAN-Y-CRAIG.

XI. 3. EDWARD, third son (base) of David ap Hopkin of Ynis-Dawe, by Nest, d. of Jevan ap Thomas of Nether Gwent, m. Maud, d. and h. of Jevan ap Madoc of Dan-y-Craig ap Jevan ap Griffith Gethyn. [Margaret, d. of Rees Thomas ap Hopkin of Ynis-y-Biben]. Issue :

XII. DAVID, m. Catherine, d. of Rhys ap Evan ap William [Price] of Ynis-y-Maerdy [Briton Ferry], by Elizabeth Mansel, and sister of John Price of Cwrt-y-Carnau. Issue : 1. *Hopkin*. 2. John David of Swansea, m. Margaret, d. of Robert Smith of Swansea, and had (a) *David*, (b) *Robert*, (c) *Matthew* (base), by Jacquet Richard. 3. *Matthew Davies* of Bernard's Inn, London, s. p. 4. *Edward* of Llysworney, m. Eliza, d. of Rhys Griffith of Llysworney, by a d. and h. of — Madoc, and had (a) Captain *John Davies*, a great adventurer by sea ; (b) *John*, (c) *David*, (d) *Maud*, (e) *David* (base), by Margaret d. of David Owen-ddu. 5. *Popkin*, m. Elizabeth, d. of Rees Griffith, and widow of David Griffith of Llys-y-ffronydd. 6. *Maud*, m. Morgan Rosser of Swansea. 7. *Margaret*, m. Evan John Evan of Llwyn-Eridd. 8. *Jane*, m. John Bennet of Penrice.

---

A Passage from The Genealogies of Glamorgan (The History and Antiquities of Glamorganshire and its Families) by Thomas Nicholas p. 526/7.

and set up as a lawyer before he immigrated to America and founded the American Constitution. Like Rebecca – who had a son, Thomas, and a daughter, Mary, by her marriage to Robert – the marriage between Jenkin and Mary also bore children before his death in 1734 at age 47. Whilst there is no documentary evidence to support the act of murder bestowed on Jenkin by cousin Robert Popkin, it is said that Robert admitted to his actions on several occasions during his famous drunken rages.

The Popkins Family and Others at Llansamlet 1751 - 1771.

Ynstawe House and the surrounding estates were leased to John Rhys Bevan in 1789 by Thomas Popkin of Bryn Coch for a period of 99 years. John's daughter Janet Bevan married one Zacharias Jenkin, born 12 January 1769, a connection that caused much confusion later down the line within the Thomas family as descendant Nathaniel Richard Thomas confused this Jenkin with the same individual who wed Ann Thomas, thus falsely claiming that Ynstawe House was part of the Thomas estates. This is thought to be the reason why Jenkin Zacharias wished to be referred to as 'Zachary' to avoid any confusion with his cousins. Nevertheless, the pair lived in the mansion house for the remainder of their lifetime.

After the death of Robert Popkin in 1763, the estates were bequeathed to his son Thomas Popkin who later married into the Stepney family of Llanelli, an English family originally from Stepney, London, who made their fortune from the lands surroundings the town of Llanelli in West Wales. Whilst Thomas and his wife had no male heir, they did have one daughter, Rebecca Elinora, who married Sir Watkin Lewes, a Welsh politician who later became Lord Mayor of London in 1780 after being elected alderman for the London Ward of Lime Street and Sheriff of London in 1772. One year later he was elected at a by-election as one of the four Members of Parliament for the City of London, and as a result he served as an MP until his defeat at the 1796 general election. He stood again at the 1802 general election but his bid was unsuccessful. The pair had one child, Justina Anna Lewes, who died unmarried in 1819. With the end of the line came the transfer of the estates, land and property that should have still been passed on to Ann Thomas and her descendants, into Chancery in 1831.

William Martin, an engineer and advisor to the Earl of Jersey, later purchased the Ynstawe estate out of Chancery.

```
::::::::::::::::::::::::::::::::::::::::::::::::::::::::::::::::::
Zacarian JENKINS (82PP-TR)    Born: 12 Jan 1769 Glamorganshire, S-Wales
::::::::::::::::::::::::::::::::::::::::::::::::::::::::::::::::::
1-- Zacarian JENKINS (82PP-TR)    Born: 12 Jan 1769 Glamorganshire, S-Wales
  sp-Janet BEVAN (82PP-VX)    Born: Apr 1776
  2-- John JENKINS (82PQ-80)    Born: 25 Jul 1799 Glmrga, S. Wales
  2-- Thomas JENKINS (82PQ-95)    Born: 9 Sep 1802 Glmrga, S. Wales
  2-- Jenkin JENKINS (82PQ-88)    Born: 29 Jul 1805 Glmrga, S. Wales
  2-- Felish JENKINS (82PQ-CH)    Born: 29 Nov 1806 Glmrga, S. Wales
  2-- Anne JENKINS (82PQ-DN)    Born: 8 May 1808 Glmrga, S. Wales
  2-- Phillip JENKINS (82PQ-FT)    Born: 2 Apr 1811 Glmrga, S. Wales
  2-- Rachel JENKINS (82PQ-G1)    Born: 2 Dec 1818 Glmrga, S. Wales
::::::::::::::::::::::::::::::::::::::::::::::::::::::::::::::::::
```

Janet Bevan was the daughter of John Rees Bevan who held a lease for Ynystawe given by Thomas Popkin of Bryncoch nr Neath. Lease dated 1789 for 99 years.

## THE TRANSFER OF ESTATES INTO CHANCERY

A court that had jurisdiction over all matters of equity, including trusts, land law, the administration of the estates of lunatics and the guardianship of infants, the Court of Chancery is still part of the High Court of Justice of England and Wales today and has been a defining and ever present institution in the Walter Thomas story and will be for many years to come yet.

Since the late 14th century, hundreds of thousands of disputes over inheritance and wills, lands, trusts, debts, marriage settlements, apprenticeships, and other parts of the fabric of daily life, were heard by the Lord Chancellor or his deputies. People turned to his Court of Chancery due to its status as an equity court, and the promise of a merciful justice not bound by the strict rules of the common law courts. As a result the procedures utilised here were very different from those seen in common law courts, and even today Chancery provides a major resource for social and economic history, with suits from the 15th and early 16th centuries particularly well documented. Whilst it was this difference that set the Court of Chancery apart from others, historically there were a number of attempts to fuse

Chancery with the common law courts, primarily beginning in the 1850s.

The use of trusts and the administration of estates was one area that Chancery specialised in. The common law courts did not recognise such trusts, and so it fell to equity and to the Court of Chancery to deal with them, as befitting the common principle that the Chancery's jurisdiction was for matters where the common law courts could neither enforce a right nor administer it. The use of trusts became common during the 16th century, although the Statute of Uses "[dealt] a severe blow to these forms of conveyancing" and made the law in this area far more complex. The court's sole jurisdiction over trusts lasted until its dissolution. In addition to mitigating the injustice of strict common law rules, Chancery had the power to seize estates whilst they were been administered and their ownership disputed. Administration was remitted to trustees, who were supposed to provide annual accounts to the Master, which are still held by the Supreme Court of Justice today.

The Court of Chancery also had the power to grant three possible remedies. Alongside specific performance and injunctions, a statute passed during the reign of Richard II specifically gave Chancery the right to award damages, as this extract states:

> For as much as People be compelled to come before the King's Council, or in the Chancery by Writs grounded upon untrue Suggestions; that the Chancellor for the Time being, presently after that such Suggestions be duly found and proved untrue, shall have Power to ordain and award Damages according to his Discretion, to him which is so troubled unduly, as afore is said.

This mission to combine the common law courts with Chancery was finally achieved with the 1873 and 1875 Supreme Court of Judicature Acts, which dissolved the

Chancery and created a new unified High Court of Justice with the Chancery Division – one of three divisions of the High Court – succeeding the Court of Chancery as an equitable body.

• • • • • •

It was Sir Watkin Lewes, who served as an inmate at Fleet Street Prison prior to his death, who acknowledged the strength of the claim held by Jenkin Zacharias and his descendants, as this extract from The Old Green Book of Ezekel Thomas (1866) explains:

> The rents of the estate had more than cleared the mortgage and paid the Trustees for their troubles. The heirs at law viz; these poor people the descendants of Jenkin Zacharias could not fail to recover the estate without any encumbrance thereon, if they produce their claim. The Trustees however, one of whom was the notorious Mr Berrington, solicitor of Swansea, made it appear in the Court of Chancery that they had various claims against the property among which they had pretended to have advanced considerable sums of money to Sir Watkin Lewes in his lifetime: and in accordance with the adage so might overcome right, these treacherous Trustees actually succeeded in getting an Order from the Court of Chancery in defiance of these poor people, the heirs at law, to sell one particular portion of the estate (which had been possessed by their forefather old Jenkin Zacharias) to pay this pretended debt.

> In order to manage matters best suited to his own advantage whilst not only depriving but bidding defiance to the real heirs at law, Mr Berrington, the principal Trustee, having the family papers in his possession kept the marriage settlement and all other important documents from the said heirs and managed to make an heir of one Major Evans of Highmead in Cardiganshire.

> The estates were subsequently purchased out of Chancery by various procurers after 1917.

# 6. THE REPOSSESSION OF THE DRYMMA

**UNBEKNOWN TO MANY,** the bloodline of Walter Thomas I was about to come into focus once more. Before his death, Jenkin Zacharias' marriage to Mary Lloyd, daughter of Mary Lloyd and John Lloyd of Peterswell and Llangennech Carms, produced three daughters. Eldest Ann – named after his mother and Walter Thomas II's surviving heir, Ann Thomas – was born in 1706 but died a child in 1715. Their second daughter Matilda was born in 1717 and four years later third daughter Joan was born, however, like Ann she also died young.

Once of age, Jenkin's daughter Matilda married her cousin Richard Thomas, son of Thomas Edward Thomas of Llwn Crwn Uchaf, Llansamlet, and a descendant of Hopkin Thomas, Vicar of Llandeilo, Talybont and Llansawel, Briton Ferry, in 1733. Hopkin Thomas was actually the second son of Walter Thomas I and younger brother of William Thomas I. As well as the union bringing the Thomas family name back into the fold for another generation, as a married couple Richard and Matilda remained close to the estates that should have rightly been theirs. The family leased a farm called Llwncrwn Ucha in Llansamlet from the second Bussey Mansel of Margam, godson of the first Bussey Mansel of Briton Ferry and son of Thomas Mansel of Margam.

From their farm in Llansamlet, Matilda and Richard had six children – namely Morgan, Jenet, Thomas, Matilda, Elizabeth and Anne – one of which was illegitimate.

Their eldest child, Matilda, was my wife's ancestor. She married William Pommer of Llangyfelach in 1757, and both were involved in the early copper works in Morriston, however latter generations have moved out of the area, mainly to Nat-y-Glo and Blaenavon to work in the early ironworks, a trade that dominated the area during the early 20th century. Many of Matilda's descendants lived on Coal Tar Row, Ellick Street and Queen Street, areas renowned for their poverty and hardship. In fact, my wife's grandmother, also called Matilda, was one of ten children occupying a one up, one down property and enduring squalid conditions. The family later moved out of the area however, to continue their story in the hamlet of Brithdir New Tredegar, an area where they laid down their roots and still reside to this day.

Individually, despite descending from the great Walter Thomas I himself, like many of the Thomases of this generation and the last, Richard had very little wealth and was effectively dealt the same card as the disinherited Ann Thomas, inheriting nothing of any significance from his ancestors. As a result, the family lived simply and whilst eldest son Thomas Richard Thomas was already the rightful heir to the Drymma Estate, which was formed of Drymma Fach and Drymma Mansion and Brithdir Farm, by 1734 these vast areas of land were in the hands of the Morgan family of Birchgrove and Gwernllwnchwyth (Gwernllwnchwith), a family also related to Walter Thomas, but how this came about is unknown.

The history of Gwernllwnchwyth itself was the subject of an article entitled 'The End of an Elegant House.' Included in the journal Gower – Vol. 23 (1972), author Prys Morgan offers an account of the rise and fall of what was a great house.

The history of Gwernllwynchwyth is not very well-documented, apart from the history of the house in the Tudor period given by Mr. W. C. Rogers in his account of Kilvey in this Journal (Gower IV, 1951, pp. 35-41).

The recently demolished house is difficult to date

No.10 Upper Colliers Row, Birthplace of John Richard Thomas and his sister Margaret.

Drymmau House, Cadoxton Juxta nr Neath.

precisely. Mr. Rogers mentions the celebrated Dafydd ap Sion Fychan of Gwernllwynchwyth, who died in 1574, the so-called "Hector of Kilvey", who feuded fiercely with his ambitious Swansea neighbours, the Herberts, despite the fact that his own niece, Jenet of Cilybebyll, was married to the son of the great Sir George Herbert of Swansea. Clark, in the *Limbus Patrum,* gives Dafydd a pedigree which goes back to the late medieval Dafydd ap Gwilym Gam of Kilvey. Dafydd's son, John, had three daughters, one of whom was married to Richard Herbert, and the second to Hopkin Popkin

of Danygraig. Herbert, not needing a second Swansea home, sold Gwernllwynchwyth (which he held through his wife) to his brother-in-law, Hopkin Popkin.

Popkin, in turn, had no sons, but only two heiresses. Catherine, who had Danygraig, married Walter Thomas of Swansea (who was so prominent as a Royalist in the Civil War at Swansea). The other, Mary, had Gwernllwynchwyth, and married William, son of Lleisian Evans (of the great family of the Gnoll). In default of a male heir, Walter Thomas's property went to Bussy Mansel, and thus Llansamlet came to be held by the Mansel, Vernon, Villiers and Jersey estates. Gwernllwynchwyth went to the Evans line however.

The family's impoverished existence however didn't prevent Richard Thomas from acquiring a mortgage from Henry Basset Thomas in 1757, an event that may have been a move to reclaim some of the estate that had been so callously defrauded from his family and that of Matilda's.

The father in law of one of his daughters, Elizabeth, Henry Basset Thomas orchestrated the purchase of the Drymma Estate – which at the time consisted of three areas Drymma Proper, Drymma Fach (Tir Trymme) Ycha, and Brithdir (Brithdyr) Farm – after the estate was bought by him from then-owner Thomas Morgan, a descendant of David Evans, a transaction detailed and confirmed in the Gabriel Powell Survey dated 1764. The purchase went ahead giving the family control of part of the estate that was once lost to them and was once held by Zacharias Jenkins and Ann Thomas under a free rent lease. However, before the property was purchased by Richard Thomas in 1757, a move that returned the land to its rightful owners, a 1650 survey showed that the freeholder of this property was Jenkin Hopkin, father of Zacharias Jenkin.

An extract from the Manor of Kilvey, a survey for 1686, also shows the possession and transfer of lands throughout the family.

The same for Tir Trymme now in the hands of Mault Thomas Widdow [wife of Jenkin Hopkin]

…

The same for Clyn Cadwgan now in the hands of Zacharias Jenkin

The same for Tir Hopkin Rosser Vaine in the hands of said Zacharias

The same for Tir Howell ap Even Jenkin now called Trymme ycha being the late Lands of Jenkin Hopkin now

in the hands of Owen John Sampson

Richard died in 1788, long after Matilda, who had passed away in 1760, leaving the Drymma Estate, which he had successfully purchased from Henry Basset years earlier, to his son Thomas R Thomas.

Thomas, like many of the purchasers who had held the estate before him fraudulently or otherwise, capitalised on the Drymma property well. A success that gave him the funds to establish claims on various parts of the lost estates in the years that followed.

The jewel in the crown of the lost Thomas estates, the Drymma (Ty-trymme, Drumma, Drumme, Drummau) itself has a long, colourful and lucrative history. The estate once formed part of the Manor of Cadoxton, a house that sits in a mountainous position above Skewen and later became a lunatic asylum as detailed here in the *Glamorgan County Lunatic Asylum/Glamorgan County Mental Hospital /Glanrhyd Hospital records:*

The Briton Ferry estate was also subject to 'rationalising' and 'modernising' whilst in the hands of Louisa Barbara Vernon's godson, George, Earl of Jersey. To ensure that the estates and the parties that owned and leased them were on a surer footing financially, according to the West Glamorgan Archive Service, George made his tenants renew their leases,

## DAVID AP GWILIM GAM OF CILVAE AND GWERNLLWYNWHITH.

X. 3. DAVID, third son of Gwilim Gam, m. Elizabeth, d. of John ap David ap David ap Hopkin Popkin, of Llysnewydd, ap Griffith ap Sir Madoc ap Rhys ap Howel, &c., from Rodri Mawr, and had

XI. JOHN ap David, m. Denis, d. of Rosser John of Duffryn-wysg, and had

XII. JOHN-YCHAN of Cilvae, m. Joan, d. of William Lloyd of Caermarthen, and had: 1. *David.* 2. *Rosser,* ancestor of a CADET BRANCH. 3. *Owen.* 4. *Robert.* 5. *Thomas.* 6. *John.* 7. *Elizabeth,* m. Evan ap Harry of Llangevelach. 8. *Catherine,* m. Jenkin John of Cilvae. 9. A *dau.,* m. Morgan John Howel Ddu.

XIII. DAVID JOHN-YCHAN of Llansamlet, m. Alice, d. of William Raglan of Llantwit-Major. They had: 1. *John.* 2. *Hopkin.* 3. *William.* 4. *Thomas.* 5. *Morgan.* 6. *Thomas,* and six other *sons.* 13. *Margaret,* m. Lewis Griffith of Cilibebill.

XIV. JOHN ap David John-ychan, of Gwernllwynwhith, m. Mary, d. of John, elder son of Rees ap John of Glyn Nedd. They had: 1. A *dau.,* m. Richard Herbert of Cardiff, fifth son of Matthew Herbert of Swansea. They had *William Herbert* of the Friars, and *Mary,* m. Samuel Cadrond. 2. *Catherine.* 3. *Alice,* m. 1st Rees Morgan of Iscoed, 2nd William Gibbon.

XV. CATHERINE, co-h., m. Hopkin David ap Edward Popkin of Danygraig. They had: 1. *Catherine,* who had Danygraig, and m. Walter Thomas of Swansea. 2. *Mary.*

XVI. MARY, had Gwernllwynwhith, and m. William, third son of Lleisan Evans of Neath, by Mary Herbert of Swansea. They had: 1. *David.* 2. *Mathew,* ob. cœlebs. 3. *Lleisan,* m. Ann, d. of Miles Basset of Eglwysbrewis. 4. *William,* ob cœlebs. 5. *Hopkin,* m. Catherine, d. of William Thomas of Neath, mercer. 6. *Catherine,* ob cœlebs. 7. *Margaret,* m. Edward Thomas of Llangevelach. 8. *Mary,* m. Hopkin Llewelyn of Altwen in Gower.

XVII. DAVID EVANS of Gwernllwynwhith, m. Ann, d. of David Jenkins of Hensol. She died with her only child.

A passage from The Genealogies of Glamorgan (The History and Antiquities of Glamorganshire and its Families) by Thomas Nicholas p. 214.

and cut down and sold huge quantities of timber. In a bid to settle a mortgage dating back to 1693, George also sold outlying parts of the estate, thus reducing its overall size by half. As a result of George's acumen, it is estimated in the 1873 return of owners of land that the then Earl of Jersey owned 7,110 acres of land in Wales (all in Glamorgan), a vast area that accumulated a rental income of £36,928.

The 19th century also brought a period of transformation for the Briton Ferry estate, as whilst initially it had been known as an area of quiet rural uplands, inclusive of rivers and deserted mudflats, the industrialisation of the Swansea and Neath valleys saw the estate and its inhabitants take

The ruins of Clyn Cadwgan, Ynystawe - Home of The Zacharias – Jenkin & Ann Thomas.

advantage of the recently improved transport system and the abundance of naturally occurring materials, as this extract from Archiveswales.org.uk explores:

Factories such as the Albion Steel Works, the English Crown Spelter Works and the Baglan Bay Tinplate Works sprang up on low-lying ground towards the sea and new terraces were built to house the factory workers. In 1840 an area of about 750 acres of land in Cwmavon was leased for 99 years to John Vigurs and subsequently passed to Wright, Butler & Co. Ltd, then to Baldwins Ltd. The terraces of houses built on this land were sublet for the remainder of the term of this lease in 1897 and 1898. When the lease terminated in the 1930s many of the houses were declared unfit for habitation and were either improved or demolished. As the railway initially attracted businesses, so the businesses in their turn created the need for more railways. The Rhondda & Swansea Bay Railway and the South Wales Mineral Railway both leased and bought land from the Briton Ferry Estate and the Great Western Railway Company continued to rebuild and expand their lines in the area. In the 1850s the newly formed Briton Ferry Floating

Dock Company set the wheels in motion to build the Briton Ferry Docks, purchasing land from the Earl of Jersey. The company later went bankrupt and was taken over as a going concern by the Great Western Railway. In 1951 portions of the estate were sold to the Principality Property Co., Estateways Builders, John Oliver Watkins, the City & Provincial Housing Association and Gwalia Land & Property Developments Ltd.

Whilst we now know that the claims made by some sources that the Drymma Estate was held by successive generations of the Popkin family before being purchased by John Birch Paddon are untrue and a matter of fraud, very little was documented regarding the history of the Drymma, apart from its impressive reputation within the coal mining and ironworks industries, which the History of the Vale of Neath by D. Rhys Phillips further explores, with an insight directly pointing to part of the estate previously mentioned.

The "Cambrian" newspaper announced, 25 April 1807, "Veins of excellent sweet binding coal" to let, the colliery being at the mouth of Neath river. Another appears in the issue of May 18, 1816.

*Brithdir.* – There are a number of old levels from Maesmelyn to Drymma but the chief of them is the Brithdir – worked since the 3rd quarter of the 18th century by various parties (particularly the owners of the Neath Abbey drift and pits since the middle of the last century). There was a railway coal-siding and passenger station at Mooretown, until recent years.

The Walter Thomas estates' profitability wasn't lost on Bussey Mansel all those years earlier either, and his dealings were heavily chronicled across a number of publications as well as being a bone of contention for many onlookers. His activity in the Llansamlet and Llanwerne Collieries drew

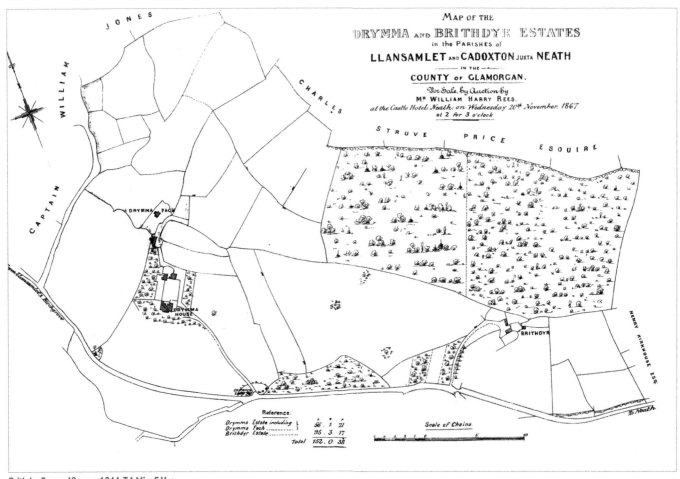

Brithdyr Farm - 49 acres 1844. T.A Miss E Vye

particular attention. Situated on the east bank of the River Tawe near Swansea, the collieries extended as far up the coast as Briton Ferry, a prominent position that caught the gaze of one Mansel. Like many sites in Wales during this era, the areas that could be worked were of considerable size and therefore in constant employ. According to Estate Papers, more specifically a letter from the steward of St Donat's Castle to Lady Mansel Stradling, dated 30 June 1717, a vast majority of workings in Llansamlet were 700 to 800 fathoms long with the entire length of the passages enclosed in brick. The area was so abundant that the number of pits present and levels worked were continuously increasing.

• • • • • •

*how the Earl of Jersey's (76) Came to Llansamlet*

*Walter Thomas of Swansea married Catherine daughter of Hopkin David of Danygraig and had issue William who married Catherine daughter of Anthony Mansel of Britonferry William had several daughters and two sons Walter and William. died young, the said Walter appointed his mothers brother, and son of Anthony Mansel whose name was Bussy Mansel as a Trustee mentioned in his Will his son Thomas Mansel was after his father [1st] Bussy and after Thomas his son [2nd] Bussy Mansel and and after above said Bussy. his daughter was Lousia Barbara appointed his successor as Trustee ⋅ Lousia Barbara Mansel married George Vinables Vernon. Buron Kingston county Chester and after her death, she gave the Trusteeship to Thomas Earl of Clarendon, who spent his life out in Foreign Country and died without issue And was succeeded by the 5th Earl of Jersey who assumed the additional name of Childs by Loyal Lisence in 1812 and died in 1859, he was succeeded by his son George Augustus Frederick 6th Earl of Jersey born 1808 married 1841 succeeded and died the same Month October 1859. and was succeeded by the present Victor Robert George Childs Villiers 7th Earl of Jersey born March 20th 1845 succeeded in October 1859 when he was only 14 years of Age Bussy Mansel 3rd son of Thomas Mansel was at Death of his brother Christopher in 1744 was elevated as Lord Mansel of Margan*

Copy of 'The Earl of Jersey Came to Llansamlet'.

## THE BIRTH OF COAL MINING AND IRON PRODUCTION IN WALES

Mining provided a significant source of income for the economy of Wales and whilst much is said about its role during the 19th and early 20th century, better known as 'The Industrial Revolution," the birth of coal mining and iron production was much earlier.

Long before the burgeoning of these key industries in the Industrial Revolution, there is evidence of mining in the Blaenavon area going back to the 14th century, as well as further documentation to support the existence of mine workings at Mostyn dating as far back as 1261. The South Wales Valleys in particular offered a prime location for industrialisation years before the revolution took hold with Welsh coal maintaining an enviable reputation since Roman times and iron works dotted along the landscape that had been in operation for years. Despite being small in scale the early iron works of South Wales set the scene for the country becoming a primary innovator in production alongside its coal mining successes. When it came to coal, as with early iron production, there had been small scale mining in existence in the pre-Roman British Iron Age, but despite this extraction would have been undertaken on an industrial scale under the Romans, who completed their conquest of Wales in 78 AD. Substantial quantities of gold, copper and lead were extracted, along with lesser amounts of zinc and silver. Mining would continue until the process was no longer practical or profitable, at which time the mine would be abandoned. The extensive excavations of the Roman operations at Dolaucothi provide a picture of the high level of Roman technology and the expertise of Roman engineering in the ancient era.

In addition to capitalising on the profitability of these two defining industry sectors, in the north, business was also booming for slate quarries. Again the slate industry began during the Roman times in Wales, a period where slate was used to roof the fort at Segontium, now Caernarfon. With the growth of the coal and iron production industries, so too was the expansion of the slate industry, which in turn exploded during the early 18th century. North-west Wales was a particularly important slate producing area, home to the Penrhyn Quarry near Bethesda, the Dinorwic Quarry near Llanberis, the Nantlle Valley quarries, and Blaenau Ffestiniog, where the slate was mined rather than quarried.

• • • • • •

The Economic History Review, under a chapter entitled *Iron and Coal on a Glamorgan Estate, 1700-1740* by A.H. John, offers an account on Bussey Mansel's dealings in such collieries, needless to say his reputation precedes him.

If conclusive proof were required that Mansel was not a gentleman turned business man it could be found in his attitude towards the sale of his coal and iron. The steward's letters repeatedly show how sensitive the area was, although geographically remote, to influences affecting trade. Buying at the fairs, for example, fluctuated with the latest news from the war front, while in 1721 unrest was felt by the small trading community in Swansea at the 'Fall in gold.' Mansel failed to appreciate these conditions and consequently issued instructions which were often impracticable, especially with regard to the sale of iron.

The natural market for this product was Bristol which, until the advent of the railways a century later, was the 'Welsh Metropolis' whence the gentry and the well-to-do obtained 'every article of consumption both in and out of the house.' The September Fair at Bristol was a time 'when all the people of this country are called upon to discharge their shop debts' and as this included the itinerant 'Scotchmen' and linen drapers, most of the people in south Wales were affected to some degree. There were, it is true, other markets open to Welsh ironmasters. 'In my thoughts' wrote Burroughs, 'Gloucester is a better place to send pig iron than Bristol, being in the middle of ye forges', and the 'Birmingham

customers who must have great quantities of iron to keep on their workmen.' But Mansel discovered that obtaining sales in the midlands required more time and humility than he was prepared to give to the selling of iron.

As the steward stated, 'the fault in the affair don't lie in he making of either pig or barr iron but in ye manner of accepting and refusing the opportunities of disposing it.' Benevolent despotism, unquestioned in other spheres, was keenly resisted when applied to a close and well organized trade. This was especially true of Bristol where trade competition was keenest; where Lancashire iron competed with that from other furnaces and forges in south Wales, Gloucestershire and the west of England. It is clear, too, that iron trade was well organized, for the merchants appear to have held meetings 'before ye fairs to determine ye rate of iron', while a little later south Wales ironmasters were forming agreements for the allocation of timber in various areas. It is probable that Hanbury's antagonism induced him to exert his great influence in the trade against Mansel, for Burroughs refers to the latter's anger at the methods adopted to prevent the sale of Melynycwrt iron. The result was that Mansel 'abominated all Bristol traders.'

Bussey's reputation in the ironworks industry and his unsuccessful attempt at casting cannon earned him no favours, forcing him to sell to small consumers for lower prices, on the other hand his natural monopoly (however deceptively gained) brought him more success in the coal trade.

The Rhyddings Estate (also referred to as the 'Rhedin'), which now lies within the Parish of Blaenhonddan, is often mentioned in the same breath as the Drymma thanks to its links with disputes regarding the earlier generations of the Thomas family. The soon to be mentioned Richard Seys was renting the Rhedin from William Thomas I, however this estate was later sold to the Tennant family by Lord Vernon. As this extract from the Chronicle of Cadoxton by Keith Tucker portrays:

> One of the earliest mentions is again found in the Elizabethan document of 1598 where the 'Rhedin' is assigned to Jenkin John Penry. The estate was acquired by a Richard Seys who had married Catherine, daughter of Walter Thomas of Dan-y-Graig Swansea. She has previously been the wife of Evan John Evan of Eaglesbush, before his death. By Catherine, Richard Seys had a son William who inherited.

> There is some confusion as to whether the Seys family owned the estate or merely tenanted it from the Thomas family at this time. Control passed solidly to William Thomas, a brother to Catherine Says. William Thomas married another Catherine, this time the daughter of Arthur Mansel of Briton Ferry. Four sons resulted, Edward, John, Walter and William. Walter who inherited but died without legal issue, and William who devised the estate to his uncle Bussy Mansel (mother's brother) when he also died without legal issue.

As with the rest of the estates meant for Walter Thomas II's daughter Ann and wrongly bequeathed and passed down by Bussey, the Rhyddings Estate ended up in the hands of the Earls of Jersey before being sold by the ninth Earl, George Child Villiers, in 1951.

While the estate was later sold on in the mid-20th century by the Earl of Jersey, the journey of Tir-y-Mynydd Drymma to this point involves many famous families and a number of historical transactions, some that can be evidenced, others that can't due to their fraudulent nature. However, the possession of Tir-y-Mynydd Drymma is best summed up here in this excerpt, developed via information gathered from

Aberpergwm House (Neuadd Pergwm) 1995. Ancestral home of the Lords of Glyn-nedd (Einon ap Collwyn)

Appendix I of the *Survey of Kilvey, Glamorgan and Swansea, Calendar Vol. II* by W.C. Rogers.

> Grant of January 1340 from Gronow ap Cradoc for Drumme in Kilvey. To Sir Robert De Penres.

> The Drumme formed part of the large Fforest Estate which also included Gwernllwnchwith.

> The Fforest Vycan Estate which it was later called was the lands of the above Gronow ap Cradoc descended from Einon ap Collwyn. Up to the year 1574 the estate was held by John David ap John Yuchan, descendant of the above, nicknamed the Hector of Kilvey. After his death in 1598 the estates passed to his daughters, one who married Richard Herbert and the other marrying Hopkin Popkin of Danygraig, otherwise known as Hopkin David Edward (Popkin). Gwernllwnchwith was given to the daughter married to Richard Herbert who later sold it to Hopkin David Edward. After the death of Hopkin Popkin in 1626, the estate was divided between his two daughters, namely Mary, who married William Evans of Eaglesbush, who received Gwernllwnchwith. Catherine

Margaret, who married Walter Thomas of Swansea, received Danygraig together with various other portions of the Fforest Estate which included the Drummau. Where Hopkin David Edward had his coal works, these coal works were bequeathed to David Thomas, first son and heir of Walter Thomas, David died young and Walter's second son William Thomas inherited as confirmed in the Composition Papers 1646 and also Hopkin Popkin's Will of 1627.

The journey of the Drymma Estate doesn't end there, as further described in Ownership of Lands in the Parishes of Cadoxton Juxta Neath and Kilybebyll by former Steward of the Manor Richard J Thomas.

The Fforest Estate or Tir-y Drumma

The estate at one time belonged to the Popkin family for several generations. John Bennett Popkin was the last in line of the junior branch of Thomas Popkin of Fforest Farm's cousins to the senior line of Popkins of Ynysdawe and Danygraig. In the year 1749 John Popkin, a son of Thomas Popkin, died 1752, of Fforest purchased Tir-y-Mynydd Drumma from Louisa Barbara Mansel who had married Lord Vernon, Earl of Jersey. It was her ancestors Bussey Mansel of Briton Ferry, died 1699, and Thomas Mansel who were trustees according to the terms of the Will of the last Walter Thomas, died 1667.

The Fforest Estate extended from Tir-y Drumma in the south east to Glais Clydach and Ynyspenllwch and Gellionen in the north west, which was a very substantial area. Popkins of Fforest Farm were relatively small land owners and it was not until after the death of Walter Thomas in 1667 they started acquiring large tracks of lands from the Mansels of Briton Ferry, lands formerly owned by William and Walter Thomas, and Hopkin David

Edward (Hopkin Popkins).

The claim on Drymma lands as part of the Fforest Estate was referenced much later in an agreement between Thomas R Thomas and family members and their solicitors in London in 1822, which in turn acknowledges the account given by Richard J Thomas above, a credit given by Nathaniel Richard Thomas and his forefathers before the story became distorted by a lack of evidence and the missing documentation. This aforementioned claim may have been the very last bid heard in court to re-secure the estates that were lost to the Thomas family, but it certainly was not the first.

Of the rest of the children of Richard Thomas and Matilda Zacharias not much detail is known. Morgan, their second son, married Eleanor David in 1769, a union that produced children. He lived in Morriston near Llansamlet after leaving the family home and worked within the copper industry. Jenet married and moved to Plymouth, whilst Ann, Richard Thomas' illegitimate child married one David Harry, had issue and was said to be leasing Tir John Thomas from Lord Vernon Earl of Jersey, a farm formerly owned by Walter Thomas. Elizabeth married Basset Thomas and lived in Ty-Llwyd Farm, Cadoxton Juxta Neath Abbey. Their grandson was the famous mining engineer David Thomas, who, once of age, immigrated to the United States to make his fortune.

• • • • • •

## DAVID THOMAS: THE FATHER OF THE AMERICAN IRON INDUSTRY

The Evans family weren't the only family to have a famous and renowned export... Born in Cadoxton, Neath, David Thomas is sadly referred to as the only success story of the Thomas family in light of their doomed standing and the lost estates.

After working on his father's farm for much of his childhood and studying at a school in nearby Alltwen, David wasn't satisfied with staying put and working for the family business. Once of age, he heavily pursued his ambitions of working in the iron industry, a burgeoning sector just about to explode in Wales due to the Industrial Revolution. After becoming one of the foremost ironmasters in the whole of the UK during his adult life, taking up employment at the Yniscedwyn Works in Ystradgynlais, Swansea Valley, he developed a process that would dramatically advance the iron industry and further revolutionise the smelting of iron ore and anthracite coal in Wales and beyond. The hot blast was a brand new procedure that made the production of anthracite iron – a type of iron popular during this period – much easier.

Whilst early hot blast stoves were troublesome, as thermal expansion and contraction were liable to cause breakages in the pipes, an idea, independently conceived by both George Crane and David Thomas of the Yniscedwyn Works would transform the process and make these problems a thing of the past. Instead of using leather to make the connection between the blast pipes and tuyeres, the incoming blast air would be preheated using waste heat from the flue gas to ensure efficient production when using either the Cowper stove or the open hearth furnace.

Taking news of his new technique with him, David relocated to Pennsylvania in 1839 along with his son Samuel, a move that signalled the owners of the Lehigh Coal and Navigation Company in Lehigh County, a region renowned for being rich in both anthracite coal and iron ore, to commission him to build a furnace for the production of anthracite iron. As well as establishing a reputation for himself stateside and becoming a key figure in the birth of the Industrial Revolution

Cottage at Blaenavon Iron Works. Griffith Davies, great great-grandfather. Died in 1868 at nearby Coal Tar Row.

in the U.S., his forward thinking obviously brought him great wealth, wealth that he shared throughout the community leading to him and his wife, Elizabeth, being frequently addressed as 'Mother and Father Thomas.' In addition to being responsible for the installation of the first public water system in the area, founding the town's first fire company and serving in the coveted role as first burgess, David used his wealth to build a series of homes, many of which are still standing today. Alongside these achievements, David was also named the first president of the American Society of Metallurgy and was one of the founders of the American Association of Industrial Engineers.

• • • • • •

# 7. MRS VYE

THOMAS RICHARD THOMAS leased the Drymma Estate to Phillip Thomas, a weaver residing in Llansamlet, in 1772-3 for a term of 99 years as many land owners had done before him. The majority of title deeds found in deed bundles are in the form of a lease and release. The lease and release was the most popular and widespread way to record simple sales of property from the 17th century up to 1845. The lease and release format was also used to convey property for the purposes of mortgages and settlements.

The 'lease' and the 'release' are two separate documents, and it is quite usual for one of them to have become separated from the other over time. However, there are clues within the text which make it clear that the deed forms part of a lease and release transaction. Whilst the use of lease and release documents was prevalent from the 16th century, in 1841, the Conveyance by Release Act made it possible to convey land by release only. As a result the lease and release became obsolete and was replaced by a 'statutory release.' Releases were themselves abolished in 1845 and replaced by a simple 'grant', later known as a 'conveyance.'

Prior to this time, and as is likely to have been used in the leasing of the Drymma Estate to Phillip Thomas by Thomas Richard Thomas, lease and release records were written in the past tense and usually dated a day before the release to detail what had been done to transfer the property. From the 16th to the 19th century conveyance by lease and release was a two-stage process. First, a leasehold interest in the land was conveyed from A to B by means of a bargain and sale ('the lease"). This bargain and sale did not have to be enrolled, because it did not transfer freehold property, it was essentially not a real lease as the intention was to follow it with a release in order to convey the freehold. The term of the lease, the consideration of money and the rent specified in the lease were all nominal. Usually the land was bargained and sold for a term of six months or one year for a nominal consideration of 5 shillings, and a rent of one peppercorn per year.

• • • • • •

## THE PRICE OF A PEPPERCORN

The term 'peppercorn rent' in the modern day causes much confusion, however, it was regularly used in legal terminology during many common law cases throughout history. A metaphor meaning a 'very small payment or nominal consideration', the price of a peppercorn was used to satisfy the requirements for the creation of a legal contract.

In English law, and other countries with similar common law systems, a legal contract requires that both sides provide consideration. In other words, if an agreement does not specify that each party will give something of value to the other party, then it is not considered a binding contract, and cannot be enforced in court. This requirement does not exist in contracts with civil law systems. Based on this premise, for a one-sided contract to be deemed valid and legally binding, the contract will generally be written so that one side gives up something of value, while the other side gives a token sum such as one pound, dollar, or literally one peppercorn.

Whilst prominently used throughout history, there are still many instances where the price of a peppercorn applies, with this token price tag being used to put a value on major, multi-million pound enterprises with equally impressive turnovers and hundreds if not thousands of staff to call their own. An extract from a recent *BBC News* article entitled 'How does a company cost £1?' explains how the peppercorn theory has been, and still is, applied today:

> The token sum is a symbolic but important part of the contract, showing that "some consideration" has been paid. It needn't be a pound, it could be any sum, as long as it shows that something has been handed over in payment.
>
> "It's the glue which binds the contract," says James Stonebridge, restructuring partner at law firm, Norton Rose.
>
> "It used to be called 'peppercorn' – which was the nominal consideration for which a sale went through, which could be one pound, five pounds or whatever change someone had in their pocket," he said.
>
> There are alternative ways of transferring ownership, he says, but in principle, the handing over of a pound is a sign of the taking over of ownership. Such small purchase prices often happen when firms are in financial trouble – and buying the firm also means accepting responsibility for liabilities, such as debts.
>
> "In these instances it's not about how much the price is, but where the liability will rest after the sale goes through – that's the key aspect of it," says Mr Stonebridge.
>
> There have been previous high-profile examples of the company pound shop. Ken Bates bought Chelsea football club in 1982 for £1, while taking on debts of £1.5m. When Barings bank collapsed, after the Nick Leeson rogue trader scandal, it was bought for £1 by the Dutch financial group, ING. And when German car company, BMW, sold Rover, the Phoenix consortium paid £10. The fortunes following such sales can also vary sharply. When Ken Bates sold the club to Roman Abramovich in 2003, the deal was worth £140m, and Chelsea has gone on to premiership triumphs.

In addition to the use of the peppercorn theory in business, in property law the term was also regularly utilised. A peppercorn rent was and still is often used as a form of nominal ground rent where a potentially substantial premium has been paid on commencement of a particularly long lease, often ranging from 99 to 125 years. Known commonly as a 'virtual freehold', the notional collection of the annual peppercorn rent helps to maintain a formal landlord-tenant relationship between the two parties, precluding the risk of a claim for adverse possession from the tenant arising.

• • • • • •

The words used to form a lease during the era would be as follows:

> [A] hath bargained and sold [or hath granted, bargained and sold] … from the day next before the date of these presents for and during and unto the full end and term of one whole year [or six months] … to the intent and purpose that by virtue of these presents and by the force of the Statute made for transferring Uses into possession, that the lands are in actual possession of B …
>
> At some point afterwards – usually the next day, but not always – A conveyed the reversion of the lease, that is, his right to the freehold property, to B or his trustee

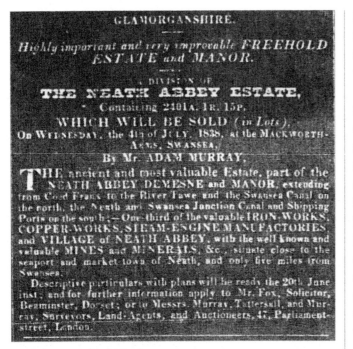

**Notice of Sale of the Neath Abbey Estate**

('the release'). At this point the real consideration money for the property was paid. B was now the owner of the freehold. Releases often involved a number of different parties, especially if they were drawn up as part of a family settlement. It can be quite hard to determine exactly what part each party was playing in the transaction.

Whilst a vast area of the estate would have been leased to Phillip Thomas using a document based on the format shown above, sub-letting was also common place, particularly where the management of large estates like the Drymma were concerned. In 1775, Phillip Thomas sub-let the Drymma Estate to Thomas Griffiths, a solicitor working and renowned within the local area of Neath, a lease that is now

held by the family. After his death, Thomas Griffiths passed on his leases first to his wife, who upon her death gave the same leases to her niece Elizabeth Sherbourne, a woman who would later become known as Mrs Elizabeth Vye.

Mrs Vye had just one daughter, also named Elizabeth and referred to across much of the documentation gathered and/or constructed by The Walter Thomas Inheritance Association as 'Miss Vye.' After the death of her mother and the subsequent receipt of the leases, Miss Vye conveyed the farm adjacent to the Drymma property, namely Brithdir Ucha, from Henry Charles Tennant, the owner of the Neath Abbey Estate, who had previously acquired the estates from the Earl of Jersey. The Neath Abbey Estate crops up a number of times throughout the story of the lost Thomas estates. An extract from Hanes Morganwy offers just one example of the estates' close connection with the Drymma, an area which was even sold as part of the same lot by the Earl of Jersey. The land was subsequently purchased by George Tennant.

> In the British Museum there is a copy of the newspaper called "The Sun" dated September 2nd 1836 and in this newspaper, there is an announcement as follows: – "Glamorgan, Neath Abbey Estate about 6,000 acres of land comprising of the lordship and Manor of Neath Abbey situate in the hamlets of Coedfrank, Duffryn Clydach, Blaenhonddan and Ynysmond in the Parish of Cadoxton &c. To be sold by Adam Murray (in one lot)

The property and associated farmland of Brithdir Ucha spanned an area of 95 acres and consequently added more weight to the already acquired lands and properties of the Drymma as sub-let by her great uncle Thomas Griffiths.

Miss Vye died a spinster in 1863, but after her death, despite the recent leasing of the Brithdir Ucha property four years earlier, no documentary evidence to substantiate her title to the Drymma and the holding of Brithdir Ucha could be

Colliers Row, Birthplace of John Richard Thomas and his sister Margaret.

No.10 Upper Colliers Row, Birthplace of John Richard Thomas and his sister Margaret.

Drymmau House, Cadoxton Juxta nr Neath.

found. However, this lack of evidence didn't stop her next of kin Richard Backhouse and John Birch Paddon stating their claim on the coveted pieces of land, and as a consequence, a result of perhaps a momentary lack of judgement from the courts, the pair were awarded a moiety of Brithdir Ucha Farm. As if this was the plan all along, Drymma Fach and Drymma House were purchased out of Chancery some time between 1873 and 1890 by John Birch Paddon.

Whilst Thomas Richard Thomas I had died years earlier,

his grandson Thomas Richard Thomas III had a somewhat strained relationship with tenant Miss Vye during her lifetime. This accumulated with him making a stress for rent in 1840, arrears which amounted to £40. The sum of outstanding rent was eventually awarded to him, she subsequently paid £15 initially and agreed to pay the remainder a few days later. It was Miss Vye's death that saw him begin proceedings to reclaim the Drymma Estate, a job that he never finished due to his own death.

John Richard Thomas, Thomas III's eldest son and heir, resumed proceedings and in 1865 he was granted possession of the estate by Judge Baron Pollock. The reinstatement of John Richard Thomas as land owner however was not entirely supported as this copy from an original letter describes:

Dear Sir,

I enclose according to promise the Amount stated one Guinea. Hoping you are quite well, I have to inform you that John Thomas of Court Herbert near Neath, the person working the Coal under Drymma Estate, put a lot of Colliers into Drymma house last Saturday. Mr Fox's

# GLAMORGANSHIRE.

## Parishes of Llansamlet and Cadoxton-juxta-Neath.

## PARTICULARS

AND

# CONDITIONS OF SALE

OF IMPORTANT

# FREEHOLD RESIDENTIAL ESTATES,

CALLED AND KNOWN AS

## DRYMMA, DRYMMA FACH, AND BRITHDYR UCHA,

SITUATE IN THE PARISHES ABOVE NAMED, WHICH, WITH THE

## MINERALS UNDERLYING DRYMMA, AND DRYMMA FACH,

WILL BE

# SOLD BY PUBLIC AUCTION,

# BY MR. WILLIAM HARRY REES,

## AT THE "CASTLE HOTEL," NEATH,

ON WEDNESDAY, NOVEMBER THE 20TH, 1867,

*AT TWO FOR THREE O'CLOCK IN THE AFTERNOON, PRECISELY.*

Copies of these Particulars, with Plans, may be had on application to Messrs. PEARSE & CROSSE, Solicitors, South Molton, Devon; Messrs. RICHARDSON, BRANDWOOD & DOWLING, Solicitors, 18, Wood Street, Bolton-le-Moors, and 26, King's Street, Manchester; Messrs. ATTREE, CLARKE & HOWLETT, Solicitors, Brighton; or to Mr. REES, at his Auction, Estate and Insurance Offices, Charlesville Place, Neath.

---

## PARTICULARS.

LOT 1.—ALL THAT DELIGHTFULLY SITUATED

# FREEHOLD RESIDENTIAL PROPERTY,

## CALLED AND KNOWN AS "DRYMMA,"

Situate in the Parishes of Llansamlet and Cadoxton-juxta-Neath, distant from the Town of Neath about two miles, from Swansea, about five-and-a-half miles, from the Llansamlet Station of the Great Western Railway one mile, and about the same distance from the Neath Abbey Station of the Vale of Neath Railway.

## THE PREMISES KNOWN AS DRYMMA PROPER,

COLORED PINK IN THE PLAN,

### COMPRISING THE SPACIOUS FAMILY RESIDENCE,

WITH ITS LARGE AND

## HIGHLY PRODUCTIVE WALLED FRUIT AND VEGETABLE GARDEN,

Extensive Outbuildings, Lawn, Shrubbery, Plantation, Entrance Lodge, and Gardener's Cottage,

## FINE PARK-LIKE PASTURE AND ARABLE LANDS,

COMPRISE

## AN AREA OF THIRTY FOUR ACRES, OR THEREABOUTS,

ALL, WITH A TRIFLING EXCEPTION, WITHIN A RING FENCE.

The Mansion, called Drymma House, on this Estate is capacious, of modern erection & situated on a commanding elevation, Partly surrounded by its Shrubbery and Plantation, having a fine Southern aspect affording a

## DELIGHTFUL PROSPECT OF SWANSEA BAY, THE BRISTOL CHANNEL & THE ADJACENT COASTS,

The House and its offices are conveniently arranged, and embrace large glazed Entrance Porch & Hall, Drawing Room, Dining Room, Breakfast Room, Library, Eight Bedrooms and Dressing Room, Butler's Pantry, China Pantry, Servants' Hall, Large Kitchen, Wash-house and Laundry, and other conveniences, with capital Cellarage in the basement, the Outbuildings are Extensive and comprise Coach-house, capital 6-stall Stable, Saddle and Harness Room, Lock-up House, Spacious Paved Court Yards, Large Barn and Fowl House, together with an extensive Lawn, Shrubbery and Plantation, Large Walled Kitchen and Fruit Garden,

## THE GARDENER'S COTTAGE AND THE LODGE AT THE ENTRANCE TO THE PROPERTY.

IN ADDITION TO THE FOREGOING THERE WILL BE INCLUDED IN THE SALE

## THE FREEHOLD FARM LANDS, CALLED DRYMMA FACH,

(Colored Green in the Plan,) situate in the Parishes of Llansamlet and Cadoxton-juxta-Neath, containing

## TWENTY-TWO-AND-A-QUARTER ACRES, OR THEREABOUTS, OF PASTURE, ARABLE, AND MEADOW LAND,

INCLUDING THE FARM BUILDINGS, &c.

The whole forms a most compact property, and requires but a small outlay to render it one of the most desirable Residential Estates in the County.

## THE VALUABLE SEAMS OF COAL, AND OTHER MINERALS, UNDERLYING THIS ESTATE,

And included in the Sale thereof, are of great value; they are now let to the Dynevor Coal Company, who are working the upper vein only, and the Royalty derivable therefrom will pass to the purchaser of this lot.

LOT 2.—COMPRISES ALL THAT HIGHLY IMPROVABLE

# FREEHOLD ESTATE, CALLED BRITHDYR UCHA,

Situate in the Parish of Cadoxton-juxta-Neath, adjoining Lot 1, colored Yellow in the Plan, containing about

## Ninety-five Acres, Three Roods & Seven Perches of Pasture, Arable, Mountain and Woodland,

NOW LET TO A HIGHLY RESPECTABLE TENANT.

## THE DWELLING HOUSE ON THIS PROPERTY IS MODERN, CAPACIOUS AND IN EXCELLENT ORDER,

And contains Parlour, Kitchen, Back Kitchen, Small Store, with four Bedrooms above, there is also a good Two-roomed Cottage attached, the whole being covered in Carnarvonshire Slate.

## THE FARM BUILDINGS ARE OF A SUBSTANTIAL CHARACTER,

Recently built with Stone, & roofed with Tiles & Slates, they comprise a large Barn, Cowhouse & Carthouse combined, capital Stable, Piggeries, &c.

This compact property is also admirably situated on an eminence facing the South, commanding a fine prospect, while on the North and North-East ample shelter is secured by the Mountain, which with

## THE WOODLANDS AFFORD SPLENDID COVER FOR GAME,

And the whole being peculiarly adapted for a Residential Estate, cannot but command itself to persons of moderate competency, who contemplate retiring, as a delightful, pleasing and healthy retreat.

The Standing or Growing Timber on this Estate is included in the Sale, but the Minerals thereunder (except the Quarries of Stone, and Slate), do not belong to the Vendors and are therefore reserved.

Conditions of Sale of the Drymma Estate.

## CONDITIONS OF SALE.

First.—The highest bidder for each Lot shall be the purchaser thereof; and if any dispute arise as to a bidding the Lot in dispute shall be put up again at a former bidding and resold. No person shall advance less at any bidding than such sum as shall from time to time be named by the Auctioneer, or retract his or her bidding. The Vendors reserve the right of bidding by their Agent for each Lot.

Second.—Each purchaser shall immediately pay down a Deposit in the proportion of £10 for every £100 of his or her purchase money into the hands of the Vendors' Solicitors, and sign the subjoined agreement, and pay the remainder of his or her purchase money to the Vendors on the 25th day of March next, at the office of Messrs. Prance and Couve, Solicitors for the Vendors in South Molton, in the County of Devon, at which time and place the purchases are to be completed.

Third.—The purchasers shall be entitled to the possession or to the rents and profits of their respective lots from the 25th day of March next, up to which time all outgoings shall be cleared by the Vendors, or their tenants, or the person or persons liable for the same.

Fourth.—The property now offered for Sale belonged to Miss Elizabeth Vye, of Ilfracombe, who died a spinster and intestate on the 2nd day of April, 1853. [...]

Fifth.—Upon payment of the purchase money at the time and place above mentioned, the Vendors shall convey the Lot or Lots which shall be sold to the purchaser or respective purchasers thereof, and the conveyance or conveyances of the same lots respectively shall be drawn and prepared at the expense of the respective purchasers, and a Draft thereof be sent to the office of the Vendors' Solicitors for perusal three weeks at least before the time fixed for completion. [...]

Sixth.—If the purchaser of either Lot shall neglect or fail to comply with the above Conditions his or her deposit money shall be actually forfeited to the Vendors, who shall be at full liberty to re-sell the Lot or Lots bought by them, him, or her, either by public auction or private contract, and the deficiency (if any) in the price on such second Sale together with all expenses attending such second Sale shall immediately thereafter be made good to the Vendors by the defaulter or respective defaulters at this present Sale, and in case of the non-payment of the same the whole thereof shall be recoverable by the Vendors as and for liquidated damages, and it shall not be necessary previously to tender a conveyance to the purchaser.

Seventh.—If consistently with the foregoing Conditions either purchaser shall make any objection, or requisition, whether on the Title to or description of the respective lots, or otherwise which the Vendors shall be unable or unwilling for reasonable cause to remove or comply with, the Vendors shall be at liberty, notwithstanding any intermediate negotiation or attempt to remove or comply with such objection or requisition, to cancel the Contract or Contracts which shall thereupon be delivered up and be at an end, and the deposit money returned without costs or compensation on either side.

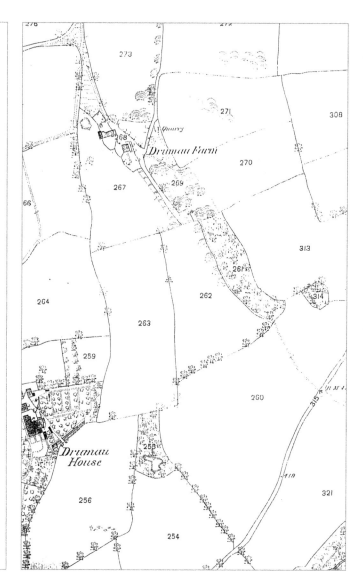

Conditions of Sale of the Drymma Estate.

## WESTERN MAIL. SATURDAY. JULY 10. 1897.

### Sales by Auction.

NOTICE OF POSTPONEMENT OF SALE.
LORD SWANSEA'S ESTATES, GLAMORGANSHIRE,
Situate at Lletyrafel, Llangyfelach, and Oyster-
mouth, near Swansea and Neath.

MESSRS. CHINNOCK, GALS-
WORTHY, AND CHINNOCK beg to
announce that the Sale of these Properties, advertised
to be held at Swansea during this month, has been
POSTPONED UNTIL NEXT SEASON.
Offices, 11, Waterloo-place, London, S.W.
L14320

*Sales by Auction feature in The Western Mail, 10th July 1897.*

# The Cambrian

## SWANSEA. FRIDAY. JULY 2, 1897.

*Sales by Auction feature in The Cambrian, 2nd July 1897.*

## SWANSEA

### TO BE SOLD BY AUCTION

IN LOTS
By Mr. J. DAVIES,
(By order of the Trustees of the Will of the late Henry Smith
of Gwernllwynwith, Esq.)

At the MACKWORTH ARMS INN, SWANSEA, on TUESDAY, the
18th day of JUNE, 1833, at twelve o'clock, unless in the mean
time disposed of by private contract, of which due notice will
be given, the following

*LEASEHOLD PROPERTY, viz.:*

THE FARMS respectively called GWERN
LLWYNWITH, LANYBRWDA, COEDSAISON-ISSA
GLYNYGORSE, PENYRHUSON, HENGARTHOUCHAN
TYRYVRON, TALYCOBA ISHA, TIR ROBERT POWELL
TIR NEST, GWERNLLESTE, LLWYNCRWN, TALY
COBA UCHAF, and HAFOD. Also the WATER GRIS
MILL, called The POTTERY MILL, the HAFOD PIP
WORKS, and the several WHARFS, called The HAFOD
WHARFS, in the respective occupations of Messrs. James an
Aubrey, Messrs. Treacher and James, John Parsons, Esq., Mrs
Martha Martin, and Mr. John Berlase Jenkins. Also other Pro
perty underlet to his Grace the Duke of Beaufort, Messrs. Vivia
and Sons, and the Middle Bank Copper Company. And also
FREEHOLD FARM, called TYDRAW.

The above Property is situated in the parishes of Lansamle
and Saint John-juxta-Swansea.

Printed particulars may be had at the Office of the Auctione
and at the Mackworth Arms Inn, Swansea; and of Messrs. Row
land and Young, Solicitors, 29, Princes-street, Bank, London.

*Auction notice for sale of the estates in Swansea.*

## SWANSEA.

THE LEASEHOLD ESTATES of the late
CHARLES and HENRY SMITH, of Gwernllwnwith, Esquires,
situate in the parishes of Lansamlet and Saint John's (including
the valuable HAVOD WHARFS on the Swansea River), and a
FREEHOLD TENEMENT, called TYDRAW, in the parish of
Lansamlet, will soon, by direction of the Trustee, be offered for
SALE by AUCTION, at Swansea.

Particulars will appear in a future Cambrian; and further in-
formation may in the mean time be obtained, by application to
Messrs. Rowland and Young, Solicitors, 29, Princes-street, Bank,
London. 7

notice to Miss Vye having expired on the Twenty-fifth inst. Drymma is a beautiful Mansion with park and pleasure grounds in front of it likewise a very nice garden in the back with Wall Fruit Trees etc, he has turned a lot of horses into the Park running over the pleasure grounds destroying the appearance of the Place. The said John Thomas turned a woman out of the Lodge, we told her to stop there, but he turned her out, he has been very anxious to get possession of Drymma Lands, I am given to understand that John Thomas would give Mr Fox's Two Hundred Pounds for repairs and expenses laid out on the house. I think myself it was a made up thing between them to keep the right owners from it. Now wish you to get an Injunction served as soon as possible on this John Thomas of Court Herbert near Neath who is now working the Coals under the Drymma Estate and please let me know the amount and I will send it by return of Post, my Cousin has been in the Duke of Beauforts office and seen a Copy of the Lease on the Minerals under Drymma it runs as follows. A Lease granted to Arthur Prichard of Cardigan on the Drymma Minerals by me Evan Davies of Peneralth Carmarthenshire who was Agent for the Family Where it remains or to any of those who has a Claim to Jenkin Zacharias Minerals like-wise an under-Lease Granted by Arthur Prichard Esq to Joseph x Martin Esq Ynistawe House near Swansea for 21 years which expired 9 years ago. He had also a few of some old Maps where it mentions on the Maps the Drymma Farm the property of Jenkin Zachariah. This beautiful Mansion was at one time a farm house. Please do not delay as we shall be anxiously waiting your reply.

Yours

Mrs Snow

Ferry Side near Red House

Unfortunately, the recovery was short lived, and in a matter of months John was ejected from the property later discovering that the court that had originally granted permission and so brutally took it away had been purged. The court was in fact unaware at the time the verdict was given and the property reinstated to John that there was a receiver in place for the estate of Miss Elizabeth Vye, an action that would see her beneficiaries, John Birch Paddon and Richard Backhouse, wrongly profit. Despite his grounds for possession and judgement at law being deemed as good, the fact that John Richard Thomas had taken possession of the estate without the sanction of the honourable court meant that his removal was unavoidable. Determined to resume the recovery of his family's estates once more, John spent the next two years gathering evidence to support his claim, but in 1867, it was John's own solicitor, William Rogers of Swansea, who disappeared with the all-important documents he needed to proceed, namely the counterpart leases and other vital evidence relating to the estate. Whilst Rogers returned to Swansea bankrupt and broken, the documents have never been found.

Not long after the disappearance of William Rogers, the Drymma Estates were put up for sale, only to be withdrawn due to objections made by Nathaniel Richard Thomas, son and heir of the late John Richard Thomas. The conditions of sale state that a receiver had been appointed to handle the estate of the late Miss E Vye based on the principle that Mr Robert Jennings Crosse declared the aforementioned died in fee simple. The guilt of committing concealed fraud was evidently a hard burden to bear for Crosse as he later took his own life.

Before his death, the proceedings didn't just take their toll on John emotionally, financially he was also struggling to foot the bill for vast legal costs relating to the recovery of the estates. Due to the strength of his claim however, his employer Mr Crawshay offered to finance the next leg of the legal battle in exchange for mineral rights once the case had been won, an offer that John respectfully declined. Despite his initial refusal, he later revisited the offer made by Crawshay, however, he had unfortunately changed his mind. He was subsequently declared bankrupt and died in 1886 in a mining accident at Cwm Pit, Merthyr Tydfil, where he was living at the time.

· · · · · ·

## MERTHYR TYDFIL'S MINING PAST

Situated just 23 miles north of Cardiff, Merthyr Tydfil is one town that has made a name for itself in the mining industry. Named after, according to legend, Saint Tydfil, a daughter of King Brychan of Brycheiniog, the town along with many other areas in north and south Wales was an important part of the country's advancement during the Industrial Revolution, and whilst many of the mines in other towns have closed their doors long ago, Merthyr is very much still a modern mining capital. Its proximity to reserves of iron ore, coal, limestone, lumber and water makes it ideally located for iron production, and whilst small scale works, in iron and coal, had provided a vital yet seemingly insignificant source of employment for the township before the early 19th century, with the birth of the Industrial Revolution came the rapid expansion of Merthyr's iron operations.

The development of the Vale of Neath Railway cemented Merthyr Tydfil's status as a growing industrial leader of the era, as this citation from the History of the Vale of Neath documents:

When the railway through the Vale of Neath was projected, some of the older inhabitants viewed its advent with fear and trembling. An old manservant of Ynysygerwn prophesied that the cows would withhold their milk and the calves would die: The landlord of the " Plough " inn at Abertwrch bemoaned, with serious brow, the possibility that the smoke of the locomotives passing so close to his house would destroy the horses in the stables ; and Sian Glover, occupying a cottage at Pont-walby, feared that the puff of the engine would sour the contents of the milk-pails from Llanfaglan to Pencaedrain.

The originator of the railway was a native of the district-Mr. H. S. Coke, town clerk of Neath. His first action was to proceed to London, in the summer of 1845, in order to put the project of a Neath to Merthyr line before the Earl of Jersey, the Directors of the South Wales and Great Western Railways, etc. So great did the engineering difficulties appear at the outset that Mr. Stephenson, "whose name was European," declared before a House of Commons Committee, "that it was impossible to make it a line adapted to the transit of minerals-that the difficulties were insurmountable " !Mr. I. K. Brunel, the famous engineer who designed the railway, proved this prediction wrong. Wooden bridges were thrown over the river and canal at Neath and Aberdulais, and from thence to Pontwalby construction was not difficult. The Glynneath-Hirwaen gradient of one in fifty, the splendid viaduct of Cwm Gwrelych consisting of four bays each of about 43 ft. span and 60 ft. high and the tunnel at Pencaedrain, all tested the capacity of the constructors. The line was laid double on the " broad gauge " (7 ft.) and stations were erected at Neath, Aberdulais, Resolven, Glyn Neath, Hirwaen and Abernant. The terminus at Merthyr was finished after the opening of the main railway.

By the peak of the revolution, the districts of Merthyr housed four of the greatest ironworks in the world, namely Dowlais, Plymouth, Cyfarthfa and Penydarren. These companies were mainly owned by two dynasties, the Guest and Crawshay families, who famously supported the establishment of schools for their workers. Whilst their support of education certainly paid off, producing a bevy of diligent workers, life for the miners of Merthyr was difficult as famous Scottish philosopher, satirical writer, essayist, historian and teacher, Thomas Carlyle, commented on after visiting the district in 1850:

> [The town was filled with such] unguided, hard-worked, fierce, and miserable-looking sons of Adam I never saw before. Ah me! It is like a vision of Hell, and will never leave me, that of these poor creatures broiling, all in sweat and dirt, amid their furnaces, pits, and rolling mills.

Living conditions in China, the name given to the slum in the Pont-Storehouse region of Merthyr Tydfil, were more than tough and inhabitants were even seen as a separate class, of which people living in more respectable areas would refer to as the 'criminal class.' The conditions in Merthyr obviously did not go unnoticed, and after the Industrial Revolution, the depression resulted in a number of uprisings. Whilst the revolution saw a steep decline in the number of young men working on farms and in other agricultural settings, instead being attracted to the higher wages associated with work in the iron industry, the non-existence of workers' rights caused revolt. From 1829 onwards, the depression meant that workers in Merthyr and beyond had no job security, with sudden dismissal, wage reductions and short term contracts a part of everyday life. The Merthyr Rising of 1831 was the result of years of hardship already endured by the people of the town. Those working for Crawshay took to the streets calling for reform, and whilst the exact figure of participants is unknown, records suggest that some 7,000 to 10,000 people marched throughout May. The protesters called for "caws a bara" – translated as cheese and bread – and "I lawr â'r Brenin" – down with the king – and sacked the courts destroying account books that contained the details of debtors. The violent events of that month led to 26 arrests, many of which were sentenced to imprisonment or penal transportation to Australia and two of which – Lewis Lewis and Dic Penderyn – were sentenced to death by hanging for robbery and assault. Lewis (referred to in records as Lewsyn yr Heliwr) had his sentence downgraded to a life sentence, whilst Penderyn was hanged at Cardiff market on 13 August 1831, however to this day, many people dispute whether he was responsible for the stabbing and before his death 11,000 people signed a petition demanding his release.

In the following years the coal and iron industries went into slow decline, and whilst several large companies were set up in Merthyr after the Second World War, leading to the resurgence of employment in the area, particularly of women, mining in the area is certainly not extinct. Building on its legacy of industrial heritage, in 2006, a large open-cast coal mine, which will extract 10 million tonnes of coal over a period of 15 years, was approved. The mine will be based just east of Merthyr as part of the Ffos-y-fran open-cast site.

• • • • • •

The receiver who claimed the priority of the possession later made a statement admitting that John Richard Thomas had been legally put in possession of the estates by the then Sheriff on 6 September 1865 and even stated that he was at a loss to why John never pursued the matter, clearly unaware of his bankruptcy.

This is a copy of the letter sent to Mrs Snow, a family member, from William Rogers, solicitor to John R. Thomas.

It appears to me that William Rogers was holding the estate documents while awaiting payment for his services, which it seems he did not receive; therefore he retained the documents which were never returned.

11 Museum Street

Bloomsbury

London

10th December 1873

Dear Mrs Snow,

Your letter was duly received and considered. I had given you all the information you required before I left Swansea. But you appear to treat the matter as if there was only one suit we commenced in the name of John Richard Thomas. Whereas there was two to recover the Drymma Estate. The other, a 3$^{rd}$, was an administration suit, in the court of chancery, by heirs-at-law, of the late Miss Vye, who claimed the Drymma Estate, as her freehold up to the time of her death, supposing she had purchased it in her life time. But it appears to be quite the reverse and the 2 claims of John Richard Thomas and the same time they came to collision; but John Richard Thomas, having obtained a judgement in ejectment and put in possession by the Sheriff of the county under an execution. I found, out of His Majesty's

Court of Exchequer of pleas he continued in possession at the time Thomas Thomas the receiver first claimed the Drymma as the estate of the late Miss Vye which appears to be fraudulently done to shut out John Richard Thomas, the rightful heir-at-law. Thomas, receiver having falsely deposed, by affidavit, that the Sheriff had not given possession of Brithdyr Farm; part of the estate at the time; he gave notice to John Richard Thomas of Miss Vye's claim. There being numerous persons present when the notice was given, to prove the contrary. It appears, therefore, necessary, that the proceedings in Chancery, should be obtained and examined, as I have mentioned, to you and Mr Davies before to instruct counsel, upon affidavit, to make an application, to the court. The late Miss Vye, having no title, or legal claim, to the freehold, of the Drymma; and there is every appearance that Divine Providence has ordered it to be so, by taking away the life of the receiver when he was endeavouring to carry it out in London, upon the false affidavit he made drawn by Mr Randall of Neath; a solicitor ever since afflicted with lunacy. I trust you will not keep me here longer, waiting for copies of papers which are ready upon payment of the money which you promised to get collected. I will give you every satisfaction on my return.

I remain dear madam in haste.

Your respectfully

W Rogers

Page 209      Trevelyn Versus Charles

4.J. Reports   Law Journal Reports, Vol 4, New Sriss

Vol. 13. Pt 1-4          Court consisting of H.

As to the question of time which the defendant will no doubt rise against the plaintiff the following case which is only one out of many which can be cited and which counsel is in no doubt well aware of will override any objection which may be made. It is fitting that those who appropriate the property of others should be assured that in this court that no time will secure to them the fruits of their dishonesty, but their children's children will be compelled to return the property of which their ancestors have fraudulently possessed themselves. Time is no bar except the party having full information of his injuries and his rights allows time to elapse without seeking relief.

| No. | When and Where Born. | Name (if any). | Sex. | Name and Surname of Father. | Name and Maiden Surname of Mother. | Rank or Profession of Father. | Signature, Description, and Residence of Informant. | When Registered. | Signature of Registrar. | Baptismal Name if added after Registration of Birth. |
|---|---|---|---|---|---|---|---|---|---|---|
| 439 | Twentysecond May 1868 Cefn Vaynor | Nathaniel Richard | Boy | John Richard Thomas | Ann Thomas formerly Jones | Coalminer | John Richard Thomas Father Cefn Vaynor | Twenty-eighth June 1868 | Edwd Martin Registrar | |

**Certificate of Birth.** Superintendent Registrar's District of *Merthyr Tydfil*

1868 BIRTH in the Sub-District of *Upper Merthyr Tydfil* in the County of *Glamorgan & Brecon*

I, Superintendent Registrar of Births, Deaths, and Marriages, for the District of *Merthyr Tydfil* in the Counties of *Glamorgan & Brecon* do hereby Certify that the foregoing is a true Copy of an Entry in the Register Book of Births for the Sub-District of *Upper Merthyr Tydfil* within the said District; and I further Certify that the said Register Book is now lawfully in my custody. Witness my Hand this 17th day of August 1889.

Book No. 62 Entry No. 439 Page 88

John Davies Dep Superintendent Registrar.

Birth certificate of Nathaniel Richard Thomas.

# 8. NATHANIEL R. THOMAS

**AS BRIEFLY MENTIONED** John Richard Thomas had just one son, Nathaniel Richard Thomas, a figure that is held in high esteem and provided an essential and accurate insight into the wider history relating to the Thomas family to the members of The Walter Thomas Inheritance Association. Whilst similar to the foundation of The Walter Thomas Inheritance Association, many family associations have been formed over the years, all with one sole objective in mind like their forefathers Thomas R Thomas I, Thomas R Thomas III and John Richard Thomas. Attempts to finance the case however have often only been met by closed doors, despite the final attempt in 1917 by Nathaniel offering a turning point in regards to providing conclusive evidence and correcting the flaws that had so commonly caused former cases to collapse.

After watching his father's endeavours to re-establish a claim on the Drymma Estate fall into failure, Nathaniel wasn't deterred from launching his own campaign of recovery. It was in 1887 that Nathaniel made his very first attempt as recorded in an account published in The Bridgend Chronicle on Friday 23 September 1887 under the headline 'Wilful Damage at Neath':

> At Neath Police Court before Messrs. J.H. Rowland, G.H. Davey, J. Leyson and the Revd. Walter Griffiths, Mr. Paddon, of Drymma, near Neath, summoned a man named Thomas, of Pontypridd and three others for wilful trespass upon his property and cutting down two oak trees. Mr. David Lewis, barrister, of Swansea, instructed by Mr. James Kemphorne, solicitor, Neath, appeared for the plaintiff; and Mr. Spickett, junior, Ponty-y-pridd, for defendants. The evidence went to show that this man Thomas committed the trespass on a pretended claim of the right to the property. But, Mr. Paddon proved that he had been in undisturbed possession for upwards of twenty years, and never heard anything of the present defendant until the alleged trespass. Mr. Paddon's title unimpeachable having been declared valid by a decree of the Court of Chancery more than twenty years ago. The justices fined Thomas the sum of twenty shillings for damage done and costs including advocates fees or fourteen days imprisonment.

This wasn't the last attempt by Nathaniel. From as early as 1896, he worked tirelessly to raise the funds he needed to take his case to court, and realising his resources were limited even sought publicity to secure the financial backing he required to proceed as this article from Merthyr Express, dated 5 December 1896, shows:

> An action has been entered in the High Court of Justice and will shortly, says a contemporary, come on for trial, the hearing of which, consequent upon the stupendous issues involved, will create an interest throughout South Wales such as has not before been paralleled. This case is one in which Mr. Nathaniel Richard Thomas, a working collier, of Cefn, Merthyr, lays claim to the Drymma Estate, an immense property extending into three counties and embracing fourteen parishes, with an annual value computed ay upwards of £300,000. There are said to be in the case elements of romance which cap the wildest flights of fiction. Upon the property, which is located chiefly in the Swansea and Ogmore Valleys, there are a large number of collieries, several tin-plate and copper Works, numerous railways, and other gigantic undertakings.

## A GREAT WELSH LAWSUIT.

### CEFN COLLIER'S ROMANTIC CLAIM.

### AN IMMENSE PROPERTY IN DISPUTE.

### £300,000 A YEAR INVOLVED.

An action has been entered in the High Court of Justice and will shortly, it is expected, come on for trial the hearing of which, consequent upon the stupendous issues involved, will create an interest throughout South Wales such as has not before been paralleled. The case is one in which Mr. Nathaniel Richard Thomas, a working collier of Cefncoed-y-Cymmer, near Merthyr, lays claim to the Drymma Estate, an immense property extending into three counties and embracing fourteen parishes, with an annual value computed at upwards of £300,000. There are said to be in the case elements of romance which cap the wildest flights of fiction. Upon the property, which is located chiefly in the Swansea and Ogmore Valleys, there are a large number of collieries, several tin-plate and copper works, numerous railways, and other gigantic undertakings. In respect of part of the estate the tenants have for many years past paid rent into Chancery because of a dubiety as to the actual ownership, and the sum which has thus accumulated represents a colossal amount. Among the reputed owners of the rest of the property in relation to which the claim is made are mentioned the names of the Earl of Jersey, Lord Swansea, Sir John T. D. Llewelyn, Bart., M.P., Mr. J. Player, Mr. Gregory, Mr. E. Strick, Mr. W. Player, Mr. J. B. Paddon, and Mr. H. N. Miers. Thomas, the claimant, is declared to be in a position to prove direct descent from a testator under whose will the estate was left from heir to heir for ever, the genealogical evidence he is able to produce being stated to be flawless and irrefutable. By way of asserting his title he cut down some of the oaks in front of the Drymma Mansion, near Dynevor Station, upon attaining his majority, in 1887, and in 1893 he took possession of the Ynystawe Mansion, then vacant, with his step-brother, David Meredith, who is also a miner. On the latter occasion Mr. Strick is alleged to have brought a body of about 300 men to the house, and the two were forcibly ejected, each being carried out by four persons. Since then the brothers have devoted themselves exclusively to the business of working up the case so as to get it tried as soon as possible—a task in which Mr. W. Vaughan Edwards, of The Cottage, Cefn, has lent them most invaluable assistance.

'A Great Welsh Lawsuit' feature in The Western Mail, 30th November 1896.

In respect of part of the estate the tenants have for many years past paid rent into Chancery, because of a dubiety as to the actual ownership, and the sum which has thus accumulated represents a colossal amount. Among the reputed owners of the rest of the property in relation to which the claim is made are mentioned the names of the Earl of Jersey, Lord Swansea, Sir John T.D. Llewelyn, Bart., M.P., Mr. J. Player, Mr. Gregory, Mr. E. Strick, Mr. W. Player, Mr. J.B. Paddon and Mr. H.N. Miers.

Thomas, the claimant, is declared to be in a position to prove direct descent from a testator under whose will the estate was left from heir to heir for ever, the genealogical evidence he is able to produce being stated to be flawless and irrefutable. By way of asserting his title he cut down some of the oaks in front of the Drymma Mansion, near Dynevor Station, in 1887, and in 1893 he took possession of the Ynystawe Mansion, then vacant, with his step-brother, David Meredith, who is also a miner*.

On the latter occasion Mr. Strick is alleged to have brought a body of about three hundred men to the house, and the two were forcibly ejected, each being carried out by four persons. Since then the brothers have devoted themselves exclusively to the business of working up the case so as to get it tried as soon as possible, a task in which Mr. W. Vaughan Edwards, of The Cottage, Cefn, has lent them invaluable assistance.

*The party was also accompanied by cousin William Davies and other family members.*

Despite having help from high profile figures like William Nash Vaughan Edwards, who was at the time chief clerk for the County Court and Town Hall of Merthyr Tydfil, and generating an unprecedented amount of publicity for the claim, Nathaniel did not receive the financial backing he needed. He subsequently spent years gathering funds from relations, who were equally as keen to return the lost Thomas estates to their rightful owners, to finance proceedings, and despite the sudden death of step-brother David Meredith in 1900 he continued to pursue his claim up to 1916. The case was eventually heard in that year at the Court of Justice when it was brought before Mr Justice Neville.

Despite an attempt from Arthur Mathews Paddon, son of John Birch Paddon, to settle out of court. He offered an undisclosed amount of money, said to be a considerable enough sum to allow Nathaniel and his relatives to live 'very comfortably'; Nathaniel of course refused. Unfortunately the case, dated February 1917, was lost with the judge describing his efforts to recover the estates as 'frivolous' and 'vexatious', and ruling in favour of Arthur M Paddon and the Poor Law Committee purchasers of the Drymma Estate defendants. It is at this stage important to note that at the time the case was heard, said Arthur M Paddon was the freeholder after his father purchased the whole of the Drymma Estate from Chancery between 1888 and 1890 as detailed on page 52 in The History of the Vale of Neath by D. Rhys Phillips. The purchase went ahead as planned during this time, despite the new Dynevor & Dyffryn Coal Co's (a company that was formed following the suspension of the Dynevor Coal Co in 1866 according to 1866's The Engineer) refusal to renew John Birch Paddon's coal lease when the original lease expired in 1874. Paddon subsequently applied to the Court of Chancery for a lease of 21 years at a minimum rental of 5,000 and under the agreement that certain royalties were to be paid to the company during this period.

Despite generous support from family members, Nathaniel, like his father, was made bankrupt. The lack of title deeds, documentation which was stolen years earlier,

appeared to be his downfall. Whilst Nathaniel had managed to halt the sale of the estates some years earlier, the disappearance of the title deeds did come back to haunt him considerably, as the debate to whether the property was freehold or leasehold raged on prior to the case being heard in the High Court of Justice. At this time there were still no title deeds or any form of documentation available to him but a discovery in 1904 would at first appear to be his saving grace.

The original leases, as granted by the first Phillip Thomas to Thomas Griffiths for a period of 99 years, expiring in 1874, were discovered lying hidden in a metal box in the grounds of the estate after being buried there by Mary Beynon, Miss Vye's maid, who was living in Brithdir Ucha at the time. Whilst the leases discovered related to the Drymma property, not Brithdir Ucha, also part of the Neath Abbey Estate, the documents found stated the conditions of sale in reference to Miss Vye's possession and provided evidence that she was paying rent to her 'superior landlord', Thomas Richard Thomas.

An account from John Mallon, whose great, great uncle was Nathaniel Richard Thomas, provides an integral yet brief overview of the proceedings so far and an insight into the legalities behind the claim, as the following excerpt explores:

Thomas Thomas III said that he was the owner of the Drumma. In fact, a solicitor examining Nathaniel's claim said the evidence as to grandfather Thomas Richard Thomas, who died in 1865, having been the owner of the Drumma and Brithdir properties in fee simple at the time of his death appears to be ample.

Whereas Elizabeth Vye wasn't in fee simple at the time of death. This is the significant difference between Thomas and Vye.

IN RE NATHANIEL RICHARD THOMAS

OPINION BY COUNSEL

This is a claim by Mr NATHANIEL RICHARD THOMAS to an estate in Glamorganshire formerly known as TYR MINYDD DRYMMA with a coal mine beneath the surface, and formerly known as MYNYDD DRYMMA, the total acreage being      acreas or thereabouts, and the facts disclosed in these instructions, and upon which this claim is based, are as follows :-

THOMAS RICHARD THOMAS (the first) the great great grandfather of the Claimant is supposed to have granted two leases , one of the surface of the land, and the other of the coal mine, in 1773 and 1774, respectively for 99 years to one PHILLIP THOMAS, otherwise SAMUEL, and there is no doubt that PHILIP THOMAS - otherwise Samuel - did on January 13th 1775 and 1776 respectively grant two leases , one for 99 years from September 29th 1774 of the surface, and the other for 98 years from September 1775 of the coal mine to a THOMAS GRIFFITHS. These leases would therefore in September 1874. It is to be observed that these leases were granted by PHILLIP THOMAS or Samuel , as if he were Freeholder, that is , he covenants in various parts of the lease for himself, his heirs, executors, &c., THOMAS RICHARD THOMAS (the first) died in 1839. The next stage in the instructions is that at some time in 1858, rent is paid by Miss ELIZABETH VYE - a resident on the land - to THOMAS RICHARD THOMAS ( the third ) the grandfather of the Claimant, and that he levied a distress upon MISS VYE'S goods personally for rent, which however was paid before the goods were removed. A Statutory Declaration to this effect has been made by DAVID THOMAS, who is still living he swearing that he was present at the distress with one THOMAS GEORGE (deceased ). Assuming that, THOMAS RICHARD THOMAS (the third ) was the owner in fee simple of the land, subject to the reversion of the leases granted by his Grandfather to PHILLIP

receive the rent ( although there is no evidence of this) until April 3rd 1863 when Miss Vye died, and complications ensued. Shortly after her death, letters of Administration to her Estate were granted to a Mr and Mrs Brewer, and on May 23rd 1864, and action for the Administration by the Court of Chancery of her estate was brought against Mr and Mrs Brewer by a Mr Backhouse (Backhouse versus Brewer ) On April 12th of that year an Order for Administration was made, and according to the Master's Certificate made in the action, there is no trace of the leases to GRIFFITHS which afterwards came to light - no doubt they were in the possession of MARY BEYNON, as hereinafter appears - neither is there any trace of any documents of title to the land of which Miss VYE had possession, although there was document of title to land at COMBE MARTIN in DEVONSHIRE, and elsewhere belonging to Miss VYE. The significant fact is that Mr and Mrs Brewer do not appear to have found any title to the MYNYDD DRYMMA Estate, or the MYNDD DRYMMA COAL-MINE , but, according to the information given by them to the Master, Miss Vye had previous to her death been in receipt of the rents of the Mansion House and Farm and of the royalties from the Coal Mine. THOMAS RICHARD THOMAS (the third ) died on or about the      day of      1863 and on his death bed, his son, JOHN RICHARD THOMAS, according to instructions does not appear to have collected any rent, but the next transaction is that in Trinity Term 1865 he obtained Orders of Ejectment against Thomas Thomas in respect of DRYMMA FACH FARM and against MARY BEYNON in respect of BRITHDYR UCHA. Unfortunately a Receiver had been previously appointed by the Court of Chancery in the Action of BACKHOUSE versus PADDON. And on the Sheriff attempting to evict THOMAS THOMAS and MARY BEYNON, he complained to the Court with the result that on September 15th 1865 JOHN RICHARD THOMAS and the Sheriff were ordered by the Court to withdraw from the land, and on October 13th 1865 a Writ of Attachment was issued against JOHN RICHARD THOMAS upon which he apologised to the Court, and probably paid the costs of

of the application to commit him. It is difficult to see why if he knew that his Father had been in the habit of collecting the rent of the estate from Miss Vye, he did not proceed further in the matter, but the explanation given is, that his Solicitor, Mr ROGERS, had in his possession the counterparts of the leases originally granted by THOMAS RICHARD THOMAS (the first) that he afterwards disappeared with these counterparts, and the other title deeds, and was found years afterwards in a state of beggary in the Town of Swansea. I note that Mr PULLEN - the London Agent of Mr ROGERS - on the 20th of November 1867 made an Affidavit in the Action of Backhouse v Paddon, in which he says he believes that Miss VYE only had possession of the land, under the leases granted to THOMAS GRIFFITHS. An explanation is therefore necessary as to how it was that, Mr ROGERS, having in his possession the title deeds to the Freehold, and, or the counterparts of the original leases to PHILLIP THOMAS (otherwise SAMUEL ) Mr PULLEN the Agent makes no mention of the fact. I now come to a feature in the case upon which the success of the Claimant will largely depend. In an Affidavit sworn by Mr GEORGE in the action of Backhouse v Paddon on November 5th 1864 at South Molton in Devonshire, in which he sets out as the result of his enquiries, the real estate (including the land now claimed ) as belonging to Miss Vye, but no reference is made to any title deeds. He acting as Solicitor on behalf of the Plaintiff - Mr Backhouse - who was claiming to be the sole heir-at-law of Miss Vye. I think it is clear that at that time he had never seen any title deeds, nor had any reason to believe there were title deeds shewing that the land belonged to Miss Vye, because, long afterwards namely in September 1866 and nearly ten months after the decree of the Court - dividing the property between Backhouse and Paddon had been made - Backhouse and Paddon being in action (September 12th 1866 ) against MARY BEYNON, Housekeeper to Miss Vye, charging her with retaining the title deeds to the estate, but giving no particulars of those title deeds, and admitting by the Interrogatories to be administered

the Bill of Complaint in that Action - September 18th 1866 -
they allege that Miss Vye was seised in fee simple of the Drymma
Estate and the Coal Mine beneath the surface, and of the Brithdyr
Ucha Farm and the Coal Mine beneath the surface, and of the Brithdyr
Ucha Farm and the Coal Mine beneath the surface, and of the Brithdyr
Ucha consisting of 89 acres 3 r. 32 p. was conveyed by a Mr Tennant
and his Mortgagee to Miss Vye.  In 1867 the whole of this property
is put for Sale by Auction, and according to the conditions of
Sale, Lot 1, which I presume includes the surface of the Estate
excepting Brithdyr Ucha is to be sold subject to the Lease of the
Coal Mine demised by PHILLIP THOMAS otherwise SAMUEL to THOMAS
GRIFFITHS in 1776 hereinbefore mentioned.  The condition goes on to
say that by an assignment dated July 9th 1841 that Lease was vested
in a JOHN PARSONS who had paid rent and royalties to Messrs Backhouse and Paddon, the heirs-at-law of Miss Vye.  Lot 21 was
supposed to consist of Brithdyr Ucha conveyed to Miss Vye by the
deed of May 17th 1859, but apparently that conveyance was not to
be found, and a copy was supposed to be produced and a Statutory
Declaration would be provided, that it was a copy of the original
conveyance, and that the original conveyance had been properly
executed by the parties thereto.  Was this conveyance a valid or
concocted document ?  At the first sight it seems difficult to
understand - at least on the facts placed before me - that a
document bearing the name of a well-known banker as Mortgagee
should be a forgery.  On the other hand it is quite inconsistent
with the fact, that in 1775 PHILLIP THOMAS - otherwise Samuel -
granted to THOMAS GRIFFITHS a lease of the whole surface of the
land ( TYR MYNYDD DRYMMA ) for 99 years.  If it were a conveyance
subject to that lease, the fact would be mentioned .  Again the
assignment of the Coal Mine to JOHN PARSONS is not produced, only
a copy, but that might possibly be , because at that time (1867)
the lease had not expired.  But, I should have thought that if
the lease had been assigned to Parsons, it would have been handed
over to him with the assignment, whereas we know that both leases
by GRIFFITHS were in possession of MARY BEYNON at Miss VYE'S death
and secreted by her, and not delivered up until 1904 when they

were handed over by her (Mary Beynon)  nephew to the Claimant,
with a message that they were his property.  Those leases are now
in the possession of Mr William Burchell Rees, and I understand
that there is no doubt as to their genuineness.  The Sale by
Auction was forbidden or protested against, and the Auctioneer
apparently thinking there was a " flaw in the title " of the
Vendor did not proceed with the sale.  I do not propose to go into
all the parts of the case which are numerous and complicated.
Suffice it to say that the two leases after being secreted for many
years were delivered up to the Claimant in 1904.  But, it was not
until the year 1911, that owing to the perseverance and industry of
Mr Rees the above matters were brought to light.  Assuming that the
Claimant is entitled to the property, the question will arise,
against whom, and in what form, is the action to be brought.
The persons now actually in possession are the Guardians of the
Poor for the County of Glamorgan, and as they are in possession
under an Act of Parliament ( Mental Defiancy Act, 1913 )3 & 4,
George V. Cap. 78 - under which they have taken the estate
compulsorily the ordinary Action of Ejectment will not lie, but
inasmuch as they have not paid any part of the purchase money
(now £16,000 ) but are in the meantime paying interest at the
rate of 3½% per annum, it will be necessary to claim the amount
of the purchase money instead of the land.  Notice has been
given to them, both publicly and by written communications
that Mr THOMAS is the Claimant, and heir-at-law of his Grandfather.
I should like to add that it would have been impossible for me
to form an opinion as to the merits of this case, without the
assistance of Mr W.B. Rees, both from the written instructions
(which I understand were formulated by him ) and from the
verbal information given by him to me in various conferences,
as well as the benefit of his legal views on many aspects of
the case.  I see clearly however, that it will be necessary
to exercise the greatest care in collecting the evidence in
support of the claim, and I realise that the successful issue
will depend on the way, in which the evidence both of living

I understand that Mr W.B. Rees is prepared to  continue his
services in this respect.  Subject to the obtaining of the
necessary evidence, my opinion is as follows :-

FIRST  I think that the Claimant's Grandfather
died in 1863 seised in fee simple of the Drymma
and Brithdyr property.

SECONDLY - I think that the matters herein
previously set out, commencing with the
Affidavit of Robert Jenning Crosse, and
ending with the Condition of Sale, shew
that there was concealed fraud, within the
meaning of Section 76. of the Real Property
Limitation Act 1833 ( see case of Petre v Petre
1889. 1.Drew p. 397) and numerous other
cases following that decision.

THIRDLY - The concealed fraud was not discovered
and could not reasonably be discovered until 1911

Under these circumstances it is now a question of
obtaining the necessary evidence.

(Signed ) W.A. GRIST HAWTIN.

5, Essex Court,

T E M P L E.

April 18th 1916.

SOUTH WALES DAILY NEWS. THURSDAY. JUNE 17. 1915.

The Building Committee of the Glamorgan Poor Law Board and officials of the Local Government Board visit Drymman, Llansamlet, the new Glamorgan County Home for the Feeble-minded. Left to right—Mr Dyer, Pontypridd; Dr. Stephens, Swansea; Mr Trick, Neath; the Rev. E. D. Evans; Mr Harries, secretary; Mr Hugh Williams and Mr Kitchin, L.G.B.; the Rev. D. Phillips and Mr Roderick, consulting architect to the Poor Law Board.—(Chapman.)

'The Poor Law Committee' featured in The South Wales Daily News, 17th June 1915.

The dictionary definition of fee simple is 'a restriction on the transfer of ownership.'

The only reason why John Richard Thomas lost possession was due to the affidavit between Paddon, Backhouse and Crosse falsely stating that Vye had died in fee simple. Also, when William Rogers ran away he took with him title deeds regarding this property, whilst John's other solicitor vanished with various other deeds.

In addition to juxtaposing positions regarding which parties were in fee simple and which were not, Nathaniel's misinterpretation of this family's claim to the estate may have also contributed to his downfall and led to the judge's misunderstanding that his attempt to recover the Drymma Estate was nothing more than vexatious. As seen in the Brief from Counsel: Thomas Versus Paddon, dated 17 March 1911, the following extract shows an inconsistency, which, whilst it can be explained and corrected today based on our improved understanding of the facts, may have cast some doubt regarding the legitimacy of the claim when brought to court in the early 20th century.

Nathaniel Richard Thomas, son of John Richard Thomas and Grandson of Thomas Richard Thomas claims as heir at law to an estate called Drymma House and Lands and a farm called Drymma Fach, known as little Drymma, and a farm called Brythdir as show on the map marked (a) and coloured pink yellow and green. These lands are situated in the parishes of Llansamlet and Cadoxton Juxta, Neath in the County of Glamorgan, and had and have been fraudulently withheld from the late John Richard Thomas and Nathaniel Richard Thomas the present Claimant since the year 1865 by one Richard Backhouse and John Birch Paddon by design and concealed fraud for the reason that the said Backhouse and Paddon knew full well that they had no legal right or

Neath Abbey Estate.

claim to this property as freehold.

…

When John Richard Thomas, the father of the present claimant, Nathaniel Richard Thomas, heard of the death of the intestate Elizabeth Vye, he instituted proceedings in the Chancery Division of the High Court of Justice to recover against one Mary Beynon, widow, possession of about 50 acres of land with farm house, barns, stables, and outbuildings, erected thereon. The place was commonly known as Brythdir farm, situated within the parish of Cadoxton Juxta Neath in the said County of Glamorgan.

The ejectment order, or writs were made out and sent to the then sheriff of Glamorgan, William Booker, Esq., for execution.

After the said sheriff received the necessary writs of orders, the father of the claimant, Nathaniel Richard

Warrant or Writ of Possession
Glamorganshire.

To Wit,   Thomas William Booker Esq.
Sheriff of the County of Glamorgan.

To, Frederick William Armstrong James Ashbee.
Greeting. Whereas I have received a Writ of our
Sovereign Lady, the Queen in the words following.
(that is to say) "Victoria by the Grace of God of
the United Kingdom of Great Britain and Ireland
Queen Defender of the Faith.   To the Sheriff of
Glamorganshire Greeting, Whereas John Richard
Thomas lately in our Court of Exchequer of Pleas
by Judgment of the same Court recovered against
Thomas Thomas possession of all that arable
pasture and woodlands containing about 60 acres
more or less together with the messuages tenements farmhouse barns stables outbuildings and
appurtenances erected thereon and commonly
called or known as Drynna farm situate in
the parish of Cadoxton juxta Neath in the
County of Glamorgan with the appurtenances
in your Bailiwick - Therefore we command
you that you omit not by reason of any
liberty of your County. But that you enter
the same and without delay you cause the
said John Richard Thomas to have possession
of the said land and premises with the
appurtenances and in what manner you shall
have executed this, our Writ, make appear to

Witness, Sir Frederick Pollock Knight at Westminster
"The 1st day of September A. D. 1864  1865.
"Therefore I command you and each of you jointly
and severely that you omit not by reason of any
liberty in my Bailiwick, but that you enter
the same and cause the said John Richard
Thomas to have possession of the said land
and premises in the said writ specified with
the appurtenances, Hereof fail not at your peril

Given under my hand and seal of office this
4th day of September A. D. 1865

L. S.       Signed    Thomas William Booker Esq.
Sheriff.

Writ endorsed
This Writ was issued by Charles Alfred Pullen of
Chichester Chambers No. 22 Chancery Lane in the
County of Middlesex, Attorney for the said Plaintiff
(B. Ward)
(J. J. 8)
True copy.

Judge's Order
August 17. 1865.
Exchequer of Pleas Judgment Book Page A 465
John Richard Thomas Trinity A Pullen 5/B, against
Mary Beynon widow, for possession and each of Pleas
Judgment Book page 499 August 25. Pullen 57
John Richard Thomas for possession.

**Writ of Possession 1865.**

Thomas, John Richard Thomas was put in possession legally and in proper form by the said sheriff of Glamorgan on the 6th day of Sept., and the Counsel will observe that it is dated the 17th Aug. 1865

There was also an other order or writ of possession granted at this time to John Richard Thomas; this was against Thomas Thomas of Drymma Fach, in the parish of Cadoxton Juxta Neath, with all the appurtenances appertaining to Drymma Mansion. The said orders or writs were placed in the hands of the said sheriff of Glamorgan, and under the same, John Richard Thomas father of the now claimant, Nathaniel Richard Thomas, was put in possession on the 6th day of Sept. 1865.

Whilst much of the extract above and the remainder of the document contained statements backed up by evidence as required in court, the instance where Nathaniel was not clear in his claims to the estate may have planted a seed of doubt in the ruling judge's mind. His father John R Thomas and grandfather Thomas R Thomas were claiming for Brithdir Farm and its approximate 50 acres, whereas Nathaniel is claiming Brithdir Uchaf, which consists of 93 acres, an entirely different holding and one that can be substantiated by Miss Vye's claims of ownership as the aforementioned land was conveyed to her, as previously described, in 1859 by Charles Henry Tennant, who in turn acquired it from Bussey Mansel.

It was Nathaniel's previous seizure of Ynistawe (or Ynystawe) House that also caused concern when the case was brought in front of the courts years later. The confusion derives from the fact that in many instances Nathaniel only had accounts that were verbally communicated to him, many of which had been passed down from generation to generation. Many family members, both living and long gone, incorrectly pointed to an estate, which included Ynistawe

Ynystanglwst, adjacent to Ynystawe House.

Mansion, being owned by his forefather Jenkin Zacharias, however the aforementioned lands and associated properties had not been in the family any time beyond the 16th century, and were in fact purchased legally by Thomas Popkin – father of the notorious and alleged murderer Robert Popkin – from Hopkin John during the early 18th century. This information however only came to light following the recent examination of vital evidence, documentation that Nathaniel did not have access to at the time. With a strong belief that Ynistawe House was part of the lost Thomas estates, in 1893 Nathaniel and a number of his companions seized possession of Ynistawe House, holding residence there for five days in total before being forcefully removed by a mob of three hundred men. Nathaniel did not take his removal lying down, and took legal action against Edward Strick, coroner for Swansea and leader of the mob, for forcible entry.

A letter to then Prime Minister Lloyd George from Nathaniel details the plight that he faced in taking Mr. Strick to court for his actions. Whilst an indictment was initially found against Strick when the case was taken to the magistrates at Swansea Police Court, on arriving at court at a later date Nathaniel was advised that the case was already lost as the individuals making up the Grand Jury were all men living on the Ynistawe Mansion estate, as this extract from the August 1903 letter states:

> When I was there with all my witnesses, solicitor and counsel awaiting the trial, we was informed that the officials of the court had lost the bill, a fresh bill was drawned but I was advised not to appear before the Grand Jury because that they were pack jury, comprise of Gentlemen, who was holding the property which I was claiming therefore having being a poor man I have made a very little progress in the matter since but lately I was told that I can proceed under the forma pauperism that is of course if I am able to show … case.

> I would be very grateful if you would go through my papers and documents and advise me as to what would be my best step to adopt in the matter.

To this day, the site of Ynistawe House, now home to three private dwellings, is still connected to the 'Strick' name as it is said to be owned by a solicitors firm trading under 'Strick and Bellingham.' Whilst in the mid-1990s the land itself was not registered with Land Registry, its sale to the present owners of the New Ynystawe House, Mr & Mrs Edwards – the latter a former city councillor – have sold areas of the estate for use as private housing.

Page 29 of the Brief from Counsel: Thomas Versus Paddon, dated 17 March 1911, also demonstrates Nathaniel's lack of clarity regarding some parts of the case despite the statements referred to as part of Henry Sambrook's involvement, as shown in the following extract, now able to be validated.

> (3) My grandfather David Morgan Evans told me that he paid rent many times to a Mr. Thomas as owner

of the land at Skewen adjoining the old road leading from Swansea to Neath who was also the owner of the Drymma Estates including the marshes to the Neath river and at one time the owner of the monasteries on the estates which Cromwell destroyed adjoining the Neath River.

> (4) My grandfather David Morgan Evans told me the said Tomas was an old man but he had not seen him for some time and that the said Thomas was low hearted because he was being kept out of some of his estate.

Henry Sambrook's version of events offered a vital insight into life on the estate and the tenants', in this case Sambrook's grandfather, David Morgan Evan, relationship with owner Thomas. During the time of the case it was however only Sambrook's word that could be taken, but some time after statements, like the ones made in the preceding excerpt, could be confirmed. Another document for example, the Tythes for 1844, states that 'Thomas Trustee', who the Association take to be Thomas R Thomas III (Nathaniel's grandfather) and another Thomas Thomas (noted as Nathaniel's great-grandfather), were the landowners, and confirms that David Morgan and others were tenants of the land's cottages and gardens. The statement's precise detailing of the location also seems to substantiate Sambrook's account, whilst a lease granted by Phillip Samuel to one Owen David Morgan's tenement, which means Owen son of David Morgan, could now be confirmed as the grandfather of Henry Sambrook due to the Association's gathered evidence and accompanying dates.

A man of 72 years of age at the time of giving his statement, Henry Sambrook of 18 Alverton Street, Deptford, London, went above and beyond to assist Nathaniel with his case, despite fears that retribution may not be too far behind him as a result. Born in Skewen, near the town of Neath,

Henry's account was based on what he had been told by his mother and father, a tale of lost estates and concealed fraud, one that could be authenticated by his own grandfather's experiences as a Drymma tenant. Whilst his grandfather was now long gone – he is buried in the church yard of Llansamlet – what his mother and father were told and what he witnessed for himself provided vital evidence to support Nathaniel's claim. His relationship with Henry also led him to discover the missing deeds as mentioned previously in this text, the first hint of which came from a mysterious letter from London.

Dear Sir,

Having heard that you have been trying to claim the Drymma Estate and not being successful on account of the papers being missing I think I have a clue to where they can be found having been in Wales on business and hearing certain things concerning missing papers. I think it is my duty to try and find you soon and then I will tell you all I hear about them.

I remain dear Sir, your sincere friend, Henry Sambrook, 18 Alverton Street, Deptford, London.

More correspondence followed, as despite at first glance appearing to be a cruel hoax due to the information it contains being easily described as 'too good to be true', Nathaniel had no other leads so was therefore determined to discover if this one was indeed real.

My dear Sir,

I am glad to know that my letter found you as I have had a deal of trouble to find your name. I am only a poor man without means.

I left my home at Skewen and since that time I have travelled the world on the same boat as Engineer for about eight-and-a-half years. But now I have been out of work for about twelve months or I should come personally to try and find you. My dear Sir, the papers are buried in an iron-box two feet under the earth and the man that told me said he could take me to the very spot where they were buried so trusting I may be of service to you, I remain your sincere friend

H Sambrook

Another letter from Sambrook provided the assurance Nathaniel needed to journey to Deptford and obtain a sworn declaration from Henry in person, a statement that he anticipated would provide the centre piece for his claim. The letter read as follows:

Dear Sir,

I am so sorry our circumstances are keeping us apart for I could explain so much better to you if I could see you. Do you think you could go and see him if I sent you his name? He lives close to the Estate. If so I will willingly send you his name and address for he knows what's in the box and where it is buried and the two old ladies that buried it there are both dead now.

He promised them he would not say anything about it while they were alive he told me he is only waiting for someone to advertise for it. He does not know that I have been trying to find you but I thought it would be a cruel thing to keep a man out of his rights, and let me know if you will go and I will send name and address.

The name Henry was referring to was that of Lancelot Griffiths of Skewen, an individual he had been made aware of whilst talking to Benjamin Jones, landlord of the Plough & Harrow Pub, on a recent visit to the area. It was Lancelot's aunt Mary Beynon that had been Miss Vye's housekeeper and partner in crime when it came to the disappearance of the all-important title deeds. Fearing further retribution for her family – Mary was imprisoned under the charge of contempt of court for insisting that the documentation held by John Birch Paddon in relation to the Drymma was forged – Mary had sworn Lancelot to secrecy.

A declaration directed to the Commissioner for Oaths describes in detail just what Nathaniel and his companions uncovered on the instruction of Henry Sambrook, however, as you'll discover, the first search was unsuccessful:

Mr Benjamin Williams, of Langoch, Bon-y-maen upper Llansamlet near Swansea, and Mr Thomas Owen of near the Colliers Llansamlet, were engaged by me to search for the Box, which I had been informed by Mr Henry Sambrook's letters in which he sated had been buried in a Garden, and contained deeds relating to the Drymma Estate and which he said belonged to me.

The above parties searched several gardens on the Skewen, and could find nothing, and went from there to a small Farm at Crwmlyn which was occupied by one Thomas, a farmer who gave them possession to search his garden, and they actually found the hole where the box had been buried near the Pigs Stye, and the hole had been filled up with small stones and earth leaving the trace of the box in the soil. Benjamin Williams is dead, but Thomas Owen is still alive and resides now in one of the cottages near the Travellers Rest Llansamlet.

The deeds were indeed in a metal box on the estate, however, as a letter received later would reveal, were removed just before the search ensued.

Dear Sir

Just a few lines to inform you that I have received the deeds back the offer is acceptable and for me to draw the agreement the best way we can Mr Owen and Mr Williams was with me on Saturday night and we agree for you to come down on Tuesday March 29th 1904 so you can take them back with you that night and therefore

I will leave your honour myself.

So no more at present

From your dear friend

Mr Lancelot Griffiths

The exchange went ahead as planned, with Nathaniel receiving the deeds from Lancelot, for a fee of course! The experience that his father John R Thomas had with then family solicitor William Rogers made Nathaniel more than cautious when it came to the handling of documentation for the case years later, a tact that he was keen for everyone in his party to employ as this letter from William Burchell Rees – Nathaniel's solicitor – evidences:

Dear Mr Thomas,

Received your letter this morning , when I at once went to 33 Chancery Lane, where I saw Mr Roberts who informed me that Mr Ellis Davies had written to Mr Evans but had not received an answer. This I think has been very ungentlemanly on his part, in fact I went also to see how matters stood, but took a typed copy of a portion of the case of Trevelyn v Charles, and pasted it on the inside cover of the Bound Book, so that o Counsel can come to a hasty conclusion by virtue of the Limitation Act – as it is distinctly laid down there that "no time will bar the rightful owner of his rights" And I have also done the same to the Bound Book that I have just posted on to you. Please be careful with it, as it fully sets out your Claim, and do not trust any Solicitor with it, until you can get another bound book like it.

Letters from Lancelot Griffiths to Nathaniel Richard Thomas March 21st1904.

Despite his failed attempt, looking back no one could doubt that Nathaniel was, by reputation, a man of honour, a trait that inspired Sambrook to assist him in the first instance. An extract from Merthyr Historian: Volume Eleven, specifically an account entitled 'The Walter Thomas Heirs Who Lived in Merthyr Tydfil' by John Mallon, provided a vital insight into the man behind the claim in the form of two job references written for Nathaniel to support his application for the role of handyman at Pontsarn Tuberculosis Hospital, Merthyr, in 1915.

Bryn Derwen
March 28th 1904

Dear Sir

Just a few lines to inform you
that I have received the deeds
back The offer is acceptable and
for me to draw the agreement
the best way we can Mr Owen
and Mr Williams was with me on
Saturday Night and we agree for
you to come down on Tusday March
29th 1904 so you can take them
back with you that Night and
therefore I will leave to your Honer

My self
So no more at Preasant
from your Dear friend Lg.

adress
Mr Lancelot Griffiths
Bryn Derwen
Dynevor
N Neath

Letters from Lancelot Griffiths to Nathaniel Richard Thomas March 28th 1904.

Nathaniel Richard Thomas.

Nathaniel Richard Thomas, front row far right.

49, High Street, Cefn Coed, 8<sup>th</sup> February 1915. To whom it may concern.

"Mr. Nathaniel Richard Thomas, of Holford Street. Cefn Coed, is an applicant for the post of handy man at the Pontsarn Sanatorium. I have known him all my life and have always found him honest and sober. If appointed to the position he seeks he would do his utmost to satisfy his employers". Joseph Price, J.P., Cefn grocer.

Gwnfa, Cefn Coed, Merthyr Tydfil, 8<sup>th</sup> February 1915. To Gwilym Hughes, Esq., Cardiff.

"This is to certify that I have known Mr. Nathaniel Richard Thomas for nineteen years, and during that period I had ample opportunities of forming an opinion of his character. I bear willing testimony to his upright and exemplary behaviour, and to the gentlemanly way in which he conducts himself on all occasions. He is a man of QUIET, GENTLE AND STRICTLY MORAL CONDUCT, always pure and chaste in his language; also sober and honest. I have implicit confidencein him that he will do well in the situation which he now seeks. I can say that he is a superior man in many things". Jacob Thomas, Congregation Minister.

Diary entries, shown from page 55 to 57, gathered as evidence for the same title also provide a vital view of Nathaniel Richard Thomas' character.

Henry Sambrook wasn't the only individual to support Nathaniel's claim to the Drymma Estate. A distant relative, namely Matilda Thomas, was just one of the supporters to offer their honest account. She made the following Affidavit in May 1913.

I, Matilda Thomas of Heol Las, Birchgrove, in the parish of Llansamlet in the County of Glamorgan, solemnly and sincerely declare as follows:

1. I am eighty four years of age and was born in a farm house known and called Tyr Thomas Shon Thomas in the parish of Llansamlet in the aforesaid County. The farm was at one time the freehold property of my ancestors.

2. I am a distant relation of Mr. Nathaniel Richard Thomas, the claimant to the above estates. My mother took a very prominent part in this claim for many years, and I am almost acquainted with everything that has happened in connection with the same for the last sixty years or more. I was very intimate with JOHN RICHARD THOMAS who resided at Colliers Row, Merthyr Tydfil.

3. For some years prior to the death of the late Miss Elizabeth Vye I used to accompany old THOMAS RICHARD THOMAS, at my mother's request, to the Drymma and Brithdyr Farm to collect rent from Miss Vye because he was feeble in health at the time, and as far as I can remember was suffering from asthma and bronchitis. He used to stay at our farm for a few days, on each occasion that he came down from Merthyr to collect his rents; and I used to look forward to these times, as it gave me an opportunity of visiting Miss Vye and her old housekeeper, Mrs. Mary Beynon. I liked going there because I was attracted to Miss Vye, who was a very peculiar woman in appearance and dress. She was short in stature and had a big, crooked nose. She always wore a blue and white spotted handkerchief over her shoulders, instead of the customary Welsh flannel shawl and a very old fashioned bonnet. Miss Vye was very kind to Mr. Thomas and myself; and always surprised is with refreshments after settling her accounts with him.

4. I distinctly remember one occasion when we had been to the Drymma and Brithdyr Farms to fetch the rent from Miss Vye, old Thomas Richard Thomas (the third) lamenting and complaining to my mother and I of his

grandfather Thomas (Richard) Thomas of Llwyncrwn having leased these farms to Phillip Samuel Thomas, otherwise Samuel, at such a ridiculous low rental. I also remember him showing us some old maps and parchments which he said were counterparts of the leases between his grandfather and Phillip Samuel Thomas. He also said that he was looking forward to the time when the leases would expire.

5. And, I make this declaration, conscientiously, believing the same to be true and by virtue of the Statutory Declaration Act, 1835.

Nathaniel was the last direct male heir of the line of Walter Thomas I. His sister Jenet married James Davies of Neath before settling in Merthyr Tydfil, where their descendants still reside to this day.

# 9. THE SALE OF THE ESTATES

**WHILST WE HAVE ALREADY EXPLORED** how the lost Thomas estates came into the possession of the Earl of Jersey, with the line of succession beginning when Bussey Mansel of Margam, the fourth Baron Mansel, married Lady Barbara Blackett, the daughter of the second Earl, in 1729, the estates' path from the second to the ninth Earl of Jersey was generally uneventful. A fact that made their sale in 1951 even more shocking.

The vast estate, which consisted of more than 7,500 acres spanning the Swansea, Briton Ferry, Neath and Port Talbot areas, went up for sale after the ninth Earl of Jersey, George Child Villiers, was forced to sell the land due to 'tax purposes.' According to a number of statements given to the local, regional and national press at the time, the Earl commented:

> It is the usual story of rising costs and crippling taxation which has forced me to take this course.

The estates, which included a forestry area of around 1,500 acres as well as residential areas in Cwmavon (800 dwellings plus one police station and 15 chapels), Aberavan (150 dwellings) and Blaengwynfi (325 dwellings plus one police station, one school, one public hall and a selection of chapels), were sold to a Mr. J. Oliver Watkins, a Swansea based auctioneer and estate agent who was acting on behalf of three 'property owning companies.'

The land was sold for £400,000, which equates to £53 an acre, despite annual income for the estates exceeding some £90,000.

The sale of the estates were something of a surprise for many, as the family had held the land for more than 200 years, but the Earl's move to the Channel Islands three years before should have, with hindsight, offered a crucial hint.

The son of the eighth Earl of Jersey, also named George Child Villiers, the ninth Earl had a number of seats throughout the country, including his South Wales estate. He was notably responsible for the remodelling of the family seat, Middleton Park in Oxfordshire, and employed Edwin Lutyens as architect. When he tried to give Middleton to the National Trust however, they refused on the grounds that the house had been remodelled by Lutyens, whose houses they now seek in particular. The ninth Earl gave Osterley Park in Hounslow to the nation in the late 1940s before making his move to Radier Manor in Jersey shortly after. In addition to having a rather controversial love life for the era – the Earl married three times, firstly to Patricia Richards, secondly to American actress Virginia Cherrill, ex-wife of Cary Grant, and thirdly to Bianca Luciana Adriana Mottironi – unlike the malignant misfortunes suffered by the Thomas family, the Jersey family had their own disputes regarding their legal standing, one that, under one theory, makes Villiers the rightful heir to the throne via Anne Stanley, Countess of Castlehaven.

Anne Stanley, Countess of Castlehaven (died 1647) was the eldest daughter and heir of Ferdinando Stanley, fifth Earl of Derby, and Alice Spencer. According to the Will of Henry VIII and the Third Succession Act, she was heir presumptive to the English throne upon the death of Elizabeth I. However, being foreigners, Anne and her descendants were excluded from succession to the throne. After his own three children – Mary I, Elizabeth I and Edward VI – the throne was to pass to the descendants of Henry's younger sister, Mary Tudor, Queen of France. This left Anne Stanley as first in line after her grandmother's death in 1596. Whilst there

## LLANSAMLET ROMANCE

EASTWARD of Swansea, between the river-mouths of Tawe and Nedd, and from high Llansamlet to the Crumlin sea - shore, the country is not distinguished for scenic features, and when the industrial smoke hangs low in the hollows can be one of the most dreary prospects imaginable.

The traveller who hurries through by road or rail would find it hard to see a vestige of romantic colour, yet colour there is.

Most of this terrain is part and parcel of the Jersey Estate. Seeing that the Earl's seat was just across the river, at Briton Ferry, this will cause little surprise, but the story is not so well known of how these lands came into the succession.

## CIVIL WAR

THE broad acres of Llansamlet and Danygraig had their part in the Civil War, at any rate in sequel, and the account of their disposal bears out that blood, and even the ties of relationship through marriage, can sometimes be thicker than water.

When William Thomas, son of the Commissioner of Array and Governor of Swansea Castle, whose family owned most of the land between the two rivers, tried to fight back for King Charles against the strong forces of Parliament in South Wales, he was brought to heel by his brother-in-law, Bussey Mansell, of Briton Ferry House.

## BUSSEY MANSELL

GENEROUS in victory, Bussey Mansell interested himself at high level in the case of his defeated relative, and considerably ameliorated his misfortune.

After the death of William Thomas' heir the whole of the Danygraig and Llansamlet Estates were as a reward willed to the magnanimous Mansell and his heirs, from whom they passed in succession to the Jersey family.

## EARL OF JERSEY SELLS SOUTH WALES ESTATE

### 7,500 ACRES INVOLVED

BY OUR LONDON CORRESPONDENT

THE Earl of Jersey has sold practically the whole of his South Wales estate—some 7,500 acres of his estates in the industrial and agricultural properties centred chiefly in the Swansea, Briton Ferry, Neath and Port Talbot areas. The purchase price is believed to be between £350,000 and £400,000.

In a circular letter to tenants, the Earl announces with very great regret that he has been compelled to sell because of "crippling taxation and recent legislation." His family has been connected with Wales for almost 200 years.

The purchasers, it is understood, intend to retain the estate and carry on as before. They were represented in the discussions which have continued for some months by Mr. John Oliver Watkins, Swansea, chartered surveyor. Contracts have now been exchanged.

Representing the Earl were Messrs. Alfred S. Savill and Sons, of Lincoln's Inn Fields, London.

### THREE MARRIAGES

The Earl of Jersey, George Francis Child-Villiers, the ninth earl, was born in 1910, and educated at Eton and Oxford. He was formerly a major in the R.A.T.A.

He was married successively to Patricia Richards, of New South Wales, in 1932, by whom there is a daughter, Lady Caroline, born 1934; to Virginia Cherrill of Hollywood, in 1937; and to Bianca Mottironi, of Turin, in 1947, by whom there is a son, George Henry, Viscount Villiers, born in 1948.

There is a brother, the Hon Edward Mansel, born in 1913. Lady Margaret Dynevor, who married Lord Dynevor in 1898, is an aunt.

The Earldom dates back to 1697.

### FAMILIAR NAMES

The family names are familiar in the Neath area in street and house names. Even one of the family's English seats Osterley Park—a magnificent mansion—which the Earl recently decided to open to the public— is represented in this way. Villiers and Hoo are other such names, while Vernon House, besides being the estate office, also houses Ministry of Transport staff in connection with the Great Neath river bridge schemes.

Mr. Earl has made several gifts to the area, notably the areas of the extension of Jersey Park, Briton Ferry and the Recreation Ground. Briton Ferry to Neath Council to mark his extension as mayor on April 9, 1931 and followed his opening of the reconstructed golf course at Jersey Marine and the presentation of a gold wrist watch by the estate staff.

A few years ago the estate began selling freeholds privately to tenants, and in authoritative quarters it is assumed that this process has gone on steadily till a comprehensive sale was decided upon.

### SWANSEA LINKS

In Swansea the Jersey park at St. Thomas is a gift by the Earl's predecessor, made about 1900, and the Swansea and Bonymaen area have many names of estate origins. Following various sales, some of them in the Corporation, the ownerships are practically confined to the parish of Llansamlet.

The Corporation's most recent substantial purchase was the land for the Hanover-square housing scheme. The biggest was that of the site for the Tir John power station.

## 7,500-acre estate in new hands

THE Earl of Jersey has sold nearly all his South Wales estates for a figure believed to be about £400,000.

About 40 farms, industrial works and private houses are involved. But the new owners, whose names are not disclosed, will maintain the properties as before, it was stated yesterday.

"We are under a pledge not to disclose the purchasers' names," said their Swansea agent.

Industries on the estate at Briton Ferry include the Briton Ferry Steel Works, Albion Steel Works, Briton Ferry Iron Works, Gwalia Tin Works, Whitford Sheet Works, Old Villiers Tin Works and Wern Aluminium Works.

### 'Usual story'

Most of the houses, at Briton Ferry, are on ground owned by the estate. Some individual tenants, it is learned, have been granted the freehold of their properties after approaching the company.

Confirming the sale, which involves about 7,500 acres, the 41-year-old earl said at his Jersey home yesterday: "It is the usual story of rising costs and crippling taxation."

Considerable portions of the estate have been bought in the past for development by Swansea Council. Biggest is the site of Tir John Power Station.

The present Marquess of Bute's father sold a large slice of Cardiff years ago for a sum said to be £20,000,000.

## TAX FORCES EARL TO SELL LANDS

### Crippling, He Says, So Mr Watkins Steps In With £400,000 Cheque

By Daily Mail Reporter

THE Earl of Jersey yesterday announced that he has sold 7,500 acres of his estates in South Wales. "It is the usual story of rising costs and crippling taxation which has forced me to take this course," he said at his home, Radier Manor, Longueville, Jersey.

The land stretches from Swansea to Port Talbot. It includes residential and industrial sites. Many steel and iron works are in the area.

Purchaser is Mr. J. Oliver Watkins, a Swansea auctioneer and estate agent. After four months' negotiations he bought for £400,000—about £53 an acre.

The Earl of Jersey, 41, moved to the Channel Islands three years ago. Income from the estates is £90,000 a year.

His family have held estates in South Wales for 200 years. He has married three times.

### THREE SHARE

Mr. Watkins, who is attending a conference at Hastings, said last night : "I just stepped off in London on my way here and signed the deal.

"I am acting on behalf of three Swansea property-owning companies who have bought the estates as a business investment. I have not told them the deal has gone through.

"It was all very simple and I intended waiting until I got home to tell them. They will continue to run the estates as before with myself as manager."

Next week Mr. Watkins will call a meeting of the three companies to share out the property.

### JERSEY ESTATES BUYERS ARE NAMED

## INCOME FROM PURCHASE IS £20,000 A YEAR

PURCHASE of the Earl of Jersey's South Wales estates in the Swansea-Port Talbot area, announced last week, of which the transfer date is June 25, was made by three Swansea property companies.

The acreage is about 7,000 and the income about £20,000 per annum.

The acquiring companies are: Estateways Builders, Ltd., whose chairman is Mr. Harold A. Adams; the Gwalia Land and Property Development, Ltd., whose chairman is Sir William Jenkins, and the Principality Co. (Swansea) Ltd., whose chairman is Mr. Richard Thomas.

Mr. F. R. Ragg, of Alfred Savill and Sons conducted negotiations for the vendors, the Villiers Estate Co., Ltd., and Mr. John Oliver Watkins on behalf of the three purchasing companies, for whom he is to continue to manage the estates as a whole.

### SUBSTANTIAL INTERESTS

The companies have been established during the last 25 years—the youngest is some 18 years old—with Mr. Oliver Watkins as adviser, and their very substantial interests have been gradually extended till they have properties from as far west as Pembrokeshire to London, including very large holdings in the metropolis.

Past balance sheets have revealed a healthy prosperity.

### SAME STAFF

It is gathered that no development of any kind was in contemplation when purchase was decided on; that it is hoped to continue management as before; and that for this purpose the office is being continued at Vernon House, Briton Ferry, with the existing staff.

The group is to continue, in areas.

of its latest acquisition, its policy of willingness to sell freeholds to lessees, whether large or small, and it is understood that some of these Jersey lessees have already written seeking this step.

### WORKS ON LEASE

Most of the dozen well-known works included in the sale of which the largest are perhaps the Briton Ferry Steelworks and the Swansea Vale works of the National Smelting Company, are on long leases.

The portion of the estate not included in the purchase is at Jersey Marine this includes the Swansea Bay Golf course and land involved in compulsory purchase orders for the new arterial road.

### FORESTRY AREA

An area of 1,500 acres in the Briton Ferry, Michaelstone, Aberavon and Llantwit districts is included, and there are 36 farms in addition to smallholdings.

In Swansea there are works in St. Thomas and Llansamlet where the 1,000 acres being transferred included leases of some 500 houses, a school, the Kilvey parish hall, church institute and chapels.

### MOST OF CWMAVON

Also included are:
Cwmavon: Most of the township, about 800 houses, the police station and 15 chapels.

Aberavon: About 150 houses.

Blaengwynfi (parish of Glyncorrwg): Practically the whole village; some 325 houses, the police station, school, public hall and the chapels.

Other properties are in Neath, Penrhiwllan and Michaelstone.

are no descendants of Lady Anne Stanley recorded living after 1826, if her line did fail, then her right of succession to the throne of England would have passed to the heirs of her sister Lady Frances Stanley (born 1583). Lady Frances' senior descendant, William Villiers, the tenth Earl of Jersey, is said to be the heir to Lady Anne Stanley's claim to the throne, however, it has been pointed out that Lord Jersey's grandfather, George Child Villiers, the ninth Earl of Jersey, had been divorced from his first wife before he married Lord Jersey's grandmother. In the opinion of some legitimists, no English law passed since 1603 is valid as Lady Anne and her heirs were not in possession of the throne. They further claim that under the laws of 1603, the ninth Earl of Jersey's divorce was not valid, and as a result his remarriage during his ex-wife's lifetime was null and void, and the children of the latter marriage were ineligible to inherit his claim to the throne. Legitimists of this type assert that the current holder of the Stanley claim to the throne of England is Lady Caroline Ogilvy, only child of the ninth Earl's first marriage.

Despite the theory that the latest Earl – George Francis William Child Villiers, tenth Earl of Jersey – is the rightful heir to the throne of England, the title of Earl of the Island of Jersey, shortened to Earl of Jersey, is a prestigious one in itself and one that many, particularly those within The Walter Thomas Inheritance Association, feel may have restricted the story of the lost Thomas estates, and the concealed fraud that prevailed, from being told and getting the publicity and justice it deserved.

This English peerage was created in 1697 for statesman Edward Villiers. Ambassador to France from 1698 to 1699 and Secretary of State for the Southern Department from 1699 to 1700, Edward was already a protuberant member of the infamous family and by the time the peerage was created for him had already been created Baron Villiers of Hoo in the County of Kent, and Viscount Villiers of Dartford in the County of Kent. Despite the title the Earls of Jersey haven't always resided on the island of Jersey, with the stately home of Osterley Park in the London Borough of Hounslow providing a base for most of the family throughout the years. Originally constructed for merchant Sir Thomas Gresham, Osterley Park was purchased by Francis Child in 1711 before undergoing refurbishment under his grandson. Robert Adam, a renowned architect and the most fashionable in England during his lifetime, led the remodel utilising designs commandeered during a recent trip to the Portico of Octavia in Rome. To this day Osterley Park is known for its stunning use of Greek ceramics, with the house, according to the National Trust Collections, 'the principal ornament in the 142-acre flat parkland, where there is also a semi-circular garden house designed by Adam and a Doric Temple of Pan.'

Exactly why both John Richard Thomas and his son and heir Nathaniel Richard Thomas could not directly pursue a claim against the Earl of Jersey, a case started but never finished by John's father Thomas R Thomas III, relies on a number of factors.

Although both John and Nathaniel had knowledge of their ancestral grandmother Ann Thomas, the legitimate daughter of Walter Thomas who died in 1667, and that she had been dispossessed by her trustee and guardian Bussey Mansel and his son Thomas Mansel, they were never financially in a position to pursue the case. The impending bankruptcy of both John and later Nathaniel was enough to prove this, whilst the disappearance of William Rogers, the solicitor who was acting on behalf of John Richard Thomas, with vital documentation was also a defining factor.

In 1948, long after the deaths of both John and Nathaniel, the family formed an Association to raise funds for another recovery attempt to retrieve funds and bring the Jersey family to justice but the end of the war meant money was tight and efforts short lived.

The sale of the South Wales estate by the ninth Earl of Jersey however was a milestone for the descendants of the Thomas family, a transaction that made its retrieval even more of an unlikely possibility due to the lack of financial resources available to them, but determined to take their claim once again to the High Court, this time with more evidence than the previous claimant and last direct male heir of the line of Walter Thomas I ever had, The Walter Thomas Inheritance Association was formed.

## Viscount Villiers

**Heir to the Earldom of Jersey who preferred playing the guitar with the band he formed to following a career in business**

Villiers on the guitar: his band's style was 'Segovia meets the Gypsy Kings'

THE VISCOUNT VILLIERS, heir to the 9th Earl of Jersey, who has died aged 49, pursued a career as a guitarist and composer.

Both as a solo performer and with his band, George Villiers Express, he performed regularly on the concert platform and made a number of recordings.

The Villiers family first rose to prominence under James I. George Villiers, Duke of Buckingham, was a favourite of the King's. The Earldom of Jersey was bestowed on the family in 1692; the first Earl had been Master of the Horse to Mary II and later Ambassador to the States General.

For more than two centuries the family had no connection with the island of Jersey, its main family seat being Osterley Park, Middlesex. But when the 9th Earl visited Jersey in 1947, he liked it, and bought an estate at Longueville. There he bred prizewinning Jersey cows.

George Henry Child Villiers was born on Jersey on August 29 1948, the son of the 9th Earl by his third wife.

George was educated at Eton and Millfield, where he learned to play the guitar. On leaving school, he joined the 11th Royal Hussars, signing up for a three-year short service commission in 1968. However, a few weeks after he joined the Hussars, and encouraged by his fiancée, Verna Stott, the 25-year old daughter of a retired Yorkshire textile manufacturer, he considered buying his way out of the Army in order to take up music full time. But his father and his CO dissuaded him.

In 1971, by then married, Villiers left the Army to become a foreign exchange trader with Williams and Glyns Bank. After periods with M L Doxford (Jersey), European Commodities and Rouse Woodstock (Jersey), he became managing director of Villiers Trading.

But music remained his main passion. He had learned piano accordion from the age of four, piano from eight and guitar from the age of 13. He played electric guitar and bass, as well as folk-style acoustic guitar.

He began studying classical guitar aged 21 and, during his City career, made regular appearances on television and radio and at concerts. He gave classical recitals and played bass in a dance band and a jazz trio; he also wrote guitar music.

In the 1970s, he set up a "spring school" for musicians in Jersey, which so impressed the local education department that they took it over themselves.

In 1986 Villiers took up music professionally. His band, with two guitars and keyboard, played, said one critic, in the style of "Segovia meets the Gypsy Kings".

The band recorded three albums The first, *Magical Dance* (1988), contained some of Villiers's own compositions. After their second album *Dawn* (1989), they toured the country for three years, performed in the Purcell Room, and made a number of appearances on television. In 1992, the band reformed, adding bass and drums, and in 1995 recorded the album *No Dog Required.*

As well as playing and composing for his band, Villiers wrote commercial video, radio and television theme music, and music for computer games. He edited *Classic Duets for Guitar.*

Viscount Villiers was thrice married. By his first marriage (dissolved 1973) he had a daughter. He married secondly, in 1974 (dissolved 1988), Sacha Hooper Valpy; they had a son and two daughters. He married thirdly, in 1992, Stephanie Penman; they had a son.

Villiers is succeeded as heir to the Earldom of Jersey by his eldest son, William, born in 1976.

SIR — At the conference on "Labour and the House of Lords" (report, June 8), Lord Richard said that the "medieval character" of the Lords must go. This "medieval character", of course, was responsible for the development of jury trial, common law, Parliament and the Monarchy — the pillars which this Government is pulling down.

It also gave rise to the hereditary peerage, which has worked for the benefit of future generations, thus giving stability to government. The blood of the 17th-century Villiers family has been found in 15 prime ministers alone, including the Younger Pitt, Lord Melbourne, Lord Salisbury and Churchill.

L. L. BLAKE
London SW13

The Ninth Earl of Jersey, newspaper clipping.

# 10. THE FOUNDATION OF THE WALTER THOMAS INHERITANCE ASSOCIATION

**THE AFTERMATH OF THE TREACHERY** that caused the dispossession of what many individuals, family members or otherwise, refer to as the lost Thomas estates has affected a number of generations. Whilst claims have been made to rectify the situation, the last attempt being that of Nathaniel Richard Thomas in the early 20th century, the devastation and injustice has since not been forgotten.

The Walter Thomas Inheritance Association was established at a meeting in Port Talbot on Wednesday 12 July 1995 with one objective in mind – to recover any assets or benefits connected to Walter Thomas and at last, lawfully restore the lost estates to their rightful owners. To ensure the continued legitimacy of the claim, the Association didn't just invite anyone as member. Under the terms set out by the Association, each individual considered must be a 'direct descendant' of Richard Thomas (1706-1788) and Matilda Zacharias (1717-1760) or the children they shared, namely Morgan Thomas (1748-1784), Jenet Thomas (1738-1814), Thomas Richard Thomas (1739-1802), Matilda Thomas (1736-1813), Elizabeth Thomas (1735-1793) and Anne Thomas (born 1730), a connection that must be proved by documentary evidence.

• • • • • •

## THE GOOD FORTUNE

In 1994 a programme aired that would capture all of the soon-to-be Association members' gaze. Aptly named 'Good Fortune', presenter Gloria Hunniford urged cases similar to Walter's missing millions to come forward and preceded to surprise members of the public with news of unclaimed cash, property or prizes.

Solicitor Alun Thomas presented the case to the BBC shortly after, a light at the end of the tunnel for the Thomas family perhaps? To gather further evidence, the BBC set up a hotline in an effort to solve a 200-year-old murder mystery that had plagued one generation after the next.

Following months of research, led by programme researcher Alec Lom, and a terrific response from the people of Swansea, the associated programme aired in November 1994. BBC research also revealed that an estimated £20 billion was sitting in Chancery, but unfortunately not much else was revealed about the case as the family and the solicitor acting on their behalf were informed that research would be limited, most needing to be done by the family.

Despite the programme being a success, gathering unprecedented publicity for the family and its story, its airing did not inspire financial backers to come forward as was hoped. It did however inspire the foundation of Walter Thomas Inheritance Association, which took place some nine months later.

To date the Good Fortune team has handed out more than £3.5 million in unclaimed money, plus offered a chance for viewers to help solve some of the mysteries in which the beneficiaries are still missing.

• • • • • •

# Inheritance mystery gets flood of calls

### By ABI HOLLAND

SWANSEA fortune seekers have flooded a hotline set up to try and solve the mystery of a 200-year-old murder and inheritance claim.

They made the calls after watching BBC's Good Fortune programme which aims to reunite people with lost legacies and inheritances.

The programme had been contacted by Alun Thomas, a solicitor from North Wales, who believes his family was deprived of inheriting a huge chunk of land around Swansea.

His appeal was broadcast in last week's show.

Programme researcher Alec Lom, said: "In 1654 his direct ancestor Walter Thomas was a wealthy landowner who left a will itemising large amounts of property and land in the South Wales area.

"Mr Thomas believes the money was misrouted by a murder which denied the rightful inheritance."

### Response

He said the story involved Rebecca Evans and Jenkin Zachariah who lived at Ynystawe Hall, Ynystawe, and had three daughters.

Mr Thomas claims Jenkin was killed by Robert Popkin who regularly visited Rebecca.

Legend has it that Popkin then locked up their only surviving daughter Matilda who was a direct descendant of Walter Thomas.

Mr Lom said: "It is alleged Popkin siphoned off the Thomas inheritance. This involves an area of 240 square miles to the east and west of Swansea.

"When we visited the area to research it, we talked to local people who knew a lot about it.

"We had a terrific response from people in Swansea after the programme.

"We will be updating people on developments on the story tomorrow night."

☎ If you have any information relating to the Thomas inheritance then contact the BBC on freephone 0500 509950.

Article entitles 'Inheritance mystery gets flood of calls'.

As of August 1997, the Association committee consisted of the following members:

## Officers
Secretary – Malcolm Winmill
Chairman – Edward Phillips
Vice Chairman – David Williams
Treasurer – Eluned Lewis

## Committee members
William Bentley
Sonia Griffiths
Charles Jonathan
John Mallon
Jean Morgan
Lynette Morgan
David Phillips
Linda Winmill
William Williams

The Association and the aforementioned members got to work, not just to research the subject further, and build on and validate the compelling and substantial evidence already amassed, but to raise the profile of the Association, its story and the injustices that so many of their descendants had faced, as Nathaniel Richard Thomas had begun to do some 95 years earlier. Like Nathaniel, the Association were keen to gain the financial backing they needed to pursue the claim further or at least the assistance of an experienced legal professional to ensure a fair assessment of all the evidence gathered, a process that many family members before them had failed to achieve. As a result, secretary Malcolm Winmill and many other committee officers and members approached solicitors and law firms for support, a tactic that mostly saw them encounter countless closed doors despite the blatant fraud that their family and its descendants had been privy to. Many of the solicitors approached admittedly found the sheer volume of information now at the disposal of the Association

## Former nurse is related to one of the most influential figures in city's history

# Walter's fortune mystery

THERE'S nothing like tales of rich ancestors and lost family fortunes to stir the imagination. JILL FORWOOD meets a Swansea woman whose family history can be traced to one of the most influential figures in 17th Century South Wales.

**The way we Were**

MANY of us have grown up on stories about family fortunes lying in Chancery because wills mysteriously disappeared and bloodlines became too complicated to be proved.

But a Swansea woman has more proof than most that she is descended from a very rich and powerful ancestor.

Mrs Kate Williams has a copy of the will of Walter Thomas, one of the most important and influential figures in Swansea before and during the time of the Civil War.

And a fascinating document it is, because the quantity and quality of Walter's bequests make him sound like the uncrowned king of Swansea.

He left various sums of £50, a fortune in the 17th Century, together with land and mansions throughout Swansea, including Wind Street, High Street, Frog Street, Fisher Street, St Mary's Square and Whitewalls.

"He owned land as far north as Brecon and as far west as Cardigan," said Kate, an 86-year-old former nurse.

"I believe there's a fortune lying in Chancery which should have come to my family."

Kate became fascinated by Walter and his family when she gave up her nursing job at the old Swansea General Hospital to act as housekeeper to her mother and three bachelor uncles in Morriston.

"My uncles were interested in the family history and it was them who got a copy of Walter's will," said Kate. "I became fascinated as well and discovered that the family goes back to Lord Dynevor and owned several large properties,

including Drymma Hall, Plas Ynystawe and the land that is now Swansea Enterprise Park."

Walter Thomas, of Swansea and Danygraig, is a key figure in the family tree. He is fairly well documented in the history of Swansea as a leading citizen who did his best to promote the interests of the town.

Walter was a rich merchant who exported iron to Bristol and also dealt in agricultural by-products such as skins and feathers.

Twice he held the all-important office of portreeve, in 1615 and in 1625. In 1615, when local shipping needed better facilities, he started building a new quay at his own expense.

In the same year, going along with the vogue for pomp and circumstance, he ordered a pair of new maces for the town from a Bristol goldsmith. These are now in the Glynn Vivian Art Gallery.

When the turmoil of Civil War came, Walter was prominent. W S K Thomas, in the History of Swansea, explains that the town was at first Royalist, partly by the inclination of its leading aldermen, partly at the urging of their lord, the Earl of Worcester.

Charles I, who was hard-pressed for men and money, gave Walter the right to mine for coal in certain areas of Swansea and Llangyfelach on condition that for every wey mined and sold, the King received 18d.

The royal demand for 60 men from Swansea, 20 from Llangyfelach and 40 from Neath was not so welcome. Walter and his colleagues protested that they had already raised as many men as could be spared.

Already deputy steward, Walter was

**POWERFUL FOREBEAR: Kate Thomas with the will of her ancestor Walter Thomas.**

not appointed governor of the castle and the crunch with Cromwell's Roundheads was soon to come.

Kate tells me that the gateway into Swansea was the Maliphant Weir on the river Tawe. Walter, she says, bought it and placed soldiers there day and night to prevent "strangers" from entering the town.

W S K Thomas said that Swansea fell to the Parliamentarians in 1645 and, as a

result, Walter's fortunes received two severe blows. His estates were sequestered and he was deprived of his aldermanic status.

It seems this had a drastic effect on his health. The following year, when he confessed that he "did arm and array the inhabitants" of Swansea, mention was made of his great weakness and age and his being unable to stir in his bed without the assistance of two others.

He was obviously treated with some consideration because his original fine of £400 was reduced to £313.

And, as his will proved before judges in Westminster in 1654, it seems that he regained his estates.

The will, a document of several pages, not only mentions his many mansions, including his new house in Castle Bailey, but woods and meadows, water and grist mills and freehold lands in Oystermouth, Llangennith, Loughor, Pennard and Bishopston among other places.

Bequests of silver basins and ewers show that Walter lived in some style, but he didn't forget the needy. He left £5 for the poor of Swansea and £2.10s for the poor of Llansamlet, to be distributed on the Feast of the Nativity. He also left 10s for reparations at St Mary's Church where he and his family were buried.

Kate is proud of her distinguished forebear.

At the age of 86 she holds out little hope of miraculously coming into a family fortune, but as she says, "it's nice to dream of what might have been".

# History man tackling fascinating family

ONE of the most knowledgeable people with regard to Swansea local history is Eric Thomas.

Regular readers of this column might remember that he grew up on the Clyne estate at the time of Admiral Walker-Heneage-Vivian and saw at first hand how the other half lived.

Eric is in such demand as a public speaker that it's not unusual for him to give as many as half-a-dozen talks in one week.

But every year Eric gives one special lecture. It's his annual presentation on behalf of Blackpill, Derwen Fawr and Mayals Local History Club at the Vivian Hall, Blackpill.

Book the date now. It's Tuesday, August 20, at 2.30pm. Eric's subject will be the fascinating Vivian family.

Everyone is welcome, but as the hall is usually packed for this event, my advice is get there early.

The £1.50 admission fee includes tea and will go towards the Vivian Hall maintenance fund.

**HISTORY MAN: Eric Thomas.**

Catherine Williams, ancestor of Walter Thomas feature, The South Wales Evening Post, 31st July 1996.

difficult to digest and even understand, and as a result turned down the case and the Association's pleas for help.

As part of their additional research, The Walter Thomas Inheritance Association even contacted Linda Joy, Director of Communication at the Public Guardianship Office, for an insight into the current status of the monetary figure connected to the estates that still remained in Chancery. The sum calculated by previous correspondence and based on the family's own reference material stood at 96 million pounds at last count according to a letter to Linda Joy from secretary Malcolm Winmill, dated Wednesday 8 May 2002. Though this wasn't the only information to come to light as an extract from the very same letter shows:

Dear Madam

I am writing to you with reference to an enquiry made by MR DAVID MALLON of … to yourself some months ago, relating to a surplus amount of money in your Department, to be precise a figure amounting to 96 million pounds, this amount is consistent with calculations made by our family. We estimate that there is an amount of £14 million £720 pounds inclusive of interest and excluding Royalties ad Purchase money paid into Chancery for the Estate.

A trust fund was put in place in the years 1874-1878 by CHANCELLOR (VICE) MALLINS CASE 11CD.605 a Lease was granted to one JOHN NEWALL MOORE DIRECTOR OF THE NEW DYNEVOR COAL CO LTD for a period of 21 years at a minimum rent of 5,000 per annum and certain Royalties for the minerals worked beneath the Drymmer Estate Cadoxton Juxta Neath.

The letter goes further and highlights just how much information the family members and then the Association had gathered since Nathaniel's failed claim upon the estate. The fact that evidence had been gathered regarding the existence of a trust fund also gave the Association a new objective to align with their wider goal despite having all the evidence they needed to substantiate the claim. More letters, this time to Julia Lomas, dated 22 February 2001, provided an insight into the sheer volume of knowledge that the Association now had at their disposal, all they needed was support in taking their case to the High Court.

Following its foundation, the Association also sought help from local, regional and national press to spread the story of the lost estates further and possibly, as Nathaniel Richard Thomas had thought when he worked with the Merthyr Express and South Wales Weekly News almost a century earlier, rally financial backing as well as publicity for the case. The stories subsequently published were a far cry from the previously distributed, sensationalised tales surrounding the estates in the late 1980s, entitled 'Dynasty!' and 'Murder Most Foul! Secrets of the pigsty' by Charles Jones, stories that were based more on fiction than fact. The Association's work, mainly via John Mallon, with the News of the World brought the story to an international audience with an article published on Sunday 6 February 2000.

**Malcolm and the members of the Walter Thomas Inheritance Association would like to say a special thanks in particular to John and David Mallon for their input.**

The final question that is certain to be on everyone's lips is what has become of the lost estates in the present day?

Walter Thomas' estates extended from Neath Abbey and Cadoxton Juxta, in the east of Swansea, to Oystermouth and Mumbles. He also owned lands in Llanrhidian and Llandeilo Talybont, a stake that ensured his lands extended from the Mount in Swansea to the Llandore of the old copper works (White Rock) Foxhole Weir and up again to Llysnewydd Farm, Knap Coch, Llansamlet and beyond.

**Dynasty! Part Two: Fate strikes**

# MURDER MOST FOUL!

**DURING the innumerable High Court hearings, one sworn affidavit besides substantiating the Thomas claim, hints at what happened to the Jenkin Zachariah Estates. It also provides a fascinating glimpse of life in the year 1862.**

"I Owen David, of Howell Terrace, Trallwyn Road, in the Parish of Llansamlet in the County of Glamorgan, solemnly and sincerely swear as follows: I am 69 years of age and was born at a farm called Tyr Thomas John Thomas in the Parish of Llansamlet aforesaid. The said farm and lands belonged to my family but they are now in the hands of the Earl of Jersey.

"My father's grandfather and great-grandfather were also born there. And my sister Matilda Thomas nee David was the last to live there before the farm fell to ruins. Near the said farm there was an old wooden tramroad the tram rails being made of wood.

## Secrets of the pigsty

"The trams were drawn up to Gelly Gynven Colliery. Old Walter Thomases Colliery as it was then called. The Colliery situated above Gwrenllwynchwyth.

"My grandfather and my mother told me that the Colliery belonged to old Walter Thomas. They also told me that the old pond or stream situated on the Drymma Estate Llansamlet served as a canal for the purpose of carrying coal from old Walter Thomas Works in small boats down to the Malliphant Weir, Swansea, the Foxhole side, where it was put into ships lying in the River Tawe.

"This canal extended from "Pwll Mawr", "Charles Pit" and "Pwll Scot" down to the Foxhole bank wharf opposite the Malliphant Weir. The old canal which was made because there were no railways in those days is still visible in some parts, but the shafts and levels were worked by a drum and horses.

"I can also well recollect my grandfather telling me that his father and grandfather had worked at that coal works and was called by the Welsh people Gwaith Hen Walter Thomas. All my family are buried at Llansamlet. I was also informed by my grandfather that it was customary for the people living at Drymma above Gwrenlwynchwyth to pay Walter Thomas a penny for every funeral that was used over the private road at the back of our house and farm . . . "

What a harsh comparison to Illfracombe where Miss Vye certainly died impoverished but unwittingly resurrected another mare's nest of homicide, mayhem, subterfuge, legal treachery and fifty years of High Court litigation, including a House of Lord's Appeal. With judgement that convinces that the law besides being blind was, in this suit, biased as Sir Francis Drake's bowls.

### Evidence

Otherwise how could someone who never saw the tide go out in Swansea, or the sunrise over Llansamlet, against all the evidence lay successful claim to land that for centuries belonged to an ancient Welsh family? Indeed, one cannot ignore the sworn statements freely given under oath. Here is a newspaper report that appeared in 1897: "Murder Most Foul!"

"One of the Thomas family, claimants to the Drymma Estates, whilst riding to his home at Merthyr Tydfil, stopped at a roadside inn for a drink of "rye bear". Sometime afterwards his riderless horse trotted into the farmyard. A search was mounted and, his body was found in a roadside ditch. He had been strangled . . . "

From the death of the first Walter Thomas, it seems as though the family were to be dogged by malignant fate. In fact during the fifty years of the Drymma law suit, the only occasion the plaintiff's were successful was, when Judge Baron Pollock presiding over the Court of Exchequer granted recovery of possession which enabled them to stop the Public Auction advertised by John Paddon of the sale of the Drymma and Brithdyr Estates to be held at the Castle Hotel, Neath, on the 20th November, 1867.

The Sheriff of Glamorgan was also instructed to execute the said writs. But wily John Paddon wasn't so easily disposed of. Hastily he procured an Order of Attachment directed to the Sheriff of Middlesex against the plaintiff's, thus forestalling repossession.

The lynchpin of Paddon's claim to be the Drymma Estates was the sworn testimony of the Ilfracombe solicitor Robert Jennings Crosse. The only way to disprove his claim was to produce the original freehold deeds, but here the Thomases were in a quandry. Search as they may they couldn't find them. Then one morning, Nathaniel Richard Thomas now living at Cefn Coed near Merthyr Tydfil received the following letter:

"Dear Sir, having heard that you have been trying to claim the Drymma Estate and not being successful on account of the papers being missing I think I have a clue to where they can be found having been in Wales on business and hearing certain things concerning the missing papers. I think it is my duty to try and find you soon and then I will tell you all I hear about them. I remain dear Sir, your sincere friend, Henry Sambrook, 18 Alverton Street, Deptford, London."

But the subsequent letter was like something out of a

● JOHN Richard Pembridge, one of the last of the Thomas family who still lives in South Wales.

**BY CHARLES JONES**

melodrama and could well prove to be a rather crude con trick: "Mr dear Sir, I am glad to know that my letter found you as I have had a deal of trouble to find your name. I am only a poor man without means.

I left my home at Skewen and since that time I have travelled the world on the same boat as Engineer for about eight-and-a-half years. But now I have been out of work for about twelve months or I should come personally to try and

Estate Offices, 11, [illegible]

[illegible]

London, W.C.

FOXHOLE,

IN THE BOROUGH TOWN OF SWANSEA.

In the County of Glamorgan.

I hereby give you One and All, Vendors and Purchasers, NOTICE on behalf of NATHANIEL RICHARD THOMAS, Heir-at-Law of one WALTER THOMAS, Deceased, of Swansea, the Freeholder of the LAND upon which the Dwelling Houses are built, and all other LANDS now offered for Sale by Messrs. [illegible] and Son, and advertised in the "Western Mail," on November [illegible], 1910, to take place on Tuesday, November 15th, 1910.

I have to inform You, as Agent for the said Nathaniel Richard Thomas, that the Freehold Lands now for Sale are the Property of the said Nathaniel Richard Thomas, by virtue of a Will dated 1654, and by subsequent Wills.

And I further inform You that [illegible] you make any Sale or Purchase of the aforesaid Lands as advertised for Sale it will be NULL and VOID, as the Vendors have NO TITLE, and the aforesaid Nathaniel Richard Thomas will draw Ejectment, Possession and [illegible] against the Vendors and Purchasers of these Lands.

Dated this 12th day of November 1910.

WM. BURCHELL REES

find you. My dear Sir, the papers are buried in an iron-box two feet under the earth and the man that told me said he could take me to the very spot where they were buried so trusing I may be of service to you, I remain your sincere friend H Sambrook."

This seemed incredible. Was it a hoax? Or an attempt at raising some easy money? With so much at stake there was no alternative other than seeing it through.

Mr Thomas clutching at straws was about to journey to Deptford when he received yet another letter, which though highly fictional (two old ladies with spades and an iron-box. The only thing missing were moonbeams) convinced him that Sambrook was genuinely trying to help:

"Dear Sir, I am so sorry our circumstances are keeping us apart for I could explain so much better to you if I could see you. Do you think you could go and see him if I sent you his name? He lives close to the Estate. If so I will willingly send you his name and address for he knows what's in the box and where it is buried and the two old ladies that buried it there are both dead now.

"He promised them he would not say anything about it while they were alive he told me he is only waiting for someone to advertise for it. He does not know that I have been trying to find you but I thought it would be a cruel thing to keep a man out of his rights, and let me know if you will go and I will send name and address."

After receiving such an assurance, Thomas visited Sambrook at Deptford. "And fearing any accident should befall him obtained from Sambrook a sworn declaration . . . "

### Revealed

With what appeared to be the vital information in his possession, Thomas on his return contacted a Lancelot Griffiths of Skewen.

After a great deal of persuasion, Griffiths revealed that sometime previously he had retrieved the iron-box hidden in the ground. This was done in the early hours of the morning, as a pigsty had been erected over the exact spot. Yes! The freeholds were in his possession, but he was scared and didn't wish to be involved.

As his aunt Mary Beynon had been imprisoned for contempt of court "for insisting that the John Paddon deeds to the Drymma were a forgery . . . "

No wonder Griffiths was frightened. One couldn't blame him. If it became common knowledge that the deeds were in his possession, intimidation and possibly grievous bodily harm could well befall him. But in the end reason prevailed and the deeds were handed over to Mr Thomas, who for safe-keeping immediately placed them with their Family Solicitor, William Rogers of Swansea.

At long last it seemed that success was imminent, impatiently they waited for the next High Court hearing. Then it happened their family solicitor William Rogers Esq., doyen of the Local Law Society, chairman of the Board of Guardians, President of the Bible Society ABSCONDED "taking with him or destroying the genuine newly recovered Drymma and Brithdyr freehold lawsuit."

Yet again, fate in the guise of another solicitor had finally negated all hope of them successfully concluding their never ending lawsuit of concealed fraud. But still they fought on. Twenty years later Rogers in abject poverty and obviously dying, resurfaced in Swansea — though he never revealed the truth of why he absconded.

In the meantime their continuous plea for justice had reduced the Thomas family to penury, and ironically, in 1916 Nathaniel Richard Thomas was declared bankrupt. Today the direct descendants of the first Walter Thomas live contentedly and without rancour in the village of Cefn Coed Y Cymmer on the outskirts of Merthyr Tydfil.

Fate hasn't treated them kindly, but the one possession it failed to deprive them of, is their unbroken pedigree that goes way back over 350 years to 1654. Which, to say the least, is most unusual in Wales — a country prior to the First World War, was in more ways than one, regularly considered despicably alien.

© Charles Jones, 1988

## The riderless horse and a body in a ditch

## A proud pedigree that no-one could take away

'A Murder Most Foul' article, with image of John Richard Pembridge, Merthyr. (Charles Jones 1988)

# DYNASTY!

**THE following account is a factual one, and has never before appeared in print. It bears out the old adage that truth is stranger than fiction. It deals with a Welsh family whose offspring married into the aristocracy, resulting in one far-fetched royal supposition. In 1719 at Llansamlet Church a marriage took place between Elizabeth Thomas grand-daughter of one Walter Thomas to Sir John Sidney 6th Earl of Leicester.**

On his death it is purported that his brother the 7th Earl, Sire Iestyn, married Elizabeth his brother's widow and that his daughter Ann's descendants married King William the IV — while the fact is, the 7th Earl never married. Ann was his base daughter by Elizabeth.

This is just an aperitif before the main course of skullduggery; false witness, sharp practice, unscrupulous lawyers, legal-bias, racial prejudice, withholding relevant documents and sworn affidavits, an absconding solicitor possessing indisputable evidence, a buried iron chest, mayhem, murder and, the incredible behaviour of a Peer of the Realm.

Most of these accusations are in the form of signed statements given on oath, all of which are recorded in a well-documented account of the legal fight by a Welsh family for the recovery of their hereditary estates which resulted in a long, drawn-out legal wrangle entailing an appeal to the House of Lords and pleas in the High Court from 1864 to 1916.

In the year 1654, one Walter Thomas, of Dan-y-graig, St Thomas, Swansea, was the lawful owner of large tracts of land in Swansea, Llansamlet, Neath Abbey (destroyed by Cromwell) Neath, Cadoxton Juxta, as well as farmlands in Carmarthenshire, Cardiganshire and Breconshire. He bequeathed these estates to his son William but during his lifetime he made a gift of lands known as the Drymma in the Parish of Llansamlet to his grandson, John Thomas.

### Slick operators

Because John had been amply provided for by his grandfather, William made his other son Walter, so named after his grandfather, his sole beneficiary.

Walter, now a very wealthy landowner, married Catherine a sister to Lord Bussey Mansel, of Briton Ferry. Unfortunately, the children of the issue died young, with the exception of one daughter named Matilda, whom, on the death of her father, being too young to assume responsibility, trusteeship was placed in the hands of her uncle, Lord Bussey Mansel.

But such was his complete lack of personal supervision, that in no time the estates were providing easy pickings for slick operators, dishonest smallholders and quick-witted claim jumpers, and "strangers were allowed to misappropriate miles of land in different counties . . . "

This state of affairs assumed such proportions that trusteeship was transferred from Lord Bussey Mansel to his cousin, the Earl of Jersey, who held on to his trusteeship even after Matilda's marriage to one Richard Zachariah. The only child of this union was a son named Jenkin who married a Rebecca Evans, of Peterswell, in the County of Cardiganshire.

The only surviving issue of this marriage was a daughter named Matilda, who married her cousin, Richard Thomas, a direct descendant of John, to whom was given the Drymma, by his grandfather, the first Walter Thomas.

But for a murderous quirk of fate, this marriage would have reunited the family estates.

It wasn't to be. In 1734 Jenkin Zachariah, Matilda's father was brutally murdered. He was thrown from an upstairs window at his home, Ynystawe House, near Swansea — a crime that had unbelievable repercussions. The following extract appears in a written statement:

"It was a current report and believed that he was murdered by one Robert Popkin who was at the time a daily visitor at the house and who shortly afterwards circulated in the neighbourhood of Swansea that he was now married to the widow of Jenkin Zachariah, of Ynystawe House.

But although diligent search had been made no legal entry or otherwise can be found of such a marriage having taken place. Robert Popkin took management and control of the vast estates of Jenkin Zachariah of which he held and retained unto himself by virtue, as he then alleged, that he was the lawful husband of the widow of Jenkin Zachariah."

This was clearly a fraud to the daughter Matilda the rightful heir-in-law. It is noteworthy to remark that in his drunken bouts Popkin admitted to the murder of Jenkin Zachariah.

● NATHANIEL Thomas, pictured while attending a London Court hearing. So much violence had occurred, that he never ventured outdoors without his fully loaded pistol and the added protection of "Buller" his ferocious bull mastiff.

**BY CHARLES JONES**

Though openly admitting to the murder, he was never even charged with the crime. Indeed, the whole unsavoury affair reeks of subterfuge. But retribution in a most diabolical manner was soon to be enacted in this macabre real-life drama. Besides, it seems that Zachariah's widow was privy to both the crime and the acquisition of her late husband's estates.

It's evident that Popkin was no stranger to the Thomas family. In those days in Welsh-speaking Wales, the name Popkin must have been an unusual one. In the will of the first Walter Thomas, dated June 19, 1654, there's a record, of: "fields, a mill, tracts of land including Fisher Street within the Town of Swansea . . . ", all leased to one Roger Popkin.

More than likely Robert Popkin was a descendant of Roger. The record also states that he had been friendly with the Thomas family since childhood. In later years he became a daily visitor at Ynystawe House, visits that culminated in a crime passionell, and wholeheartedly aroused the public's imagination.

At every fair, villagers listened open-mouthed to itinerant bards singing and posturing mummers enacting perky high spots of the tragedy. Not since the decapitation of Charles the First had there been such a spate of titillating gossip of dark deeds and sinful cohabitation.

In the meantime, Robert Popkin, exhuberant with self confidence, but blithely unaware of what was about to happen, really believed he was master of all he surveyed. But the Earl of Jersey involved as he was with the trusteeship of the Zachariah estates, had become alarmed and decided to take action. For such an exalted personage there were a variety of ways he could remove the culprit.

Most expedient would be a simple cloak and dagger assassination but such action would result in the ownership of the estates reverting to Rebecca, Zachariah's widow. So, killing Popkin instead of removing an obstacle, would only create unavoidable barriers, which didn't suit the Earl one iota.

## A story of murder, mayhem, and the dark secrets of mysterious deeds buried in a chest

Accordingly, The Earl of Jersey fearing exposure, converted his Briton Ferry mansion into a lunatic asylum. He then had Robert Popkin kidnapped and, committed as the first and only occupant, where he remained until his death in 1763 although there is no doubt that he was perfectly sane while so confined.

So, what happened to Zachariah's vast estates? Well might you ask and, your guess is as good as mine. Although there is a clue, contained in a sworn statement, presented as evidence by a descendant of the Thomas family in the Drymma High Court "proceedings.

Which takes us to the town of Ilfracombe, where a lonely, impoverished, old spinster, Elizabeth Vye, had returned to her birthplace. For some years during the 1880s she had lived in South West Wales, having somehow or other obtained the leasehold of the Drymma mansion and estates, from one Phillip Samuel.

What an elderly lady, unable to speak the language was doing in such an alien environment, is a mystery. It wasn't as though she had ample resources. Often she had difficulty paying the ground rent and, on more than one occasion a distress warrant was served. As a matter of interest, written evidence provides a pen portrait of her.

"I used to look forward to visiting Miss Vye who was a very peculiar woman in appearance and dress. She was short in stature and had a big crooked nose. She always wore a blue and white spotted handkerchief over her shoulders instead of the customery Welsh flannel shawl, and a very old-fashioned bonnet. Very often we had to call back many times, as she was always short of money .

Perhaps, finding her debts increasing, she upped stakes and returned to her native Ilfracombe where, in 1863 she died intestate. Rummaging among her belongings a relative named John Paddon came across the leasehold deeds, which placed him in possession for the next 10 years. Firmly believing that "possession was nine-tenths of the law," he became convinced that with a little ingenuity the lease could be freehold.

### King's ransom

So, with the admirable assistance of Robert Jennings Crosse, an Ilfracombe solicitor, he was supplied, with: "A maliciously lying, false, corrupt, and fraudently designed affidavit, proving that Miss Vye's leases were indubitably freehold . . . " Furthermore, whenever a sighting of the said documents were required for scrutiny, his excuse never varied, the freehold deeds had unfortunately been destroyed in a "mysterious" fire.

For John Paddon, with the Drymma freehold duly sworn and recorded, there was no turning back. The loot was worthy of a king's ransom, comprising: "In the Parish of Llansamlet, Llwn Crwn Farm, Drymma Mansion House with Coachouse, stables and walled outoffices, gardens, plantation lawn, entrance lodge with large field and orchard, altogether about 17 acres. Drymma Fach Farm and lands, cottages and outbuildings, four fields and three pieces of meadow altogether about 15 acres and the Dynevor Coal Mine.

"In the Parish of Cadoxton Juxta and the Brithdyr Estate, Brithdyr Ucha Farm and lands, dwelling house and outbuildings. In the Parish of Neath, a public house called the General Picton, situated in Cattle Street, a yard at the rear of Duck Street, a cottage adjoining, a piece of ground in the Outer Ropery measuring from east to west 70 feet or thereabouts, another meadow in the Outer Ropery containing from east to west 460 feet or thereabouts."

● **Continued next week.**

© Charles Jones, 1988

**KIDNAPPED AND LOCKED IN A LUNATIC ASYLUM**

Nathaniel Thomas Dynasty. (Charles Jones 1988)

place furnaces, buildings, "other cottages or erections for the workers", and/or quays or additional slag banks – viz. the salt marsh which was part of Cae Morfa'r Carw, Cae Pistill near Knap Coch House (on the north side of the turnpike road from White Rock to Bon-y-maen), and other waste ground. Again, it was stipulated that the disposal of rubbish could not be allowed to obstruct navigation on the Tawe – and this clearly would be in the interest of the partners, for their right to use the dock and quay at White Rock was confirmed.

Stones for new building and for repair work could be obtained from Cwm Scethan and other quarries on such of Lord Vernon's lands, in Swansea and Llansamlet parishes, as would be shown to the partners – who were to pay the occupiers for any damage done. Similarly, earth, clay and sand could be taken for making bricks and tiles and for the furnaces; but they were not to be taken "from open and enclosed lands called Graig y Foxhole and Graig Tir y Gwl".

The whole of Kilvey, extending across Drymma mountain to engross many farms and following further into Swansea Valley through Danyogof, Ynyscedwin Rhos and Alltycam, has also been confirmed to be a part of the lost Thomas estates.

Llysnewydd, which was purchased out of Chancery some years ago, is highly recognisable today as it is now home to Liberty Stadium. A hub for the latest and greatest events in rugby and football, new roads have been laid throughout this area, whilst a number of housing developments cement its status as a desirable place to live. A large part of this area,

'Fortune Claimed' feature, News of The World. 6th February 2000.

The area referred to as Graig y Foxhole, and the prominence of the White Rock Copper and Brass Works, is described in this extract from the book Glamorgan Historian: Volume Twelve, a figure that not only references its lease from Lord George Venables Vernon in 1805-06 but also the period of works undertaken under lessees John Freeman of Letton in the County of Hereford, Esq., Richard Bright, Levi Ames, William Delpratt and William Dighton of the City of Bristol, merchants, and Joseph Blisset of Clifton in the County of Gloucester.

Permission was granted to demolish furnaces and cottages on the demised premises and to erect in their

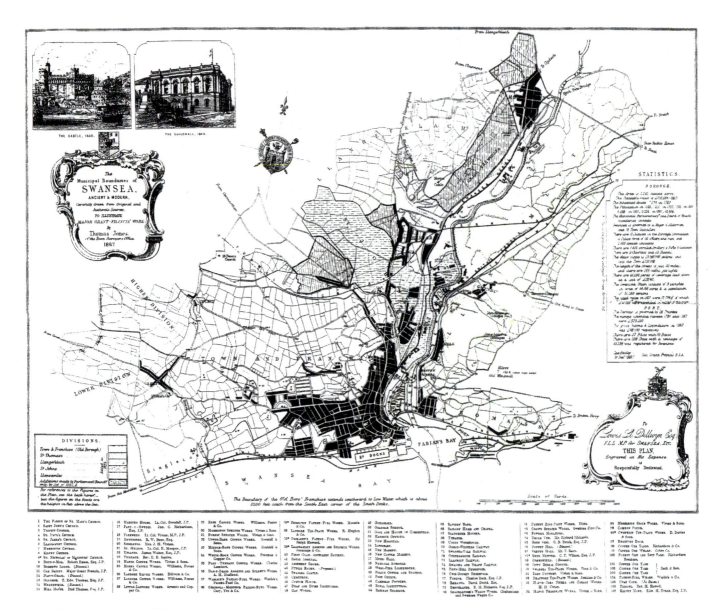

**Walter Thomas land in Swansea 1867.**

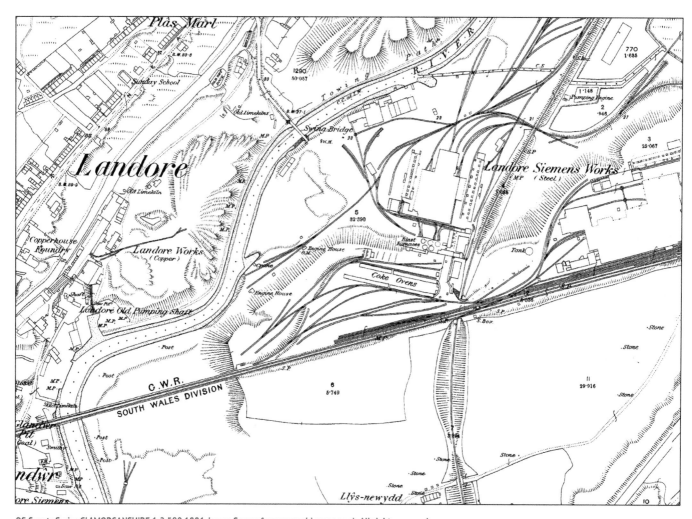

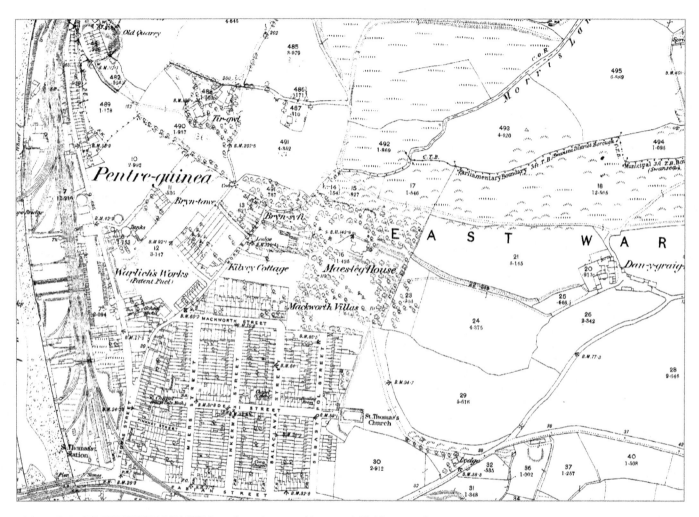

OS County Series GLAMORGANSHIRE 1:2,500 1879. Image Source from www.old-maps.co.uk.

**3.**

1693,
Dec. 5.

COUNTERPART of No. 4.

1693/4,
Mar. 2.

1.   Bussy Mansell of Briton Ferry,
     co. Glamorgan, esq.;
2.   Sir Walter Plumer of Mitcham,
     co. Surrey, bart.

MORTGAGE in the form of a demise, in
consideration of six thousand pounds,
of those messuages, tenements, and
lands called Dan-y-Graig, Llysnewidd,
and Gwern Llesty, situated in the
parishes or hamlets of Swanzey,
Llansamlett, Llangeveylach, Llandilo,
and Llangennith, co. Glamorgan,
and all other messuages, mills,
mines etc., late the estate of
William Thomas of Dan-y-Graig, parish
of Llansamlett, esquire, deceased, and
bequeathed by the said William Thomas in
his will to the said Bussy Mansell, and
which are situated in the parishes of
Swanzey, Llansamlett, Llandilo-
Tallabont, Oystermouth, Llangennith,
Llanryddyan, and Llangeveylach; also
the messuage and lands called West
Place and all other properties purchased
by the said Bussy Mansell of Sir
Edward Stradling, bart., deceased, and
situated in the parish of Coyty, co.
Glamorgan; also those messuages and
lands called Ynisvorgan and Llanghaed,
and all other lands and tenements
excepted by the said Bussy Mansell
out of the marriage-settlement of
Thomas Mansell, esquire, late eldest
son and heir apparent of the said
Bussy Mansell, since deceased, situated
in the parishes and hamlets of
Llangeveylach and Llandiloe; also those

**4.**

2.   (cont'd)

messuages and lands called Wennelt,
Cline, orchard lands, Coed Garele (sic),
and all other properties purchased by
the said Bussy Mansell of the Right
Hon. Phillipp, late Earl of Pembroke,
since deceased, and situated in the
parishes of Cadoxston, Neath, Llantwit-
iuxta-Neath, Bagland, Llangug, and
Killybebill, co. Glamorgan. The said
demise is made for the term of one
thousand years. Annual rent one
peppercorn at Michaelmas. Provision
is made that if the said Bussy Mansel
shall repay to the said Sir Walter
Plumer the sum of six thousand six
hundred pounds in portions as specified,
repayment to be completed by 3 Mar.,
1695, this demise shall be void.

119.  1697,
      Apr. 9.

PROBATE of the will of Sir Walter
Plummer, Bart, late of Mitcham, co.
Surrey, now of the parish of St. Andrews,
Holborne, co. Middlesex.
Latin.                    Attested Copy.

124.  1699,
      July 12.

PROBATE, with will attached, of Bussy
Mansel of Britton Ferry, co. Glamorgan,
esquire.  The will is dated 1699, Mar.
30.
Latin-English.

123.

DUPLICATE of No. 124.
                          Attested Copy.

**Tregrove farm being prepared for development.**

extending to Llansamlet, is now Swansea Enterprise Park. The Drymma mansion is still there, taking pride of place in what was the heart of the estates, and today the property is utilised as a home for the elderly. Drymma Fach Farm and Brithdir Uchaf also act as relics of the lost estates, whilst the old house of Drymma Issa and Drymma Fach at Birchgrove, a property that sat at the centre of many disputes – now successfully resolved thanks to a large volume of evidence – regarding which lands and properties formed part of the correct Drymma Proper, is now a private dwelling. The main dual carriageway from Swansea through Danygraig to Earlswood and Jersey Marine, more commonly referred to as Fabian Way, was given to the Swansea Corporation by the Earl of Jersey. Much of the lands surrounding the route have been transformed in recent years making way for many housing projects, hotels, factories and The new University of Wales Trinity Saint David (UWTSD) have just acquired 19 acres of prime land at SA1 for a new campus. This vibrant, waterfront setting is known as the Waterfront Innovation Quarter in SA1.

The majority of the lands in Oystermouth and Mumbles are currently housing projects, with a number of hotels and parks thrown into the mix. Many of the residential areas are home to expensive private housing with actress and Swansea native Catherine Zeta Jones and fellow Hollywood star and husband Michael Douglas owning a luxury property at Thistleboon, land once owned by Walter Thomas I. Wind Street in Swansea, which leads up from the Mount, is now the site of supermarkets, museums, hotels and public houses. Walter Thomas actually owned almost every property on Wind Street, with some of his residences occupying nearby Goat Street and Wassail Street too. As for the aforementioned lands in Llanrhidian and Llandeilo Talybont, not much is known about their current status.

The Walter Thomas Inheritance Association was disbanded after the reading of J.P. O'Sullivan's opinion (1998). Since this time, Malcolm has been working alone to build upon the progress made by the Association, the solicitors they called upon at the time – Hugh James Ford Simey of Merthyr Tydfil – and other members of the family.

*Work is still ongoing, and despite a resolution for the Thomas family and its descendants still not being in sight, this book will play an integral role in helping the story, its facts and the evidence so carefully curated by many generations, live on. Who knows a future descendant, maybe one yet to be born, may have the backing they need to restore the estates lost to the disinherited Ann Thomas…*

# GLOSSARY

**Ad infinitum**

The term *ad infinitum* is a Latin phrase. Used similarly as 'et cetera' or 'etc', when utilised in context when referring to a sequence it means 'continue forever, without limit' thus implying a non-terminating, repetitive process.

**Affidavit**

An *affidavit* is a statement, regularly required as evidence for court proceedings. The statement itself acts as verification when given under oath or penalty of perjury.

**Alderman**

The position of *alderman* relates to one held by a member of a municipal assembly or council. The position was commonplace in many jurisdictions founded throughout English law. A coveted role, the title of alderman is often taken by a high-ranking member of a borough or county council, and is chosen by the elected members rather than via popular vote.

**Annuity**

In the present day *annuity* is the name given to a financial product which gives you a guaranteed income for life. Now popularly associated with retirement income products, annuities were historically granted during the resettlement of land from one generation to the next.

**Book of Orders**

The *Book of Orders* is a publication directly associated with King Charles I. The document itself was regarded the 'centre-piece of Charles I's policies towards the mass of his subjects during his personal rule', a period which lasted from 1629 until 1640 when the Civil Wars officially took hold. The purpose of the book was to improve the management of affairs by local gentry and ultimately, according to *The Making of Charles I's Book of Orders* by B.W. Quintrell, enable 'better administration of justice, relief of the poor and reformation of disorders.'

**Chronicle of the Princes**

More commonly referred to as 'Brut y Tywysogion' the translated title *Chronicle of the Princes* is considered one of the most important primary sources of Welsh history to date. The series, of which there is several versions, provides an insight into a number of events that affected the Welsh nation, including eclipses, plagues and earthquakes, as well as records of death.

**Composition papers**

*Composition papers* offered an important historical insight into one of the great periods of unrest for England and Wales – the Civil Wars. Often referred to more specifically as 'royalist composition papers', these texts were composed as a record of economic affairs, and now provide an illuminating look into the regime that gripped three kingdoms.

**Comptroller**

The title of *comptroller* is used in our Royal Household today to describe a senior management level position of great importance. The role itself has not changed over the years with duties including the arrangement of ceremonial affairs in addition to the management of household finances.

**Convey**

When an individual is said *'to convey'* in relation to property law, they are involved in the transfer of legal title of property from one party to another. Also referred to as the granting of an encumbrance, conveying is now more commonly denoted as 'conveyancing.'

**De facto**

This Latin phrase takes on a number of translations depending on its context, however it essentially means 'in fact', 'in reality', 'in actual existence', or 'as a matter of fact', literally translating as 'from fact.'

**DWT**

Abbreviated from the term 'deadweight tonnage', *DWT* is a type of measurement used to describe how much mass a ship is carrying or, alternatively, can carry safely. The final DWT value constitutes the combined weight of the ship's cargo, fuel, fresh water, ballast water, provisions, passengers and crew.

**Fathom**

Commonly used in the old imperial and U.S. customary systems, a *fathom* is a unit used to measure length. One fathom equates to 6 feet or 1.8288 metres.

**Fee tail**

In common law, a *fee tail*, sometimes referred to as an 'entail', is a form of trust established by deed or settlement. The fee tail restricts the sale or inheritance of an estate and prevents the associated lands and/or properties from being sold. The term, which is derived from the Medieval Latin phrase *feodum talliatum*, is the opposite of 'fee simple' where no such restriction applies.

**Heir at law**

Used regularly when discussing property law, an *heir at law* relates to a person entitled to succeed to the real property of a person who dies intestate.

**Indemnity bond**

An *indemnity bond* acts as a lawful promise to indemnify the parties named in relation against losses should the individual creating the bond fail to perform. Used commonly in the present day to provide insurance for residential and commercial rental payments, throughout history it was also used to ensure the maintenance of an illegitimate child.

**Legal issue**

This term refers to the legal right that an individual has to pursue a claim. To have 'male issue' is to have the right, by law or custom, to inherit as the firstborn male child, in preference to younger sons.

**Legitimists**

The name *legitimists* is used to describe royalists in France who believe that the King of France and Navarre must be chosen according to the simple application of the Salic Law.

**Maunch**

A *maunch* represents a detachable lady's sleeve with a wide, overhanging cuff. The sleeve itself was particularly fashionable during the 13th and 14th centuries, and has since been used on numerous coats of arms to symbolise that either the bearer was popular with the ladies or loved his wife.

**Moiety**

To be awarded a *moiety* is to be given a part or portion of something. Referred to in this case as an estate, to be awarded moiety would often mean to be granted a lesser share of the lands.

**Papist**

Used as a disparaging term throughout history, and particularly popular during the English Reformation in the 16th century, *papist* is the name given to any individual who has loyalty to the Pope and the Roman Catholic Church.

**Portreeve**

Often seen in historical documents in the old English 'portrefe', a *portreeve* or port warden is a title given to an important official that has authority over a town.

**Royal Standard**

The *Royal Standard* is the name given to the personal

flag used by Elizabeth II, however the term can be used universally when referring to the flags used to display the Royal Arms. Those in support of the crown were generally said to be 'raising the Royal Standard.'

**Sequestration**

In law, *sequestration* refers to the removal, separation or seizure of land or goods from the possession of its owner.

**Tenants in tail**

Used in relation to the legal term 'fee tail', a *tenant in tail* or in possession is one that has barred his fee tail by disentailing the deeds. As a result, the tenant has a vested interest in an estate, property or land for life.

**Third Succession Act**

Introduced during the reign of Henry VIII, the *Third Succession Act* was a piece of legislation passed by the Parliament of England in 1543. The Act, formally entitled 'Succession to the Crown Act 35 Hen. VIII c.1', was responsible for returning both of Henry's daughters, Mary and Elizabeth I, to the line of succession after the death of their brother Edward VI.

**Wey**

The *wey* is an old unit of measurement used to calculate the volume of dry commodities as well as the weight of other goods, such as lead, cheese and soap.

# BIBLIOGRAPHY

Anon. (n.d.) *Bussy Mansel, MP.* Online at http://www.geni.com/people/Bussy-Mansel/6000000008872302772 (accessed 05/11/15)

Anon. (1911) *Brief from Counsel: Thomas Versus Paddon.*

Anon. (1866) *The Engineer.*

Anon. (n.d.) *James Brydges, 1st Duke of Chandos.* Online at https://en.wikipedia.org/wiki/James_Brydges,_1st_Duke_of_Chandos (accessed 05/11/15)

Anon. (1764) *Gabriel Powell Survey.*

Anon. (2004) *The Genealogy Of Iestyn: The Son Of Gwrgan.* Undisclosed: Kessinger Publishing.

Anon. (2006) *How does a company cost £1?* Online at http://news.bbc.co.uk/1/hi/magazine/5262616.stm (accessed 27/08/15)

Anon. (n.d.) *The Industrialisation of the South Wales Valleys.* Online at http://www.data-wales.co.uk/valley1.htm (accessed 20/08/15)

Anon. (1645) Letter to Sir Jacob Astley, Baron of Reading, 13 September.

Anon. (n.d.) *Margam MS. 5695.*

Anon. (n.d.) *Rhodri Mawr (Rhodri the Great).* Online at http://www.britainexpress.com/wales/history/rhodri.htm (accessed 18/05/15)

Anon. (n.d.) *Rise and Fall of HENRY JAMES BRYDGES First Duke of Chandos for whom Handel composed The Chandos Anthems, The.* Online at http://www.baroquemusic.org/chandos.html (accessed 05/11/15)

Anon. (1646) *Royalist composition papers relating to Glamorganshire.* Republished on 13 October 1888.

Anon. (1646) *Royalist composition papers relating to Glamorganshire.* Republished on 10 November 1888.

Anon. (1650) *Survey of the Manor of Kilvey A.D.*

Anon. (1686) *Survey of the Manor of Kilvey A.D.*

Anon. (1688) *Survey of the Manor of Kilvey A.D.*

Anon. (n.d.) *Warrant or Wit of Possession.* County of Glamorgan.

Anon. (1903) *The winning of Glamorgan: Introduction.* Cardiff: Cardiff Records.

'7,500-acre Estate in New Hands' (n.d.) *Undisclosed.* [Print article].

'Ann Thomas to Zacharias Jenkin' (c. 1680s) [Marriage Certificate].

'Areas of Claim Relating to Walter Thomas' Will 1654' [Map].

Banks, R.W. (1684) *The Account of the Official Progress of His Grace Henry The First Duke of Beaufort.* London: Blades, East & Blades.

Biancalana, J. (2007) *The Fee Tail and the Common Recovery in Medieval England.* Cambridge: Cambridge University Press.

Birch, Walter de Gray. (1893) *Descriptive Catalogue of the Penrice and Margam Abbey Manuscripts.*

Birch, Walter de Gray. (1897) *A History of Margam Abbey.* London: Bedford Press Publication.

Booker, T.W. (1865) *Warrant or Writ of Possession.*

Burchell Rees, W. (1908) Letter to Editor of the Daily Chronicle, November.

Burchell Rees, W. (1914) Letter to Nathaniel R Thomas, 28 May.

Burchell Rees, W. (1914) Letter to Nathaniel R Thomas, 28 July.

Bridges, J. (1668) *The Will of Sir John Bridges.*

Capwell Fox, M. (2002) *Images of America: Catasauqua and North Catasauqua.* Undisclosed: Arcadia Publishing.

Carter, E.H. (2010) *A History of Britain book IV, The Stuarts 1603 – 1714.* London: Stacey International

'Centre of Swansea, The: An extract from the Ordnance Survey' [Map]

Charles I, King of England. (1645) Letter to William Thomas I, 11 September.

'Coalmine fortune has…' (2000) *News of the World.* Written by Dominic Herbert, Published 6 February [Print article].

Clark, G.T. (1978) *Limbus Patrum Morganiae et Glamorganiae.* Utah: The Genealogical Society of Utah.

Davies, W. (1891) Letter to Harper, W, 4 February.

Davies, W. (1891) Letter to relatives, 13 July.

Davies, W. (1893) Letter to relatives, 2 May.

Davies, W. (n.d.) *Statement: In the Matter of the Drymma Estate.*

'Drumme Farm in the Parishes of Lansamlet & Cadoxton' (1777) Surveyed by John Williams [Map].

'Drymma and Brithdyr Estates in the Parishes of Llansamlet & Cadoxton Juxta Neath' (1867) [Map].

'Dynasty!' (1988) *Undisclosed.* Written by Charles Jones [Print article].

'Earl of Jersey Sells South Wales Estate' (1951) *Evening Post.* Written by our London correspondent, Published 28 May [Print article].

Edward, H.D. (1626) *The Will of Hopkin David Edward of Danygraig.*

'Emanuel Bowen's Map of South Wales of 1729' [Map].

'Family Group Record' (1996) *The Archives of the Church of Latter Day Saints (Mormons) Utah, America.* Retrieved 17 July [Ancestral file].

Gabb, G. (1986) *The Story of the Village of Mumbles.* Undisclosed: D.Brown & Sons Ltd.

Gilbert, A. (2002) *The Holy Kingdom: The Quest for the Real King Arthur.* Undisclosed: Invisible Cities Press Llc.

Glamorgan County Lunatic Asylum; Glamorgan County Mental Hospital; Glanrhyd Hospital. (1864-2008) *Glamorgan County Lunatic Asylum / Glamorgan County Mental Hospital/ Glanrhyd Hospital records.* Glamorgan: Bridgend and District NHS Trust.

'Glamorgan Sheet No. 15 S.W.' (1938) Supplied by E.N. Mason & Sons Ltd. [Map]

'Glamorgan Sheet No. 24 N.W.' (1948) Supplied by E.N. Mason & Sons Ltd. [Map]

'Great Welsh Lawsuit, A' (1896) *Western Mail.* Published 30 November [Print article].

Griffiths, L. (1904) Letter to Nathaniel R Thomas, 21 March.

Griffiths, L. (1904) Letter to Nathaniel R Thomas, 28 March.

Griffiths, R.A. (1993) *Sir Rhys ap Thomas and his Family.* Cardiff: University of Wales Press.

Hall, W. (1716) *The Will of William Hall of Peterchurch.*

Harnden, J. (1998) Letter to Malcolm Winmill, 29 April.

Hirst, D. (1990) The Lord Protector, 1653–8 in *Morrill.*

'Home for Lunatics' (1996) *South Wales Evening Post.* Published 10 January [Print article].

'Industries of the Areas Owned by the Thomas Family and Popkins (Hopkins)' (1800) [Map]

'Inheritance Mystery Gets Flood of Calls' (n.d.) *Undisclosed.* Written by Abi Holland [Print article].

'Jersey Estates Buyers Are Named' (1951) *South Wales Evening Post.* Published 6 June [Print article].

John, A.H. (n.d.) Iron and Coal on a Glamorgan Estate , 1700-1740 in *The Economic History Review.*

John, King of England, Langton, S. (1215) *Magna Carta.* British Library, Lincoln & Salisbury.

Johnson, B. (n.d.) *The Great Plague.* Online at www.historic-uk.com/HistoryUK/HistoryofEngland/The-Great-Plague/ (accessed 22/07/15)

Jones, W.H. (1922) *History of the Port of Swansea.* Carmarthen.

Lambert, T. (1990) *A Brief History of Wales.*

'Llansamlet Romance' (1954) *Undisclosed.* Published 15 February [Print article].

'Locations of Colonel Cameron's Great House at Danygraig St Thomas, Swansea' (1838-42) [Map].

Mallon, J. (2000) The Walter Thomas Heirs Who Lived in Merthyr Tydfil in *Merthyr Historian: Volume Eleven.* Merthyr Tydfil: Merthyr Tydfil Historical Society. Edited by Holley, T.F.

Mansel, B. (1750) *The Will of Lord Bussy Mansel.*

Mansell, B. (1699) *The Will of Bussy Mansell.* Document includes *Court Sentence* for the aforementioned (1700)

Mansell, T. (1684) *The Will of Thomas Mansell.*

Mansell, T. (1705) *The Will of Thomas Mansell.*

Maunsell, C.A., Statham, E.P. (1917) *History of the Family of Maunsell (Mansell, Mansel).* London: Kegan Paul Trench & Co Limited.

Matthews, J.F. (n.d.) *Constantine I.* Online at http://www.britannica.com/biography/Constantine-I-Roman-emperor (accessed 11/05/15)

McDermott, P.M. (1992) Jurisdiction of the Court of Chancery to award damages in *Law Quarterly Review.* London: Sweet & Maxwell.

'Medieval Swansea' (2014) *Medieval Swansea.* First broadcast 26/08/14 [Video].

Montague, P.W. (1986) *The Royal Line of Succession.* London: Pitkin Guides.

Morgan, P. (n.d.) *End of an Elegant House, The.* Online at http://welshjournals.llgc.org.uk/browse/viewpage/llgc-id:1272866/llgc-id:1274487/llgc-id:1274493/get650 (accessed 05/11/15)

Morganwg, D. (n.d.) *Hanes Morganwg, 227.*

'Murder Most Foul! Secrets of the Pigsty' (1988) *Undisclosed.* Written by Charles Jones [Print article].

National Trust. (n.d.) *Osterley Park and House.* Online athttp://www.nationaltrust.org.uk/osterley-park/ (accessed 05/11/15)

Neville, Mr. Justice. (1916) *Statement of Claim.*

Nicholas, T. (1874) *The History & Antiquities of Glamorgan.*

'Obituaries: The Earl of Jersey' (1998) *The Daily Telegraph.* Published 13 August [Print article].

Owen, R. (n.d.) *Undisclosed.* Online at http://wbo.llgc.org.uk/en/s-THOM-DAV-1794.html (accessed 10/08/15)

'Particulars and Conditions of Sale: Drymma, Drymma Fach & Brithdyr Ucha' (1867) *Undisclosed.* Published 20 November [Print advertisement].

Phillips, D.R. (1994) *The History of the Vale of Neath.* Glamorgan: West Glamorgan County Archive Service and Neath Borough Council.

'Place Names of Areas of Claim' [Map].

Plant, D. (n.d.) *The Irish Uprising, 1641.* Online at www.bcw-project.org/church-and-state/confederate-ireland/the-irish-uprising (accessed 05/06/15)

Polubinski, E. (1968) The Peppercorn Theory and the Restatement of Contracts in *William & Mary Law Review 10.* Undisclosed: National Welsh-American Foundation.

'Popkins Family and Others at Llansamlet, The' (n.d.) [Original notes].

Popkin, T. (1752) *The Will of Thomas Popkin of Fforest.*

Price. (1863) Letter to Mr. Charles Snow, 22 April.

Quintrell, B. W. (1980), *The Making of Charles I's Book of Orders.* London: English Historical Review XCV.

Raithby, J. (1819) *Statutes of the Realm: Volume 5, 1628-80.* London: Great Britain Record Commission.

Rogers, W.C. (n.d.) Appendix I in *Survey of Kilvey, Glamorgan and Swansea, Calendar Vol. II.*

'Sales by Auction' (1897) *The Cambrian.* Published 2 July [Print article].

'Sales by Auction' (1897) *Western Mail.* Published 10 July [Print article].

Smith, A. (1776) *An Inquiry into the Nature and Causes of the Wealth of Nations.* London: Methuen & Co.

Snow, Mrs. (1863) Letter to undisclosed, 31 December.

Steward of St Donat's Castle. (1717) Letter to Lady Mansel Stradling, 30 June.

'Tax Forces Earl to Sell Lands' (n.d.) *Daily Mail.* [Print article].

Thomas, C. (1737) *The Will of Catherine Thomas of Danygraig & Swansea.*

Thomas, E. (1866) *The Old Green Book of Ezekel Thomas*

Thomas, E. (1738) *The Will of Edward Thomas of Llansamlet.*

Thomas, J.L. (n.d.) *Rhodri Mawr: King of Wales.* Online at http://www.castlewales.com/rhodri.html (accessed 18/05/15)

Thomas, K. (1669) *The Will of Katherine Thomas.*

Thomas, M. (1847) Letter to undisclosed.

Thomas, N.R. (1914) Letter to Commissioner for Oaths.

Thomas, N.R. (1903) Letter to Prime minster Lloyd George, August.

Thomas, R.J. (n.d.) *A Short Treatise on the Ownership of Land in the Parishes of Cadoxton Juxta Neath and Kilybebyll in the County of Glamorgan.*

Thomas, W. (1654) *The Will of Walter Thomas of Swansea & Danygraig.*

Thomas, W. (1667) *The Will of Walter Thomas of Danygraig Esq.*

Thomas, W. (1677) *The Will of William Thomas.*

Thomas, W.S.K. (1990) *The History of Swansea: From Rover Settlement to the Reformation.* England, Gomer Press.

Tucker, K. (1994) *Chronicle of Cadoxton.* Wales: Historical Projects.

'Ty the App: Field Numbers' (n.d.) Supplied by West Glamorgan Archive Service [Map].

'Undisclosed' (1994) *Good Fortune.* Directed by Ben Fuller. First broadcast November 1994 [Video]

'Undisclosed' (1896) *Merthyr Express.* Published 5 December [Print article].

'Undisclosed' (1915) *South Wales Daily News.* Published 17 June [Print article].

Vernon, L.B. (1786) *The Will of Louisa Barbara Vernon.*

W.A Grist Hawkin (1826-1916) '*Opinion by Counsel*' Nathaniel Richard Thomas

'Walter's Fortune Mystery' (1996) *South Wales Evening Post.* Published 31 July [Print article].

Walter Thomas Inheritance Association, The. (1998) *Commentary on Counsels' Opinion.* Port Talbot: The Walter Thomas Inheritance Association

Walter Thomas Inheritance Association, The. (1998) *Opinion.* Port Talbot: The Walter Thomas Inheritance Association

Walter Thomas Inheritance Association, The. (1998) *Statement.* Port Talbot: The Walter Thomas Inheritance Association

West Glamorgan Archive Service. (1679-1960) *Briton Ferry Estate.* Online at http://www.archiveswales.org.uk/anw/get_collection.php?coll_id=1203&inst_id=34&term=briton%20ferry%20estate (accessed 05/11/15)

'Wilful Damage at Neath' (1887) *The Bridgend Chronicle.*

Published 23 September [Print article].

Williams, G. (1990) *Swansea: An Illustrated History.* Ireland: Davies, C.

Williams, P.N. (1995) *David Thomas: Iron Man from Wales.* Undisclosed: National Welsh-American Foundation.

Williams, S, and Denning, R. (1981) *Glamorgan Historian: Volume Twelve.* Undisclosed: Williams, S.

'Wings Over a City' (1969) *Herald of Wales.* Published 20 December [Print article].

Winmill, M. (1993-98) *The Thomas Family Tree.* Compiled with assistance from Williams, D.L.

Winmill, M. (1994-99) *The Thomas Family Tree.* Compiled with assistance from Williams, D.L.

Winmill, M. (2002) Letter to Dominic Weir of Hugh James Ford Simey Solicitors, 15 March.

Winmill, M. (2001) Letter to Julia Lomas of the Court of Chancery, 22 February.

Winmill, M. (2002) Letter to Linda Joy of Public Guardianship Office, 8 May.

Ychan, D.J. (1574) *The Will of David ap John Ychan (Vaughan).*

Ychan, J.D.J. (1598) *The Will of John David ap John Ychan (Vaughan).*

# SPECIAL THANKS TO

The Walter Thomas Inheritance Association, Swansea
Archives, National Archives, Cardiff Record Office, National
Library of Wales, The Dean and Chapter of Westminster,
Merthyr Public Libraries, The Institute of Heraldic and
Genealogical Studies, University of Swansea, Glynn Vivian Art
Gallery Collection.

## TO BE CONTINUED...

# ABOUT THE AUTHOR

Malcolm Winmill.

**MALCOLM WINMILL,** Author of *The Quest*, currently resides in the tiny village of Brithdir in the Rhymney Valley, South Wales with his wife, Linda Winmill (nee Harrison).

Born 17th January 1943 to a coal mining family, Malcolm's father hailed from Somerset, whilst his mother was born and bred in Bargoed, a town also in the heart of the South Wales Valleys. Due to the family's mining background, like many living in the Welsh Valleys, Malcolm experienced much hardship and poverty whilst growing up, but his upbringing was also built on a foundation of good values and an overwhelming sense of community, two factors that were indispensable when Malcolm and his two sisters (only one of which is still living) lost both of their parents before the age of 25.

Family means everything to Malcolm, he even considers it one of his primary interests, alongside the breeding and racing of horses. It is these family values that led to Malcolm beginning the journey behind *The Quest*, with his passion for discovering the truth and ensuring justice for his loved ones – both in this immediate and extended family – central to the story, even as work continues to this very day. He now has one son, three grandchildren and five great grandchildren.

Professionally, Malcolm has had a long and varied career. Following in the footsteps of his father, and many of his other male ancestors, Malcolm's first role was as a coal miner. He then went onto become a carpenter and builder, two vocations that made him a vital part of the local community. Following this, Malcolm decided to pursue a more customer facing career as a publican in pubs and hotels across the region. Malcolm was forced to retire early due to ill health.

Malcolm's strong work ethic continued long after his retirement however, and despite his heart problems, he spent much of his time tracing back his family history and that of his wife's. It was then that Malcolm discovered an unfortunate story of deceit, murder, mystery and missing millions. His work began in 1993 and continues up until the present day with his drive, steely determination and focus certain to mean that he will pursue his book's claims until his dying day.

What began as a hobby more than 20 years ago now becomes a legacy, which, thanks to *The Quest*, will never again be forgotten.

CPSIA information can be obtained
at www.ICGtesting.com
Printed in the USA
BVOW10*0833250816

460145BV00006B/14/P

9 780993 488672